Comparative Cultural Studies
and Michael Ondaatje's Writing

Comparative Cultural Studies,
Steven Tötösy de Zepetnek, Series Editor

Comparative Cultural Studies is a contextual approach in the study of culture in all of its products and processes. The framework is built on tenets of the discipline of comparative literature and cultural studies and on notions borrowed from a range of thought such as (radical) constructivism, communication theories, systems theories, and literary and culture theory. In comparative cultural studies focus is on theory and method as well as application and attention is on the how rather than on the what. Colleagues interested in publishing in the series are invited to contact the editor, Steven Totosy, at <clcweb@purdue.edu>.

Volumes in the series are:

Comparative Central European Culture. Ed. Steven Tötösy de Zepetnek. West Lafayette: Purdue UP, 2002. 190 pages, bibliography, index. ISBN 1-55753-240-0.

Comparative Literature and Comparative Cultural Studies. Ed. Steven Tötösy de Zepetnek. West Lafayette: Purdue UP, 2003. 372 pages, bibliography, index. ISBN 1-55753-288-5 (ebook), ISBN 1-55753-290-7 (pbk).

Sophia A. McClennen, *The Dialectics of Exile: Nation, Time, Language, and Space in Hispanic Literatures.* West Lafayette: Purdue UP, 2004. 252 pages, bibliography, index. ISBN 1-55753-315-6.

Comparative Cultural Studies and Latin America. Ed. Sophia A. McClennen and Earl E. Fitz. West Lafayette: Purdue UP, 2004. 282 pages, bibliography, index. ISBN 1-55753-358-X.

Jin Feng, *The New Woman in Early Twentieth-Century Chinese Fiction.* West Lafayette: Purdue UP, 2004. 240 pages, bibliography, index. ISBN 1-55753-330-X.

Comparative Cultural Studies and Michael Ondaatje's Writing. Ed. Steven Tötösy de Zepetnek. West Lafayette: Purdue UP, 2005. 154 pages, bibliography, index. ISBN 1-55753-378-4.

Comparative Cultural Studies and Michael Ondaatje's Writing

Edited by
Steven Tötösy de Zepetnek

Purdue University Press
West Lafayette, Indiana

ISBN 1-55753-378-4

Printed in the United States of America

Library of Congress Cataloging-in-Publication Data

Comparative cultural studies and Michael Ondaatje's writing / edited by Steven Tötösy de Zepetnek.
    p. cm. -- (Comparative cultural studies)
  Includes bibliographical references and index.
  ISBN 1-55753-378-4 (pbk.)
  1. Ondaatje, Michael, 1943---Criticism and interpretation. 2. Culture in literature. I. Tötösy de Zepetnek, Steven, 1950– II. Series.

  PR9199.3.O5Z63 2005
  818'.5409--dc22

                                        2004013298

Contents

Introduction to *Comparative Cultural Studies* and *Michael Ondaatje's Writing*

Steven Tötösy de Zepetnek

Michael Ondaatje's work represents in many ways the best of contemporary Canadian literature in English not only in the context of Canada itself but also on the international scene. In this, it is not without significance that Ondaatje is an immigrant to Canada and that much of his writing is about identity, history, and about people of "in-between." Identity, whether that of an individual or that of a people, history, and hybridity are of great relevance in the age of globalization, disappearing borders, and the migration of people whether for economic, political, or other reasons. Perhaps this is one of the main reasons why Ondaatje's texts raise much interest among readers of fiction as well as in scholarship and why his texts are of great relevance in today's world. It is a given that Ondaatje's poetry is lyrical; what is important is that his prose is also deeply poetic in content and, one could argue, also in form, and certainly so in language and this view appears to be confirmed in several of the papers presented in this volume.

The theoretical basis of the volume is that of the aims and scope of the Purdue series of Books in Comparative Cultural Studies, as follows. Comparative cultural studies is a field of study where selected tenets of the discipline of comparative literature are merged with selected tenets of the field of cultural studies meaning that the study of culture and culture products—including but not restricted to literature, communication, media, art, etc.—is performed in a contextual and relational construction and with a plurality of methods and approaches, inter-disciplinarity, and, if and when advantageous, including team work. In comparative cultural studies it is the processes of communicative action(s) in culture and the how of these processes that constitute the main objectives of research and study. However, comparative cultural studies does not exclude textual analysis proper or other established fields of study. In comparative cultural studies, ideally, the framework of and methodologies available in the systemic and empirical study of culture are favored.

The papers in the volume represent recent scholarship about Michael Ondaatje's work by scholars working in English-Canadian literature and culture in the context of comparative cultural studies. The abstracts of the papers in the volume explain the thematic cohesion of the volume, as follows.

Victoria Cook, in "Exploring Transnational Identities in Ondaatje's *Anil's Ghost*," addresses issues of identity raised in the narrative of Michael Ondaatje's novel *Anil's Ghost*. Cook's paper is a close analysis of Ondaatje's novel, paying particular attention to the way in which Ondaatje examines identity as both a "construct" and a "process." The approach used is one that draws on postcolonial theory and takes a "transnational" perspective. Cook argues that Ondaatje's text moves beyond the concept of a postcolonial literature of "resistance" into an area that requires a theory of process rather than product. Transnationalism is shown here to be just such a theory, in that it captures something of this fluidity: the analysis is underpinned, therefore, by the application of transnational theory, as put forward by critics such as Paul Giles. Names and naming are the main themes addressed in the course of this argument, with regard to the way in which they impacts on issues of identification. Finally, Cook explores in her paper issues of identity in *Anil's Ghost*, identity that traverses cultural and national boundaries and encompasses both central and marginal positions.

Beverley Curran argues in her paper, "Ondaatje's *The English Patient* and Altered States of Narrative," that Ondaatje reconfigures in his novel the "romantic" figure of the father/artist as a clandestine lover, a drug addict, or an eccentric translator, all figures with dependencies. In *The English Patient*, the father or artist's sense of source, continuity, or authority are translated into a narrative which rejects the perverse captivity demanded of the lover and the translator by fidelity or by the tenets of realistic representation. Using sex, drugs, and translation, Ondaatje deranges both time and space to reconfigure the role of the artist as a translator in an attempt to dislocate the "false rhapsody of art" or historical explanation and their authority and relocate the site of the story. Creation is less a preoccupation than contradiction and the consequences of choice in this novel, and instead of the textual strategies of realist narrative to "maintain self-other relations of dominance" to establish authority, Ondaatje applies translation to narrative in the novel so that, at the story's heart there is deferment, for a translation is never definitive.

Marlene Goldman suggests in her paper, "Representations of Buddhism in Ondaatje's *Anil's Ghost*," that at first glance Ondaatje appears to promote the idea of a Sri Lankan Buddhist faith as transcending history. Ondaatje introduces the subject of Buddhism early on in the novel, emphasizing initially the devastation wrought by imperial and colonial forces. Goldman, however, argues that subsequent references to Buddhism undermine the initial portrayal of a religion besieged by external imperialist forces. For example, at one point, the character Palipana refers to the assassination of his brother, Narada, a Buddhist monk. Narada was possibly the victim of a "political killing" and rumours suggest he was killed by a novice and thus his death recalls the historical connection between the JVP (termed "the antigovernment insurgents" in the novel) and young Buddhist monks. Goldman argues that rather than offering a sanitized account that ignores Buddhism's enmeshment in politics, Ondaatje's novel addresses the complex relationship between religion, politics, and violence in Sri Lanka.

Stephanie M. Hilger, in her paper "Ondaatje's *The English Patient* and Rewriting History" situates the novel within the long-standing Western tradition of writing about the cultural "Other," from Herodotus to Michel de Montaigne to Rudyard Kipling. Michel de Certeau's notion of history serves as a reference point for the analysis of Ondaatje's presentation of the "English" patient's story as well as of twentieth-century history. Hilger argues that the protagonist's physical mutilation is a metonymic representation of post-World War II and postcolonial consciousness. In the same way that the characters in the novel attempt to understand the mystery that is the "English" patient, Ondaatje's readers are led on a search for the understanding of a brutal and fragmented reality. While the novel questions and undermines the opposition between the "civilized" and the "barbarian," Ondaatje also suggests that certain historical realities, such as the dropping of the atomic bomb, force characters into a binary that they have been trying to deconstruct throughout the narrative.

Hsuan Hsu, in his paper "Post-Nationalism and the Cinematic Apparatus in Minghella's Adaptation of Ondaatje's *The English Patient*," discusses Anthony Minghella's cinematic version of Ondaatje's novel. In Hsu's view, Minghella and Ondaatje (Ondaatje collaborated on the film script) emphasize in the film the visual and social implications of mapmaking in order to align imperialism with the cinematic apparatus. While the film explores the workings of visual power, it also explores their adulteration by unmapped forces of desire: Almásy's and Katherine's adulterous relationship transgresses marital and national constraints, but also reinscribes them when Almásy desires to possess her body and Katherine dies immobilized looking at illuminated pictures in a cave. However, the film's narrative frame presents a more promising version of apparatus theory: Hana's relationship with Kip involves both a transnational way of loving and an "adulterated" way of seeing. Whereas nationalist ideology links knowledge to the notion of a disembodied and objective gaze, both the film's eroticism and its melodramatic evocation of tears remind us that vision is fundamentally embodied.

Glen Lowry, in his "The Representation of 'Race' in Ondaatje's *In the Skin of a Lion*," bases his discussion on the observation that critics tend to view Ondaatje's writing in terms of a progression towards complex issues of "race" and post-coloniality. In contrast, Lowry argues that the matter of "race" forms an integral aspect of Ondaatje's oeuvre and Lowry proposes that *In the Skin of a Lion* is a key site in the development of Ondaatje's engagement with issues of "race" and the cultural politics of post-coloniality. Focusing on Ondaatje's depiction of Toronto in terms of its complex history of shifting social spaces and his representation of Patrick and Caravaggio as "racialized" figures, Lowry discusses Ondaatje's engagement with whiteness as a social construct. Rather than critiquing Ondaatje's novel for an apparent absence of race-writing, i.e., writing about so-called "visible minorities," Lowry suggests that Ondaatje in fact "reverses the gaze" and throws the question of "race" back on the readers. Adding the figures of Patrick and Caravaggio to the writing of the city, *In the Skin of a Lion* undermines presumptions about the racial stability and hegemonic power of Toronto's and ethnic communities. Last, Lowry argues for a more thorough discussion of Ondaatje's critique of nationalism and multiculturalism vis-à-vis the cultural politics of reading and the construction of "whiteness."

Jon Saklofske, in his paper "The Motif of the Collector and History in Ondaatje's Work" recognizes that Ondaatje rescues Buddy Bolden from historical obscurity by elevating and complicating the musician's largely forgotten history with a self-conscious and largely fictional synthesis of memory and imagination. The liberties Ondaatje takes in *Coming Through Slaughter* with his subject to achieve this re-presentation and the ownership of the portrait that results exposes this type of authorial activity as a problematic appropriation. Saklofske suggests that to understand the implications of Ondaatje's activity it is useful to compare his efforts with Walter Benjamin's "collector" figure, who is both a selfish, destructive thief, and a careful preserver. As a collector, Ondaatje becomes the owner and an essential part of this transformed and personalised image of Bolden. Further, Saklofske argues that Ondaatje preserves Bolden's presence, actively confronts historical exclusivity, and interrupts his own authority over his subject. Although his interaction with actual historical figures decreases with successive novels, Ondaatje's personal encounter with the impersonal machine of history continues, asserting itself repeatedly as a successful strategy against destructiveness or authoritative exclusion.

Sandeep Sanghera, in her "Touching the Language of Citizenship in Ondaatje's *Anil's Ghost*," discusses questions which make Ondaatje's novel a text about postmodern identity: who is this woman Anil who lives mostly in the West, travels on a British passport, works for an international organization, and no longer has any real ties to her first home? In the paper, these questions are examined via the languages Anil adopts and abandons in the novel. Sanghera elaborates on the question of foreign-ness represented by the protagonist of the novel; however, this foreign-ness is examined in the particular context concerning the substance of family and kinship as well as language and nation. Sanghera's analysis represents the questions and thoughts of readers who are themselves migrants between languages and homes.

Winfried Siemerling, in his "Oral History and the Writing of the Other in Ondaatje's *In the Skin of a Lion*," argues that the simulation of oral narratives in *In the Skin of a Lion* imagines the conveyance of oral histories of immigrant experiences obscured by historiography. The narrative device of simulated orality—the written text casts itself as the outcome of serial story-telling—serves here to introduce erstwhile anonymous societal actors as makers of history, and emphasizes the collective production of story and history. Oral narratives emerge dreamlike like light out of darkness in this text; yet light, like writing, creates a problematic visibility whose multiple sources must be acknowledged. A critique of previous writing of history, *In the Skin of a Lion* "betrays" in both senses of the word history, silence, and darkness—by imagining necessary possibilities and necessarily omitting others. The interdependence of orality and writing and of darkness and visibility evokes in the novel the romantic valorization of darkness that inverts the classical metaphor of light as purveyor of truth. Yet, this interdependence also critiques orality: articulations of history and the "survival" of events have to cope with the lacunae created by writing *and* with the hazardous transmissions and temporalities of orality. The title of *In the Skin of a Lion* evokes the *Epic of Gilgamesh* intertextually, whose eponymous hero fails to achieve immortality because of his inability of staying awake several nights. Similarly, the oral narratives Patrick Lewis collects and conveys throughout the novel almost remain in darkness when he falls asleep at a critical moment. The "immortality" of these narratives and their silenced subjects is assured only by a listener who later keeps the speaker awake in the night, and the stories alive in a conversation that sees the light of day in a written text and its simulation of oral history.

Eluned Summers-Bremner pursues in "Reading Ondaatje's Poetry" a psychoana-lytic reading of Ondaatje's poetry based on Lacan's thought, highlighting occasions where nature and culture meet. Focusing on the volumes *Secular Love* and *The Man with Seven Toes*, Summers-Bremner explores how nature's troubled regions are navi-gated through the structural estrangement of looking for a name. In Lacanian terms, a proper name signals the contradiction of one's belonging to a biological or other kind of family, whence one's name often arises, and being a user or respondent of language, which produces meaning through its infringement or exceeding of its users' intentions, language being prototypically Other or alienating in this sense. Ondaatje's poetry en-gages nature continually, in a dynamically architectonic fashion, as a world at once em-bodied and infused with cultural and linguistic losses, a field of structural liminality whose correlatives are memory, love, and desire. The poetry's engagement of nature in the guise of a reading—as of a letter, code, or name—puts loss, as does psychoanalysis, in its proper context as the enabler which drives reading and writing subjectivity as a colloquy with these other terms.

In the final paper of the volume, Steven Tötösy de Zepetnek discusses in "On-daatje's *The English Patient* and Questions of History" the novel's "historical" back-ground followed by selected aspects of Anthony Minghella's and Michael Ondaatje's adaptation of the novel to film and the ensuing controversy after the release of the film. From the historical background Tötösy designates as the "Almásy theme" of the novel and the film, he relates Ondaatje's engagement of the protagonist—Hungarian and Cen-tral European László Almásy—to the notion of the Other as a historical and fictional concept. Tötösy argues that Ondaatje's particular rendition of the notion of the Other provides venues for a particular understanding of the historical background of the novel (the "real" Almásy) as well as its fictional presentation (the "Almásy theme"). The arti-cle also responds to readers' and viewers' and the media's interest in the novel's and the film's fictional protagonist and his "real" history.

The papers in the volume are followed by a selected bibliography of scholarship about Ondaatje's writings, a list of Ondaatje's works, and by the bioprofiles of contribu-tors to the volume. It is hoped that the work presented in the volume—with the objec-tive to render appreciation of both Ondaatje's writing and thought about his writing—will prove useful to readers, critics, and scholars alike.

—Steven Tötösy de Zepetnek
Winchester at Boston and
University of Halle-Wittenberg
March 2004

Exploring Transnational Identities
in Ondaatje's *Anil's Ghost*

Victoria Cook

Michael Ondaatje could be said to exemplify the type of transnational identity that provides the focus for this paper. Born to Dutch parents, in what was then Ceylon and is now Sri Lanka, his family ancestry has been described as a polyglot mixture of Dutch, English, Sinhalese, and Tamil; his paternal grandfather was a wealthy tea planter in Kegalle. At the age of ten, Ondaatje was sent to a public school, Dulwich College in London and at nineteen followed his older brother, Christopher, to Canada, where he took citizenship, went to university, married, and began his writing career. As a product of this somewhat "colonial" background, Ondaatje's position enables him to explore, in depth, the conflicts and contradictions of the type of identity that incorporates a colonial past and a post-colonial present.

Complex cultural backgrounds such as that of Ondaatje may be seen frequently to instigate a literature of dislocation and displacement. His latest novel, *Anil's Ghost,* provides an examination of identity reflective of the cultural clashes that are an inevitable consequence of such an interweaving of nationalities, histories, and border divisions. In his discussion in *The Location of Culture*, Homi Bhabha states that "the very concepts of homogenous national cultures . . . are in a profound process of redefinition . . . there is overwhelming evidence of a more transnational and translational sense of the hybridity of imagined communities" (5). Bhabha's work mirrors the cultural diaspora that is a result of the contemporary move towards internationalism. His reference to "imagined communities" echoes the title of Benedict Anderson's influential book of the same name, and opens up the possibility of "nation" and "nationalism" as being constructed modes of identification.

Ondaatje explores the notion of nationality as just such a construct and examines the roles played by syncretism and hybridity through the discourse of *Anil's Ghost*. This is a novel that moves beyond interpretation as a post-colonial literature of "resistance" to challenge traditional perceptions of "Self" and "Other," incorporating and transgressing boundaries in a way that invites interrogation from a transnational perspective. As long ago as 1916, the American intellectual Randolph Bourne wrote a piece entitled "Trans-National America." In it Bourne urges his readers to reject the "melting pot" metaphor, which he says will result in a culture that is "washed out into a tasteless, colorless fluid of uniformity" (1736): he envisages instead a world in which a variety of cultures coexist, "inextricably mingled, yet not homogeneous. They merge but they do not fuse" (1737). This approach—very similar to the concept of multiculturalism in Canada—defies ascription to any one national culture, thus rendering it applicable in the context of Michael Ondaatje's *Anil's Ghost*, in respect of the influence of acculturation on Ondaatje's construction of identity.

The central character of the novel, Anil Tissera, is a female forensic pathologist; born in Sri Lanka and educated in the West, she returns to the country for the first time in fifteen years to investigate "unknown extrajudicial executions" (18) on behalf of the United Nations—working with a local archaeologist Sarath Diyasena. Their discovery of a recently interred skeleton in an ancient burial ground points to a government killing, a fact that places them both in danger, but despite this Anil is determined to identify the skeleton she has nicknamed "Sailor." Closer examination of Ondaatje's construction of Anil Tissera raises a number of points, such as: she is Westernised; she has an adopted masculine name, which we learn she "bought" for herself from her brother; she is a scientist and spokesperson for the United Nations—a combination of factors which render her the antithesis of Gayatri Spivak's "subaltern woman." From a post-colonial perspective, hers is a voice that not only breaks the silence previously imposed by an Imperialist discourse, but also speaks for those silenced by the neo-colonialist ideology that Ondaatje exposes in his examination of the war in Sri Lanka. The language of transnationalism, which Ondaatje speaks through Anil, incorporates the contradictions and paradoxes that are displayed in human and cultural diversity.

Sophia A. McClennen suggests that "transnationalism renders the borders of a nation insignificant" (*The Dialectics of Exile* 25). Also Robert Gross considers there to be a need for "transnational thinking" (384) in a world where "intellectually, people cross borders as they please" (390) and national identity is no longer seen as single and unified: he describes a global culture that becomes "increasingly a transnational *mélange*" (392). In the character of Anil Tissera, Ondaatje inscribes a cultural formation that could, in many ways, be described as postmodern, in that she transgresses the conventional notions of identity and boundaries of gender and position. However, neither a postmodern, nor a postcolonial perspective or indeed the point of intersection between, is sufficient to encompass the multivalent integration of ideologies and cultures that form the fluid whole that is Anil Tissera. Hers is, more accurately, a transnational perspective; she does indeed cross and re-cross many ideological boundaries, but she does so as a migrant returning to her once colonial homeland. This is not to say that Anil is empty of any national identity at all, but rather that her multiculturalism demonstrates the possibility of a fundamental parity between various nationalist discourses, ascribing multivalency to each of the cultures she encounters. The examination of Ondaatje's work from a transnational approach uncovers some of the clashes that occur between national cultures and the ambivalence inherent in a multicultural identity such as that of Anil's.

The character of Anil Tissera occupies a "dis-located" position, in terms of her name, her nationality and her family; in problematizing notions of individual identity, Ondaatje explores the concept of "Self" as something constructed, and yet whole and realizable. In other words, Ondaatje reveals Anil's transnational nature as being a continually changing mixture of a variety of cultures, which incorporates, encompasses and contains various fragments in one unified being. He examines anxieties about the way in which we construct our own personal identity in terms of name, language and culture. Robert Kroetsch describes the problem of identity as "not so much that of knowing one's identity as it is that of how to relate that newly evolving identity to its inherited or 'given' names. And the first technique might be simply to hold those names in suspension, to let the identity speak itself out of a willed namelessness" ("No" 51). For Ondaatje, it appears that it is possible, indeed necessary, to move beyond fixed expressions of identification in order to perceive of identity in terms of a process of construction. Frank Schulze-Engler speaks of "a veritable maze of globalized spaces in-between— not between the 'West' and 'the rest', however, but between innumerable intertwined histories that—at one stage or another—have all been caught up in modernity and yet have produced a unique reality of their own" ("Changing" 13). Ondaatje focuses in his work on the complications that arise from just such a multicultural reality, exposing the gaps, but also providing structures of contact and exchange that confront the interwoven nature of an increasingly syncretized and hybridized global community. His voice is one of those involved in re-defining the boundaries, speaking from beyond preconceptions of "the Other" and "writing back" to "the West," and reconfiguring the "postcolonial" perspective into one of "transnationalism." *Anil's Ghost* provides a forum for the expression of a range of cultural identities—one in which the postcolonial voice does not simply speak from the margins, but is represented as an integrated component of a transnational identity.

Kroetsch suggests that "it is possible that the old obsessive notion of identity, of ego, is itself a spent fiction" ("Unhiding" 63), and for Ondaatje this does indeed appear to be so. He calls into question the possibility of a definitive view of identity or identification, and denies the fixity of identity that is inscribed in the neo-colonial action of naming. As Stuart Hall points out, "identity is a process, identity is split. Identity is not a fixed point but an ambivalent point" (16). For Ondaatje identity—either personal or public, individual or national—is always provisional and shifting; his work continually crosses and re-crosses the boundaries between real and fictional identification.

The characters of *Anil's Ghost* are often placed between these lines of demarcation in liminal zones of namelessness and placelessness, becoming situated paradoxically by their position as "dis-located." Clearly, names and namelessness are central to Ondaatje's problematizing of identity: he points out in the acknowledgements section of his semi-autobiographical work, *Running in the Family,* that the use of names "may give an air of authenticity" (206). In other words, names are capable of providing verification; they have the power to distinguish, substantiate and confirm, and above all they confer identity and establish identification. To be named, therefore, is to belong, to be located: Rocio Davis comments that "not to know and belong to a family or have a role in history is to be denied the very basis of identity" (267). Ondaatje confronts this denial of the foundations of identity when he examines the plight of 'the disappeared' through the text of *Anil's Ghost*. Anil feels that by attempting to establish the identity of the skeleton "Sailor" and find the family to whom he belongs, she will be locating all those who Sailor represents: "who was this skeleton? ... This representative of all those lost voices. To give him a name would name the rest" (56). In this sense to be nameless is, indeed, to be without an identity, a "lost voice" that must be "called" back into existence. "Sailor" is representative of all who cannot name themselves and who rely on others to locate them, or call them into being. Some of the implications of naming in relation to identity are fore grounded in Anil's defiant act of self-naming. Anil was not the name given to her by her parents, but one that she acquired for herself from her brother:

> She had been given two entirely inappropriate names and very early began to
> desire Anil which was her brother's unused second name. She had tried to buy
> it from him when she was twelve years old, offering to support him in all fam-
> ily arguments. He would not commit himself to the trade though he knew she
> wanted the name more than anything else.... Finally the siblings worked out a
> trade between them.... After that she allowed no other first names on her
> passports or school reports or application forms. Later when she recalled her
> childhood, it was the hunger of not having that name and the joy of getting it
> that she remembered most. Everything about the name pleased her, its slim,
> stripped-down quality, its feminine air, even though it was considered a male
> name. Twenty years later she felt the same about it. She'd hunted down the de-
> sired name like a specific lover she had seen and wanted, tempted by nothing
> else along the way. (67–68)

For Ondaatje, names and identities are not fixed entities, but cultural and ideological constructions. Through choosing a new name for herself, Anil takes on a new identity; she becomes a "stranger" to her past "self"—to the person she was before she became "Anil." We are not told the name she was known by for the first twelve years of her life. In fact, prior to becoming Anil, she remains un-identified; missing a name, she is akin to the nameless skeleton "Sailor." In acquiring her name Anil ruptures the boundary between "Self" and "Other." She does not merely take on a new mask or disguise, but is recreated, defining herself through the trade with her brother. It is significant that Anil does not choose a name at random; rather she desires one that she already has a relationship with, one that belongs both to her brother and to the grandfather she has never known. Anil's gesture is not only one that asserts her independence, but it is also a liberating and self-creating action that affirms her identification with her ancestry, and assimilates her origins into her new persona. Furthermore, it demonstrates a syncreticity and hybridity that is involved in the construction of identity, and is revealed through a transnational examination of this exploration of naming. From a transnational perspective Ondaatje constructs Anil's personal identity as one that defines the individual in terms of a "state" of "self-hood"; thus the private persona stands as a figurative representation of nation, and as such individual identity is subject to the effects of transnationalism.

In the struggle to gain her chosen identity, Anil trades that which she possesses, confirming that there is a price in the liberation from "other" into "self-hood." However, this deal is negotiated and agreed by both parties; her brother gains "one hundred saved rupees, a pen set he had been eyeing for some time, a tin of fifty Gold Leaf cigarettes she had found, and a sexual favor he had demanded in the last hours of the impasse" (68). It is clear from this quotation that this exploration of identity through the acquisition of a name has other complex elements of transgression; for example, there are indications of incest, and the challenging of constructions of gender. Anil, after all, "was considered a male name" (68) and perhaps reflects a "masculine" side to her identity that is revealed further in her choice of a career as a forensic scientist, one that is also seen as predominantly masculine. Anne McClintock suggests that in imperial terms naming is a "male prerogative" (26), and that in colonial discourse "the world is feminized and spatially spread for male exploration...explorers called unknown lands 'virgin' territory" (23–24): she points out that by "naming 'new' lands, male imperials mark them as their own" (29). As such, Ondaatje blurs the boundaries of gender in his construction of the character of Anil Tissera; by naming herself, she claims the territory of her identity, her own "state" of self-hood, in what can be construed as not only a neo-colonial, but also a gendered, masculine, action.

Anil abjures the position of Spivak's gendered subaltern through her rejection of an imposed cultural identity and the traditional role of the colonial female. Instead she claims a syncretic gender construction that assumes both male and female traits, and is transnational in nature, in that her individual "state" includes characteristics from areas that are traditionally constructed as *either* masculine *or* feminine. Thus, the concept of Anil's gendered self is one that is multiple, contradictory and fragmented in nature: in the novel, Anil makes it a point to "distinguish female and male traits as clearly as possible" (137) in her work; she loves "being one of the boys" (147) and yet also appreciates that being a woman makes her "better at dealing with calamity in professional work than men" (137). In terms of gender, Ondaatje bestows on Anil "the peculiar freedoms of ambiguity rather than the fixity of one identity" (McClintock 174). This is reflected in the fact that, in the business deal to secure the purchase of her name, Anil's behavior is predominantly stereotypically masculine, and yet part of the price she pays is a "sexual favor" that her brother demands. This act of prostitution on Anil's part serves to underline her subordinate female status prior to gaining her name, but it also reveals an ancient form of feminist resistance to patriarchal control: by bartering her sexual services for profit (her desired name), Anil gains a measure of economic power and independence.

As I mentioned earlier, Ondaatje posits here the possibility of an incestuous relationship between brother and sister, one which may be usefully examined from the perspective of transnationalism. In order to do this, it is necessary to first consider the relationship between nation and gender. McClintock points out that the etymology of the word "nation" reveals it as stemming from *natio:* to be born, and that discussion regarding nations frequently centers on the semantic field of the familial and the domestic. She describes how we often refer to our "homeland" and speak of nations in terms of "motherlands" or "fatherlands," we say that foreigners "adopt" a new country and in Britain matters to do with immigration are dealt with by the "Home Office" (357). Paul Gilroy also discusses how "gender differences" are "extremely important in nation-building"; in fact he says, "it can be a nation only if the correct version of gender hierarchy has been established" (127). Anil can be seen to have adopted both male and female traits and, therefore, in her construction of a transnational identity, to incorporate the possibilities of both "motherland" and "fatherland" and their colonial offspring. Taking the trope of nation as familial and gendered one step further, Gilroy examines the relationship between "diaspora" and "masculinism" and points out that there is a "close etymological relationship between the word diaspora and the word sperm" (126). However, he also states that the alternative "family term" for "diaspora" is the word "spore," which allows for an "asexual" method of reproduction, and he confirms that "diaspora can be used to conjure up both" (127). In the gendered "family" of nation, then, the reproductive possibilities of diaspora may be seen to inseminate nation with nation to produce a hybridized cultural identity; or to reproduce asexually, through a process of fission from the originating culture, which results in the syncretism that is an essential part of transnationalism. The incestuous act between Anil and her brother may therefore be seen in the light of the conception of a new transnational identity, one that is not prohibited from inter-relationship by any barrier or taboo.

Further, Gayle Rubin argues that according to the work of Lévi-Strauss, the prohibition of incest ensures that sisters, daughters and mothers must be given in marriage, and thus creates a "wide network of relations" (173), a group of people who are connected together by a "kinship structure" (174): moreover as a result, "the incest taboo and the results of its application constitute the origin of culture, and is a prerequisite of culture" (176). Therefore she concludes that in order to succeed, "the feminist program must include a task even more onerous than the extermination of men; it must attempt to get rid of culture and substitute some entirely new phenomena on the face of the earth" (176). As Rubin concedes herself, it is neither probable nor feasible that there will be an eradication of culture (or indeed of either men or women); however, Ondaatje demonstrates the possibility of—if not removing—at least transcending or breaching the divisions and boundaries between cultures. He does this by establishing the notion of identity as a process that involves continual cultural syncretism and hybridity, and by substituting the outmoded idea of a fixed cultural identity with the emerging concept of one that is truly transnational. The cultural anthropologist David Schneider, in his book *American Kinship*, argues that in American culture, any sexual act outside of the husband-wife relationship is defined as "morally, and in some cases, legally, wrong"; he states that "between blood relatives such an act is "incest and prohibited" (38). Although this argument relates specifically to "Western" American culture, it is applicable here in that Anil's transnational identity incorporates her complicity with the West. By making an incestuous act a prerequisite for the purchase of Anil's name, Ondaatje indicates that the origination of her transnationalism is the breaking of a taboo; to become transnational involves the transgression of the boundaries that differentiate between us and them, insider and outsider, national and international.

Ramón Gutiérrez suggests that to have American nationality one must either be "born into the nation (the order of nature)" or enter it "through a legal process (the order of law) and become citizens through a process we call 'naturalisation'" he confirms that "nature and law thus create citizens" (255). Ondaatje demonstrates that a transnational identity, such as that of Anil Tissera's, is not created through either "nature" or "law" but comes into being outside of the accepted order that is required for belonging to a single nationality. In order to gain transnational "citizenship" Anil moves beyond the traditional modes of national identification. As a "Trans-national" then, Anil provides a figurative representation of the feminized nature of the land as an object of desire, the "earth mother"; and in taking possession of a male name she also subsumes something of the patriarchal role: "she'd hunted down the desired name like a specific lover she had seen and wanted, tempted by nothing else along the way" (68). In his book of poetry, *Handwriting*, Ondaatje describes "the way someone's name holds terraces of character, contains all of our adventures together" (55). Anil's name, her demand to define herself within and through that name, to name herself, reflects this poetic representation; viewed from a transnational notion of syncretism, her name "holds" her character. In this context it is significant that Anil has a fascination with names: her favorite rock star is "The Artist Formerly Known As…" (37), a celebrity who replaced his name with a symbol; and her questioning of her lover, Cullis, reveals that his middle name is Biggles, "as in *Biggles Flies East* and *Biggles Wets His Bed?*" (37).

These two book titles, one genuine and one obviously fictitious, may be seen as indicative of some of Cullis's characteristics; the true title, *Biggles Flies East,* alludes to Cullis's involvement with Anil, while the invented one not only connotes him as being false and untruthful in nature, but also evokes a sense of childishness and insecurity. Here Ondaatje's problematizing of identity through naming takes on a playful irony in terms of a postcolonial, or more particularly a transnational perspective. "Anil had courted foreignness" (54) both literally and figuratively in her affair with Cullis Biggles Wright, named (as Anil points out) after the central protagonist "Biggles" from the series of books by Captain W. E. Johns: these are boys' adventure stories which were very popular in the early part of the twentieth century.

Cullis's namesake "Biggles" is a stereotypical representation of an English pilot and hero who fights for his country in the First World War: Anil's association with Cullis therefore represents her ambivalent relationship with the West, in that she conducts a relationship with him and appreciates some of his qualities, but at the same time she refuses to be controlled or contained by him. Ironically it is Anil who constructs her own identity in the rejection of her original name and the appropriation of her new one; Cullis, on the other hand, accepts the identity given to him by his parents—he is named Biggles as his "dad grew up on his books" (37). Ondaatje's reversal of the roles of colonizer and colonized is one that demonstrates the way in which power and control are no longer necessarily negotiated in line with traditional hierarchies and systems of authority. Anil and Cullis can be seen, therefore, to form a transnational relationship, which bears further analysis in that it spans the cultural delineation between East and West. Ondaatje empowers Anil through a transnational identity that encompasses both Western order and Eastern disorder; her Western proclivity towards naming and appropriation, and Eastern passion and impulsiveness leave her free to plunder Cullis both physically and emotionally. Cullis's lack of freedom is implied in the "carefulness" and worry that he wears as protective clothing which Anil attempts to "strip off" and "unbuckle" (263–64). The car in which he sits and his marriage, stand as metaphors for the constraints imposed on Cullis by a fixed cultural identity, boundaries that Anil's transnationalism has no difficulty in transgressing. In the self-construction of her identity, Anil is complicit, then, in allowing herself to be "colonized" by Western culture. However, in exploring the effect of acculturation on individual identity, Ondaatje exposes some of the dichotomies between Eastern and Western cultures in the conflicts that Anil experiences. Anil's brief, unsuccessful marriage to a Sri Lankan whilst studying in England is a significant episode in this context. Her husband is a controlling and jealous character: "at first this presented itself as sexual jealousy, then she saw it as an attempt to limit her research and studies. It was the first handcuff of marriage, and it almost buried her" (144). Anil's treatment of her marriage "as something illicit that deeply embarrassed her" (144) is paralleled in her subjugation of her Eastern cultural identity in favor of the West. However, Ondaatje highlights acculturation as being an evolutionary process, rather than a product, in Anil's subsequent return to Sri Lanka. It is notable that Anil's husband remains nameless throughout the narrative and after the marriage is over Anil "would never say his name out loud" (144). By refusing to name her husband, Anil erases him from the cartography of her life in an action reminiscent of the imperial map-makers that Ondaatje refers to in his mimetic reproduction of the *National Atlas of Sri Lanka* (39). The "extract" from the Atlas concludes *"There are pages of isobars and altitudes. There are no city names . . . There are no river names. No depiction of human life"* (40–41). Here Ondaatje exposes the map as an usurpative imperialist tool, which may name "a territory into existence while simultaneously making the native population invisible" (Renger 112): the suggestion being that naming, like mapping, is an act of "cognitive appropriation" that has "never been innocent" (Jacobs 4). The effacement of her husband contrasts strongly with Anil's desire to name the skeleton of the Sri Lankan victim that she calls "Sailor." Thus in the action of naming, in Anil's emulation of imperial methods of control, Ondaatje demonstrates the construction of an individual's transnational identity as being one of transgression, process, and fluidity.

In conclusion, through his novel *Anil's Ghost*, Ondaatje problematizes notions of either individual or national identity as being fixed and immutable, adopting instead a perspective that considers such boundaries as both flexible and permeable. It is possible to conclude that Ondaatje offers a tri-phasic model of the process of acculturation, as examined through the construction of Anil Tissera's personal and cultural identity. Anil is initially dependent upon the cultural and individual identity given to her by her parents; however, she moves into an independent phase signaled by her desire for another name and her adoption of a different culture. Finally, Anil moves into the third phase of interdependency, when she returns to Sri Lanka developing a multicultural perspective that is transnational rather than global or universal in its construction.

WORKS CITED

Anderson, Benedict. *Imagined Communities: Reflections on the Origin and Spread of Nationalism.* London: Verso, 1995.

Bhabha, Homi K. *The Location of Culture.* London: Routledge, 1994.

Bourne, Randolph. "Trans-National America." 1916. *The Heath Anthology of American Literature.* Ed. Paul Lauter. New York: Houghton Mifflin, 1998. Vol. 2, 1732–43.

Gilroy, Paul. *Between Camps: Nations, Cultures and the Allure of Race.* London: Allen Lane, The Penguin Press, 2000.

Gross, Robert A. "The Transnational Turn: Rediscovering American Studies in a Wider World." *Journal of American Studies* 34.3 (2000): 373–93.

Gutiérrez, Ramón. "The Erotic Zone: Sexual Transgression on the U.S.-Mexican Border." *Mapping Multiculturalism.* Ed. Avery Gordon and Christopher Newfield. Minneapolis: U of Minnesota P, 1997. 253–62.

Hall, Stuart. "Ethnicity: Identity and Difference." *Radical America* 23.4 (1991): 9–20.

Jacobs, J.U. "Exploring, Mapping and Naming in Postcolonial Fiction: Michael Ondaatje's *The English Patient.*" *Nomina Africa: Journal of the Names Society of Southern Africa* 8.2 (1994): 1–12.

Kroetsch, Robert. "The Canadian Writer and the American Literary Tradition." *The Lovely Treachery of Words: Essays Selected and New.* By Robert Kroetsch. Toronto: Oxford UP, 1989. 53–57.

Kroetsch, Robert. *The Lovely Treachery of Words: Essays Selected and New.* Toronto: Oxford UP, 1989.

Kroetsch, Robert. "No Name Is My Name." *The Lovely Treachery of Words: Essays Selected and New.* By Robert Kroetsch. Toronto: Oxford UP, 1989. 41–52.

Kroetsch, Robert. "Unhiding the Hidden." *The Lovely Treachery of Words: Essays Selected and New.* By Robert Kroetsch. Toronto: Oxford UP, 1989. 58–63.

McClennen, Sophia A. *The Dialectics of Exile: Nation, Time, Language, and Space in Hispanic Literatures.* West Lafayette: Purdue UP, 2004.

McClintock, Anne. *Imperial Leather: Race, Gender and Sexuality in the Colonial Contest.* London: Routledge, 1995.

Ondaatje, Michael. *Anil's Ghost.* London: Bloomsbury, 2000.

Ondaatje, Michael. *Handwriting.* London: Bloomsbury, 1998.

Ondaatje, Michael. *Running in the Family.* London: Macmillan, 1984.

Renger, Nicola. "Cartography, Historiography, and Identity in Michael Ondaatje's *The English Patient.*" *Beings in Transit: Traveling, Migration, Dislocation.* Ed. Liselotte Glage. Amsterdam: Rodopi, 2000. 111–24.

Rubin, Gayle. "The Traffic in Women: Notes on the 'Political Economy' of Sex." *Toward an Anthropology of Women*. Ed. Rayna R. Reiter. New York: Monthly Review P, 1975. 157–210.

Schneider, David M. *American Kinship: A Cultural Account*. Chicago: U of Chicago P, 1968.

Schulze-Engler, Frank. "Changing Spaces: Globalisation, Migration, and the Post-Colonial Transition." *Borderlands: Negotiating Boundaries in Post-Colonial Writing*. Ed. Monika Reif-Hülser. Amsterdam: Rodopi, 1999. 3–15.

Spivak, Gayatri Chakravorty. "Can the Subaltern Speak?" *Marxism and the Interpretation of Culture*. Ed. Cary Nelson and Lawrence Grossberg. London: Macmillan, 1988. 271–313.

Ondaatje's *The English Patient* and
Altered States of Narrative

Beverley Curran

In his discussion of translation, George Steiner recalls Saint Jerome's representation of that process as "meaning brought home captive by the translator" (Steiner 298). From both within and without, former European colonies have been seen as "translations" of a distant and idealized original whose standards have been transplanted and reduced to "imperfect copies, characterized by absence or imitation" (Brydon and Tiffin 57). In a search for origins, we will find not a source but absence, dispersal, and loss. In Australia, alongside the more potent legend of Ned Kelly is the story of Eliza Fraser, a "captivity narrative" of "first contact" operating as a key myth in the process of translating nationhood into being. Like that of Ned Kelly, the Eliza Fraser story inspired a series of paintings by the Australian modernist Sidney Nolan. Nolan's images, in turn, provoked the imagination of Sri Lankan Canadian writer Michael Ondaatje, who rewrote the story in his early long poem, *The Man with Seven Toes* (1969) inspired only by "the account in the paintings" (Barbour 220) and Colin MacInnes's succinct and rather snide version of that story that appears in the catalogue of the 1957 Whitechapel Gallery exhibition, Nolan's first major retrospective, and which Ondaatje includes as an afterword to his long poem:

> Mrs Fraser was a Scottish lady who was shipwrecked on what is now Fraser Island, off the Queensland Coast. She lived for 6 months among the aborigines, rapidly losing her clothes, until she was discovered by one Bracefell, a deserting convict who himself had hidden for 10 years among the primitive Australians. The lady asked the criminal to restore her to civilization, which he agreed to do if she would promise to intercede for his free pardon from the Governor. The bargain was sealed, and the couple set off inland. At first sight of European settlement, Mrs Fraser rounded on her benefactor and threatened to deliver him up to justice if he did not immediately decamp. Bracefell returned disillusioned to the hospitable bush, and Mrs Fraser's adventures aroused such admiring interest that on her return to Europe she was able to exhibit herself at 6d a showing in Hyde Park. (*The Man with Seven Toes* n.p.)

According to Kay Schaffer in her examination of the Eliza Fraser stories, gaps in that captivity narrative facilitate speculative supplements like the MacInnes version. There is an absence of verifiable data concerning both the characters and circumstances: there are no records of birth or death for Eliza Fraser—she may have been born in Ceylon—nor convincing evidence to confirm the details of the shipwreck, captivity, or rescue. What can be verified is that Fraser's "captivity" lasted six weeks rather than months, and that "the popular Queensland version of her rescue and sexual liaison during a lengthy trek back to Moreton Bay with the convict David Bracefell did not occur, although historians still speculate that Bracefell may have been involved as a helpmate to her official rescuer . . . and his 'contact' with Mrs Fraser may well have been sexual" (Schaffer 136).

In writing his long poem, Ondaatje was not interested in investigating the historical account of the Fraser story nor in explaining it to his readers: "It had to be brief and imagistic because the formal alternative was to write a long graphic introduction explaining the situation, setting, characters, and so on. All the geographical references in the book are probably wrong and I'm sure all Australians think that the book is geographically ridiculous, just as the people of the south-west might think *Billy the Kid* is" (Solecki 20). Just as "the cul-de-sacs within the sweep of history" (Ondaatje, *The English Patient* 119) were sought out by Herodotus in *The Histories*, MacInnes's modulated version of the Fraser story interests Ondaatje as "the supplementary to the main argument" (119), as do the obscured "historical" figures of Billy the Kid and Buddy Bolden, or the elusive desert topography of the American Southwest or the Sahara. *The English Patient*, I suggest, reconfigures radically the nebulous representation at the core of these narratives as a translator who exists in and as the dead centre of powerful cultural tensions. Whereas Douglas Barbour contends that for Ondaatje, the father appears as a writer, as a "kind of romantic artist [that] is a paradigm of all such figures one encounters in the poet's work" (76), including Billy the Kid and Bolden, it would seem that in *The English Patient*, creation is less a preoccupation than contradiction and the consequences of choice, and that the "romantic" figure of the father/artist is being re-read as a clandestine lover, a drug addict, or an eccentric translator, all figures with dependencies. Instead of the textual strategies of realist narrative to "maintain self-other relations of dominance" to establish authority, Ondaatje's application of translation to narrative in *The English Patient* means that, at the story's heart there is deferment, for a translation is never definitive, "a knowledge derived from displacement" (Clifford 53) and from multiple "sources." Ondaatje does not begin with historical accuracy or a character to write *The Man with Seven Toes*; from the dozen versions of Eliza Fraser's story, he takes Nolan's paintings and the deliberately skewed version by MacInnes. In *The English Patient*, the father or artist's sense of source, continuity, or authority are translated into a narrative which rejects the perverse captivity demanded of the lover and the translator by fidelity or by the tenets of realistic representation. If there are a hundred different images of Isaiah's face, the "English patient" is too damaged to be identified.

In "Traveling Theory," Edward Said outlines four stages of the transportation of ideas: first, a "point of origin, or what seems like one;" next, "a distance transversed, a passage through the pressure of various contexts" . . . followed by conditions of acceptance or resistance to the "transplanted" theory or idea, and finally, the transformation of the idea by its "new uses, its new position in a new time and space" (226–27). These four stages could just as easily be applied to the process of translation, and indeed, the translation is one way in which ideas travel. But alongside the movement of ideas over time or space, there are other considerations such as speed: the particular displacement and mobility of information and communications technology disturb and redefine the process of translation and how it is represented or understood. In this regard, it is interesting to locate the Eliza Fraser story at the dawn of the Victorian era in the 1830s and then to consider the seemingly unassailable position England would occupy over the next sixty years as a wealthy and confident nation with an extensive empire and remarkable record of cultural and scientific achievements.

However, by the 1880s, Britain was losing control of the industries and technologies that had been so instrumental in its progress, importing chemicals from Germany and calibrated tools from America. "The 'civilizing mission' of imperialism, so readily subscribed to earlier in the century, so inspiring to thousands of idealistic best and brightest colonial administrator-missionaries, had become a cynical exercise in trade and despotism" (Blaise 226). The "dreadful progress" was subverted in art, culminating in the "touchstone literary confirmation" of the derangement of temporal order in Joseph Conrad's *The Secret Agent*, where, based on an actual incident which took place in 1894, anarchists attempt to terrorize the complacency of mercantile British society by blowing up the Greenwich Observatory. The touchstone text for this particular paper is Ondaatje's *The English Patient*, which uses sex, drugs, and translation to derange both time and space in an extreme complication of the captivity narrative, and to reconfigure the role of the artist as a translator in an attempt to dislocate both the "false rhapsody of art" (Ondaatje, *The English Patient* 241) and its stern authority. Resisting the established rules of personal, national, or literary relationships can be seen less as betrayal than "the desire of another life" (239), a notion in keeping with Said's "Traveling Theory Reconsidered" essay, in which the sense of remedy or reconciliation implied in the fourth stage of theoretical travel in the earlier essay assumes a more transgressive posture: the translation or "transformation" of an idea by new uses now "flames out [and] restates and reaffirms its own inherent tensions by moving to another site" (438).

Both the captivity narrative and the translation are genres linked to colonialism and national identity, "used in all kinds of ways to perpetuate the superiority of some cultures over another" (Bassnett and Trivedi 17). They also share an interesting publishing history. By the end of the eighteenth century, English translations, particularly of Eastern erotica and gothic novels, had gained enough prestige and commercial credibility to create a demand for forged translations. While literature moved toward realism, translation moved away. Translators "did not hesitate to change titles, delete entire pages and introduce new elements with a view to pleasing the reader and conforming to sensibilities that were dominant at the time" (Delisle and Woodsworth 212). At the same time, however, pseudo-translations of Eastern erotica attempted to appear as authentic academic studies through fictitious footnotes, glosses and bibliographies in order to camouflage their sexual content as scientific research (see Schick 182). In fact, imitation became more important and more attractive than the importation of actual foreign views or values, or the cachet of an original text.

There was a similar hunger for captivity narratives. About seven hundred of them were published in America between 1682 and 1800 (Schaffer 49) and by the late eighteenth century, pseudo-captivity narratives were appearing in England. Captivity narratives, too, had concerns about fidelity; a version of Mrs Fraser's captivity was promoted, for example, as a "plain, unvarnished tale, exaggerating nothing, but recording truly and faithfully the particulars" of her ordeal (Schaffer 53–56). While pseudo-translation assumed the guise of scholarship, the pseudo-captivity narratives borrowed stylistic devices from the sentimental novel until "the 'truth'-effects of the genre were so challenged by melodramatic embellishments, exaggerations and improbabilities, as well as frequent plagiarism, rhetorical and illustrated borrowings from one event to another, that disbelief was the likely result of publication" (Schaffer 49). While there were claims to historical accuracy in prefaces that "would feed the ethnographic interest of scientists and historians" (Schaffer 57), there was also a facetious tone which assured readers that along with information there would be (sexual) excitement. In other words, the popularity of accounts of captivity narratives and translations of Eastern erotica in the nineteenth century are evidence that the sexual metaphors of travel and imperial conquest can probably not be overstated.

Running alongside nineteenth-century versions of these genres were accounts of natural science and geographical exploration, which eliminated all emotion from their accounts. This was the legacy of a Victorian colonialism in which, as Clark Blaise describes it in *Time Lord*, "nature was only to be studied, not to be worshiped" (119) and even sermons were "crafted documents, listened to and judged not on their emotional content, but on their intellectual and moral merit" (119–20). This detached tone, for example, was used in accounts prepared for the Royal Geographical Society, and, in Ondaatje's novel set decades later, in the accounts of their desert explorations written by Count Ladislaus de Almásy and Madox. Nevertheless, these men each carried a translation, Herodotus's *The Histories* and Tolstoy's *Anna Karenina*, respectively, as a literary talisman that countered and informed the disembodied voice of the explorer.

Perhaps it is his choice of talisman that allows Madox to suspect not only Almásy's love and adulterous relationship with Katharine Clifton, in spite of his friend's attempts at camouflage, but also to recognize the larger dangers of that liaison. While for Almásy and Catharine, "there was only one person to avoid being seen by" (237), namely Catharine's husband, Geoffrey, Madox, through his "continual rereading [of Tolstoy's] story of romance and deceit" (237) knew the complexity and extent of the web in which the two lovers had been caught: "Geoffrey Clifton was a man embedded in the English machine. He had a family genealogy going back to Canute. The machine would not necessarily have revealed to Clifton, married only eighteen months, his wife's infidelity, but it began to encircle the fault, the disease in the system. It knew every move ... from the first day of the awkward touch in the porte cochère of the Semiramis Hotel" (237). This strange translation of a captivity narrative extends far beyond the rules of fidelity demanded by marriage and "the boulder," Almásy and Katharine "had placed between themselves for some social law neither had believed in" (171), to reveal the tense connection between history and contingency despite the fact that there is no mention of "adultery in the minutes of the Geographical Society"; and that the site of lovemaking "never appears in the detailed reports which chartered every knoll and every incident of history" 145). Obsessed with Katharine while writing his book, "unable to remove her body from the page" (235), Almásy nevertheless resists dedicating the monograph "to her, to her voice, to her body" (235), choosing instead a king. And yet, in his commonplace book, it was his own identity that he would obscure: "He bought pale brown cigarette papers and glued them into sections of *The Histories* that recorded wars that were of no interest to him. He wrote down all her arguments against him. Glued into the book—giving him only the voice of the watcher, the listener, the 'he'" (172). All the texts they read, too, in one way or another, contain echoes of their lives.

It was "the habit of social graces" (97) that prevented Katharine from admitting her love for Almásy to her husband or anyone else. The "English" patient did not want to admit his emotion and made up for it with an excessive politeness that was rude. In the Villa San Girolamo, another unlikely love was enacted in even less certain terms than that in the desert. The tender love between the mad, young, sad Hana for the "English" patient is one of psychic survival and somatic care. As a nurse, her coping mechanism for deep melancholy—the war, the death of soldiers, the loss of her father and her unborn child—was reductive: her possessions were minimal; she used the same name ("Buddy") to address everyone, including herself. She focuses her attentions on caring for the English patient and the only way that he can get Hana to communicate is to ask her to read to him. Hana's intimacy with the English patient is indeed one sustained by sharing books and administering morphine.

In *The Man with Seven Toes*, an intimacy is established tentatively between the lady and the convict who guides her through a terrible geography of swamp and desert to "the city" (19). It is a drugged landscape with "night birds / who clawed the barks of trees / sucking out cocaine, so one could catch them / staggering in the sand at dawn / their nerves clogged and rotted with drug / feathers caked with a red vomit" (28). This "ridiculous" desert geography of the poem was the site of a "love story" remembered later by an anonymous "lady" in the final poem as she sleeps in the Royal Hotel, "her burnt arms and thighs/ soaking the cold of the sheets" (41), recalling the convict's mouth as "a collyrium that licked burnt eyes" (40). The historical character of Eliza Fraser has lost her name and become "she" or "me" in that long poem; Bracefell had found a new one (Potter). In *The English Patient*, Almásy's intimate geography has been burnt to anonymity, recalling the desert in his own seared somatic state and through his memory, as he mediates between the nurse, thief, and sapper that share the provisional space of the abandoned Tuscan villa in the waning days of the Second World War. And it is the desert evoked by morphine and memory, a place rather than a time or an image, that holds the secrets of the titular English patient's identity in Ondaatje's novel, and never really relinquishes them.

The English patient is a reservoir of information and a pool of memory, "a translated subject, a liminal figure, not someone who has 'gone native' . . . but someone whose identity has become terminally displaced through cross cultural experience" (Jay 421); and his stories of the desert are fragments of an immense and fluid interweave of narrative whose pieces no longer fit snugly together in an assured and sturdy way. This is a sabotaged narrative; body parts of the text are missing. Thus a subtle echo of earlier moments in the history of conquest and contact are heard in the opening pages of the novel when the anonymous English patient recites his stories: "They found my body and made me a boat of sticks and dragged me across the desert . . . The Bedouin knew about fire. They knew about planes that since 1939 had been falling out of the sky . . . They could recognize the drone of a wounded plane, they knew how to pick their way through such shipwrecks" (5).

The novel also reminds us that the desert experienced an averting of Western eyes for hundreds of years after Herodotus, from 425 BC to the beginning of the twentieth century: "The nineteenth century was an age of river seekers. And then in the 1920s there is a sweet postscript history on this pocket of earth, made mostly by privately funded expeditions and followed by modest lectures given at the Geographical Society in London" (133). Love and war and endless emotion charge the explorations, but in the name of scientific objectivity, these are erased in the process of writing, much in the way that "the truth of lived communal (or personal) experience has often been totally sublimated in official narratives, institutions, and ideologies" (Said, "Opponents, Audiences" 147), or technology airbrushed out of the wilderness in order to differentiate between the corruption of Civilization and the purity of Nature. Almásy entered the Libyan Desert as an explorer in 1930 and gradually become nationless, nameless. For him, the desert "could not be claimed or owned—it was a piece of cloth carried by winds, never held down by stones, and given a hundred shifting names long before Canterbury existed, long before battles and treaties quilted Europe and the East" (138–39). As an explorer, he thought he was acting alone, or in concert with a group of men who cared only for the land, although one wanted a sand dune named after him, another a village. In the reports delivered to the Royal Geographic Society, "all human and financial behaviour [lay] on the far side of the issue being discussed—which [was] the earth's surface and its 'interesting geographical problems'" (134). But his eye had been fooled by the pseudo authority of the West, for even as Almásy registered "the brightness and faith and colour" (261) of a desert illuminated by the "communal book of moonlight" (261), he only belatedly realized that "the ends of the earth are never the points on the map that colonists push against, enlarging their sphere of influence. On one side servants and slaves and tides of power and correspondence with the Geographical Society. On the other the first step by a white man across a great river, the first sight (by a white eye) of a mountain that has been there forever" (141).

The English patient knew the desert before he had ever been there, "knew when Alexander had traversed it in an earlier age, for this cause or that greed" (18). The act of reading had served as a means of transport to places never seen. In the wake of his seduction in and by the desert, the attraction to that geography is in the re-reading, turning the pages backwards and "retreat[ing] from the grand story . . . stumbl[ing] accidentally upon a luxury, one of those underground pools where we can sit still. Those moments, those few pages in a book we can go back and forth over" (Ondaatje, *Skin of a Lion* 148); in the English patient's case, the story of his illicit love for a married woman. But like a book, the desert is also "crowded with the world" (*The English Patient* 285), and with the aid of books in code to guide spies and armies across it, the desert has been "raped by war and shelled as if it were just sand" (257). Caravaggio, the thief, sums it up: "The trouble with us is we are all where we shouldn't be" (122). Europe is fighting wars in the "vast and silent pocket[s]" (134) of the Libyan Desert; Kip, a Sikh, is in Italy, dismantling German bombs and fighting English wars.

Kirpal Singh, or Kip, is aligned with the English patient through a mutual affinity for machines and affection for Hana. In his own mind, the Indian sapper, whose own name has been erased and individual identity rendered invisible by his brown skin, has aligned the English patient with his teacher, Lord Suffolk: "He was most comfortable with men who had the abstract madness of autodidacts, like his mentor, Lord Suffolk, like the English patient" (111). Lord Suffolk, who had taken Kip under his wing in order to train him as a sapper, was a font of eclectic local knowledge and he introduced "the customs of England to the young Sikh as if it was a recently discovered culture" (184). Prior to his wartime preoccupation with dismantling bombs, Lord Suffolk's "passion" had been "the study of *Lorna Doone* and how authentic the novel was historically and geographically" (185). His interest in authenticity and authority marks a cleavage in the similarity between him and the English patient. Unlike Katharine, who loved words for their clarity and reason, Almásy, although a reader and polyglot, "thought words bent emotions like sticks in water" (238). Clarity was something more valued by Hana. Although she had elected to have no interest in anything but the present, she grounded herself in relationships of her personal past: "In her life there was her mother Alice her father Patrick her stepmother Clara and Caravaggio. She had . . . admitted these names to Kip as if they were her credentials, her dowry. They were faultless and needed no discussion. She used them like authorities in a book she could refer to on the right way to boil an egg, or the correct way to slip garlic into a lamb. They were not to be questioned"(268).

And indeed this is also the way that Kirpal Singh had thought of "British civilization," something certain down to the smallest detail of haberdashery. Standing over the "English" patient in the wake of news of the bombing of Hiroshima, condensing all of England into the symbol of the burnt body lying on the bed, Kip speaks of his conversion by the missionary rules and traditions that replaced those of his own country: "Your fragile white island that with customs and manners and books and prefects and reason somehow converted the rest of the world. You stood for precise behaviour. I knew if I lifted a teacup with the wrong finger I'd be banished. If I tied the wrong kind of knot in a tie I was out. Was it just ships that gave you such power? Was it, as my brother said, because you had the histories and printing presses?" (283). Kip's explosive reaction to the bomb is a surprise to all, not just because he has already implicitly questioned the national identity of Almásy by noticing that the way the patient sucks condensed milk is not the way the British do. Kip has operated, like the English patient in the "slipstream," understanding the power of invisibility; wanting "not to belong to anyone" (139). Thus he had been patient with his brother's defiance of British rule, and took no offence at the treatment he himself had received as a recruit in the British army.

Kip chooses the vantage point of the periphery—from his cold professional position, "everything . . . apart from danger, was periphery" (126)—where he can see the relationship between things, but not be sucked into responsibility. While he dismantles bombs effortlessly in the realm of straightforward choices, he is dismayed to find himself being drawn into love. During the war, the sapper had found statues to sleep with, grieving stone angels to watch over him: "he had giving his trust only to a race of stones" (104). But Hana had drawn him inside something "like a painting" (104), and it "annoyed" him that, by staying with him when he had defused a bomb in the garden, she had "made him owe her something. Making him feel in retrospect responsible for her" (104). His youth lets her sleep with him and engage in tender games, but "his body allows nothing to enter him that comes from another world. A boy in love who will not eat the food she gathers" (126), preserving the "hardness and clarity" of gem cutters" (110). Stone angels and gem cutters bring to mind the thoughts of Walter Benjamin and his melancholy gaze and "gesture of attentiveness" which "fundamentally and resolutely resists incorporating the other" (Hanssen 162).

There are other echoes of Walter Benjamin in this novel, as well. The "English" patient Almásy lies dying in a bed in a ruined villa in Tuscany whose name, Villa San Girolamo, summons thoughts of Girolamo Savonarola and his "bonfire of the vanities." The room in which he lies fools the patient—he thinks it is one in the Villa Bruscoli—but evokes Savonarola in association with Poliziano, the Renaissance translator of Homer and a poet whose verse inspired paintings by Botticelli and Leonardo da Vinci. The Renaissance seems, like Hana's adolescence, "a place rather than a time" (90), the resonance of its bold turn from the limited but certain dogmas of the medieval through a re-reading of Plato and other classical works to a "natural" inquiry into the study of man and the universe. This search for another origin recalls Benjamin's interest in "natural history," but moving in another direction, namely, towards an "*Ursprung* or 'primal leap' . . . no longer of the order of the Greek *arche*, the foundation of Western epistemology and ontology" (Hanssen 4) and his project for a new historiography and reappraisal of idealism through a theory of allegory that would de-limit "the human subject through a reading of the figures of stones, animals, and angels" (4). Benjamin was interested in the debris of history, rather than its skeleton, as Hanssen describes it, and chose allegory as a way to expose "the incontrovertible historicity that defines all human acts of signification" (15), and translation as the operation by which "the agent or power that symbolized" was turned into "the symbolized by hitting on the stratum of language that at once erased meaning, intention, communication" (35). The painted angels of the Renaissance haunt Ondaatje's novel with their sad beauty, but hovering too is the modernist image of Paul Klee's *Angelus Novus*, the angel of history, whose face "is turned toward the past. Where we perceive a chain of events, he sees one single catastrophe which keeps piling wreckage upon wreckage and hurls it in front of his feet" (Benjamin, "Theses" 259). It is a figure which Ondaatje evokes in his description of Almásy carrying Katharine from the Cave of Swimmers, "her body facing back, over my shoulder" (171), the way he had held her in his arms when they had been lovers, "her arms out, fingers like starfish" (171).

Nolan's *Woman in Mangroves*, inspired by the rock art of Aboriginal artists, might well be in there, too, at least in the modernist sensibility it asserts in exploring its subject from a multiple of perspectives. In the 1957 painting, the figure of Mrs Fraser is "splayed across a rock...as the convict emerges from the cave" (MacInnes, qtd in Schaffer 148). MacInnes's recapitulation of the Fraser captivity narrative portrays Eliza Fraser as betraying the convict who had saved her, sending him back into the bush. This is ignored in Ondaatje's long poem, as is "the paintings political theme of betrayal" (Barbour 34). But the theme is of importance in *The English Patient*, tied to issues of personal identity and national allegiance, as well as translation. It is pursued by the thumbless thief Caravaggio, who constructs a raft of morphine to let the English patient drift and identify himself and explain what he was doing in the desert during the war, why he guided the German spy Eppler across the desert. Caravaggio's appearance in the novel makes an intertextual reference to Ondaatje's *In the Skin of a Lion*, and his name sounds a wider cultural resonance. In the earlier novel, he was a convict, who escapes from prison by making boundaries uncertain. "Demarcation," he says "is all we need to remember" (497). Applying blue paint to his body he walks across the blue roof he was painting and disappears, invisible to the guards "who look up and saw nothing there" (498).

In the desert of *The English Patient*, too, "it is easy to lose a sense of demarcation" (18). Just as Kirpal Singh dismantles a bomb, "reestablish[ing] the maze of wires into its original pattern" (193), so Caravaggio shares ampoules of morphine with Almásy in order to "unthread the story out of him: "Each swallow of morphine by the body opens a further door...When Almásy speaks [Caravaggio] stays alongside him reordering the events. Only desire makes the story errant, flickering like a compass needle" (248–89). The drug "implodes" time and geography "the way maps compress the world onto a two-dimensional sheet of paper" (161) and Caravaggio later realizes that this map constructed of morphine has not after all been drawn for his desire. On the contrary, he now believes that "Almásy has used him and the morphine to return to his own world, for his own sadness" (251). Almásy, in his turn, challenges Caravaggio to reveal his own hidden stories: "You must talk to me Caravaggio. Or am I just a book? Something to be read, some creature to be tempted out of a loch and shot full of morphine, full of corridors, lies, loose vegetation, pockets of stones" (253): the guide has changed places, the subject has shifted. The desert's hazy architectures built within the mirage of drugged memory suggest rather than reveal the complex tangle of translation and transnationalism.

In another book, a woman follows a dog into her captivity; a man with seven toes leads her back. Jackals guide the dead, and translators, books, into an afterlife in a melancholy act of liberation. Ondaatje's *The English Patient*, saturated in sadness, guides the reader away from the containment of fidelity to authority and origin and the captivity of self absorption to a narrative that admits its dependencies as a communal strategy for survival: the linguistic association of a needle under the skin, the guiding needle of a compass, and the needle skipping on the record of history are played out in narrative postures as troubling, irreconcilable and vital as the task of the translator.

WORKS CITED

Barbour, Douglas. *Michael Ondaatje*. New York: Twayne Publishers, 1993.

Bassnett, Susan, and Haresh Trivedi, eds. *Post-Colonial Translation: Theory and Practice*. New York: Routledge, 1999.

Benjamin, Walter. "Theses on the Philosophy of History." *Illuminations*. Trans. Harry Zohn. New York: Harcourt, Brace and World, 1968. 255–66.

Blaise, Clark. *Time Lord*. Toronto: Vintage Canada, 2000.

Brydon, Diana, and Helen Tiffin. *Decolonizing Fictions*. Sydney: Dangaroo P, 1993.

Clifford, James. *Routes: Travel and Translation in the Late Twentieth Century*. Cambridge: Harvard UP, 1997.

Delisle, Jean, and Judith Woodsworth, eds. *Translators through History*. Amsterdam: John Benjamins, 1995.

Hanssen, Beatrice. *Walter Benjamin's Other History: Of Stones, Animals, Human Beings, and Angels*. Berkeley: U of California P, 2000.

Jay, Paul. "Translation, Invention, Resistance: Rewriting the Conquest in Carlos Fuentes's 'The Two Shores'." *Modern Fiction Studies* 43.2 (1997): 405–31.

MacInnes, Colin. "Introduction." *Sidney Nolan: Catalogue of an Exhibition of Paintings from 1947 to 1957 Held at the Whitechapel Art Gallery, London: June to July 1957*. London: Whitechapel Art Gallery, 1957.

Ondaatje, Michael. *The Man with Seven Toes*. Toronto: The Coach House P, 1969.

Ondaatje, Michael. *In the Skin of a Lion*. New York: Quality Paperbacks Book Club, 1997.

Ondaatje, Michael. *The English Patient*. Toronto: Random House of Canada, 1992.

Said, Edward W. "Traveling Theory." *The World, the Text, and the Critic*. By Edward W. Said. Cambridge: Harvard UP, 1983. 226–47.

Said, Edward W. "Opponents, Audiences, Constituencies, and Community." *Reflections on Exile and Other Essays*. By Edward W. Said. Cambridge: Harvard UP, 2000. 118–47.

Said, Edward W. "Traveling Theory Reconsidered." *Reflections on Exile and Other Essays*. By Edward W. Said. Cambridge: Harvard UP, 2000. 436–52.

Schaffer, Kay. *In the Wake of First Contact: The Eliza Fraser Stories.* Cambridge: Cambridge UP, 1995.

Schick, Irvin Cemil. *The Erotic Margin: Sexuality and Spatiality in Alteritist Discourse.* London: Verso, 1999.

Solecki, Sam. "An Interview with Michael Ondaatje (1975)." *Spider Blues: Essays on Michael Ondaatje.* Ed. Sam Solecki. Montréal: Véhicule P, 1985. 12–27.

Steiner, George. *After Babel: Aspects of Language and Translation.* Oxford: Oxford UP, 1975.

Representations of Buddhism in Ondaatje's *Anil's Ghost*

Marlene Goldman

Critical response to Michael Ondaatje's depictions of war-torn Sri Lanka have been po-
larized and politically charged. Early on, Arun Mukherjee condemned Ondaatje in the
strongest terms for his supposed preoccupation with aesthetics at the expense of more
pressing issues such as history and politics. Ondaatje, she contends, "does not get drawn
into the act of living, which involves the need to deal with the burning issues of his
time, such as poverty, injustice, exploitation, racism, sexism, etc., and he does not write
about other human beings unless they happen to be artists—or members of his own
family" (34). Similarly, Suwanda H. J. Sugunasiri in an essay entitled "'Sri Lankan'
Canadian Poets: The Bourgeoisie that Fled the Revolution" categorizes Ondaatje as an
Eurasian or bourgeois and claims that he has adopted a mode of artistic expression that
allows him to be creative "without being committed to history, legend, culture or ideology" (64). In the end, Sugunasiri argues that the designation "Sri Lankan" is "inappli-
cable" not simply because writers such as Ondaatje "were a bourgeoisie that fled the
revolution," but also because "they are ignorant of history, culture and the myth of the
land and its people, and seem unable to relate to such sensibility" (75). Other critics, responding for the most part to Ondaatje's *Running in the Family*, have been more sym-
pathetic to Ondaatje's treatment of Sri Lanka, particularly in light of the author's complex position as a bourgeois. "Probing one's identity is problematic in the best of
situations," Chelva Kanaganayakam writes, "let alone in the case of one who is seen as
both the agent and victim of colonial hegemony" (35). Analysing the fate of the middle-
and upper-class society after Sri Lanka's independence in 1947, Ernest MacIntyre explains that, unlike the Tamils and Sinhalese who found themselves engaged in "a tryst
with destiny," the bourgeoisie, "the local descendants of the previous Dutch Empire . . .
were to enjoy an entire mortality of heightened unreality, a surreality, because they
wouldn't be provided with even a humbug of 'a tryst with destiny' at midnight in 1947"
(315). As Kanaganayakam asserts: "To be refused a role in history is to be denied the
very basis of identity"; in his eyes, this explains Ondaatje's "need to establish a niche
for himself in Sri Lanaka, which appears time and again with obsessive insistence in his
work" (34). However, Kanaganayakam still finds fault with the author for refusing "to
be drawn into issues that surface in any serious discussion of the country," an apolitical
stance that makes it impossible, regardless of "the author's angle of vision or aesthetic
sensibility" for Kanaganayakam, to refute Mukherjee's observations (Kanaganayakam
36).

   As the critical responses indicate, a fundamental question about Ondaatje's fiction sparks continuous debate, namely, what kind of engagement with Sri Lanka is
forged within his texts? Far from receding, this question has loomed even larger with
the publication of *Anil's Ghost*. Some critics continue to insist that the portrayals of Sri

Lanka in *Anil's Ghost* remain apolitical and ahistorical. Kanishka Goonewardena argues, for instance, that history "is much less evident in *Anil's Ghost*, which (just like *Running in the Family*) can be and has been appreciated without any awareness of the political upheavals in Sri Lanka (1). In his eyes, the attenuation of history and politics here is more striking than it is in *Running in the Family*, if only because *Anil's Ghost* is full of characters "obsessed with history and telling the truth, along with human rights and wrongs" (1). Goonewardena, in the end, condemns the novel on the grounds that Ondaatje "only deals with the symptoms of the Sri Lankan crisis, as he paints a picture of the everyday life there in a time of terror" (2). "To caricature crudely," Goonewardena writes, "*Anil's Ghost* reads like a story about people dragging a constant flow of dead bodies out of a river that has no hint of what's happening upstream. Who is throwing the bodies in? Why? Is that not worth knowing?" (2).

Responding to the same supposed dearth of historical and political detail, Qadri Ismail argues pointedly that this oversight supports the cause of Buddhist Sinhala nationalism: "nowhere in the entire novel," says Ismail, "do we find any engagement with the Tamil claim to being oppressed, or with the liberal/human rights/leftist argument that Sinhala (Buddhist) nationalism in Sri Lanka has an extremely repressive, criminal, perhaps even genocidal record" (25). Ismail observes further that all of the main characters are Sinhala; moreover, "all of the men have names that resonate deeply within Buddhist iconography" (24). As far as he is concerned, this can mean only one thing: "When all the significant actants in a story about Sri Lanka are Sinhala, when in addition all the place names noticed by the text when it sees the National Atlas of Sri Lanka are Sinhala ones" (39), and "when the novel's only list of the Sri Lankan disappeared contain exclusively Sinhala names" (41), "its country begins to seem very like that of Sinhala nationalism" (24). Ismail goes on to insist that it is "axiomatic to the left that the oppression of the minorities has been carried out in Sri Lanka in the name of the Sinhala Buddhist majority" (25–29). But that possibility, that "Sinhala Buddhism may bear some responsibility for Sri Lanka's misery, does not even merit Ondaatje's consideration" (25). Discussing the significance of the conclusion of the novel, which deals with the reconstruction of a statue of the Buddha, Ismail once again reads it in the light of the novel's supposed bias. As he says, this final scene is "clearly a metaphor for restoring a pure Buddhism in war torn Sri Lanka" (28).

In contrast to the critics cited above, I argue that Ondaatje's novel does indeed address "the burning issues of its time." More specifically, far from advocating the restoration of "a pure Buddhism," as we will see, the narrative calls into question the longstanding ties between Buddhism and Sinhala nationalism. In *Anil's Ghost*, a human rights organization pairs a Sri Lankan archaeologist, Sarath Diyasena, with Anil Tessera, a Western-trained forensic specialist originally from Sri Lanka, to investigate claims of organized murder on the island. At one point, Sarath tells Anil: "'I want you to understand the archaeological surround of a fact. Or you'll be like one of those journalist who file reports about flies and scabs while staying at the Galle Face Hotel. That false empathy and blame'" (44). As a Western critic, my aim is to convey a sense, to borrow Sarath's words, of the "archaeological surround" of the references to Buddhism in Ondaatje's fiction. Locating these references in a broader historical and cultural context will enable readers to appreciate how Ondaatje's fiction gestures toward the problematic fusion among religion, history, and politics in Sri Lanka.

At first glance, Ondaatje's novel seems to promote the idea of a unified Sri Lankan Buddhist faith that transcends history. The novel introduces the subject of Buddhism early on in the Miner's folk song referring to the "life wheel": "Blessed be the scaffolding deep down in the shaft/ Blessed be the life wheel on the mine's pit head/ Blessed be the chain attached to the life wheel" (1). The song describes an actual piece of mining equipment and simultaneously alludes to the universal symbol of Buddhism (the "life wheel" is a metaphor for the hoist, the machine used to raise and lower the miners' cage in the mine shaft; the use of the term "pit head" suggests further that the fiction is referring specifically to a coal mine). As scholars explain, a central tension exists in Theravada Buddhism between the wheel of power and the wheel of righteousness. At its worst, "the tension collapses either into a usurping of power by temporal authorities, normally by the state though sometimes even by elements within the Sangha [the monkhood] or into an indifference toward matters temporal through a misconceived notion of *Nibbana*" (Obeyesekere 1972, 1; Tambiah 1976, 41–47). Subsequent references to Buddhism in the novel, including the surgeon Gamini's gesture of reaching out to touch the small Buddha in the niche of the hospital wall (119) and *the raksha bandhana*, the thread tied around Anil's wrist during *a pirit* ceremony (19), reinforce the association between Buddhism and notions of sacred protection and unity.

The term *pirit* is, in fact, derived from the word *paritta*, meaning "protection." *Pirit* (or *paritta*) is a collective term designating a set of protective chants sanctioned by the Buddha for the use of both laymen and monks (see *Pirit* <http://www.accesstoinsight.org/lib/bps/wheels/wheel402.html>). Pirit chanting is a popular ceremony among the Buddhists of Sri Lanka, the ceremonial recital of which is regarded as capable of warding off all forms of evil and danger; no important function can be considered complete without this ceremony. In Ondaatje's novel, the initial associations forged among Buddhism, protection, and unity are immediately challenged, however, by the narrator's early account of the plundering of Cave 14, "the most beautiful site in a series of Buddhist cave temples" (12). As the narrator explains, the Bodhisattvas in Cave 14 "were cut out of the walls with axes and saws. . . . This was the place of a complete crime. Heads separated from bodies. Hands broken off" (12). In this instance, references to Buddhism emphasize the devastation wrought by imperial and colonial forces. We are told, for example, that in the few years following its discovery by Japanese archaeologists in 1918, the Bodhisattvas were "quickly bought up by museums in the West" (12). As Palipana, the infamous Singhalese epigraphist in the novel, tells his archaeology student Sarath, "the 'ascendancy of the idea' [is] . . . often the only survivor" (12).

To complicate matters further, subsequent references to Buddhism undermine this portrayal of a religion besieged solely by external imperialist forces. At one point,

Sarath relates the story of Palipana's brother, Narada, a Buddhist monk, who was shot in his room while sleeping. Sarath acknowledges that Narada was possibly the victim of a "political killing" and that rumors suggest he was killed by a novice (47–48). Narada's assassination recalls the historical connection in the late 1980s between young Buddhist monks and the Janatha Vimukti Peramuna (JVP or Peoples Liberation Front, termed "the antigovernment insurgents" in the novel). In the 1980s, as S. Tambiah explains, the JVP recruited the monk "as another foot soldier in the revolutionary struggle" (1992, 88). Tambiah goes on to assert that many of the JVP monks, "faced with what they construed as abandonment and even betrayal by their senior monks ... became condoners of, even collaborators in, acts of violence against senior monks" (1992, 98). As Tambiah states:

> The phenomenon of the late eighties may be seen by some observes as the final shift of "political Buddhism" from a more localized religiosity of earlier times primarily enacted among monk-laity circles in villages and towns in terms of ethical teachings, moral concerns, and gift-giving (dana) to a vocal and sloganized 'religious-mindedness,' which has objectified and fetishized the religion and espoused a "Buddhist nationalism," even as regards the monks themselves, so that important tenets of their religion regarding detachment, compassion, tranquility, and non-violence and the overcoming of mental impurities are subordinated and made less relevant to Sinhala-religio-nationalist and social reform goals. In this changed context, Buddhism in its militant, populist, fetishized form, as espoused by certain groups, seems to some observers to have been emptied of much of its normative and humane ethic ... and to function as a marker of crowd and mob identity, as a rhetorical mobilizer of volatile masses, and as an instigator of spurts of violence. (1992, 92)

Similarly, although David Little cautions that "it is important not to overrate the role of the monks in politics or to give the impression that the militants and the activists are more representative of the outlook of most monks than they are," he, too, concurs that "it would be impossible to provide a complete description of Sri Lankan political history ... without highlighting the impact of the bhikkhus" (107). In Ondaatje's novel, Palipana warns Sarath and his co-investigator, Anil, that monks in Sri Lanka have never been able to transcend politics. Citing a story from the ancient Pali chronicles, Palipana relates how a group of monks fled the court to escape the wrath of the ruler, but the king "followed them and cut their heads off" (87). At bottom, this story and the novel as a whole emphasize what a number of contemporary critics have observed, namely, that "Buddhism has never stood outside the dynamics of power" in Sri Lankan society (Kapferer 108). In keeping with this realization, rather than offer a sanitized, apolitical and ahistorical account that ignores Buddhism's enmeshment in nationalist politics, Ondaatje addresses in his novel the complex relationship between religion, politics, and violence in Sri Lanka. By outlining the fate of Palipana, a nationalist who dared to offer a radical interpretation of the Buddhist historical chronicles and was ostracized for his crimes, Ondaatje gestures to the real-life controversies concerning nationalist readings of sacred chronicles and other ancient artifacts and inscriptions. As the narrator explains, Palipana, was "for a number of years at the centre of a nationalistic group that eventually wrestled archaeological authority in Sri Lanka away from the Europeans. He had made his name translating Pali scripts and recording and translating the rock graffiti of Sigiriya" (79). Yet, later in life, Palipana had "been turned gracelessly out of the establishment," owing to his publication of a series of interpretations of rock graffiti that "stunned archaeologists and historians" (81). These interpretations, which explained, supposedly, the "political tides and royal eddies of the island in the sixth century" had seemed at first to "have ended arguments and debates by historians"; the work was "applauded in journals abroad and at home, until one of Palipana's protégés voiced the opinion that there was no real evidence for the existence of these texts" (81). The supposed evidence was exposed as a fiction, "a forgery by a master" (82).

Some readers might wonder why the author of the novel makes such a fuss about mythic inscriptions written in the dim past. To dismiss the depiction of the controversy as tempest in a teapot, however, is to misunderstand entirely the roots of contemporary Sri Lankan nationalism and the country's ongoing ethnic conflicts. As Bruce Kapferer declares, interpretations of myth and history are vital in the ethnic consciousness of both Sinhalese and Tamils: such interpretations are "not the stale meal of academic fare; they are alive in processes that can generate the suffering of homelessness and bring about sudden and violent death" (38). Sri Lankans today look back on a 2,500 year past, but the important point is not that the Sri Lankan past is so ancient but that it is so present, a presence that derives from the practice of chronicle-keeping, centred on the Mahavamsa. Referred to nowadays as Sri Lanka's "national chronicle," the Mahavamsa is a work in Pali verse written by Buddhist monks from the sixth century AD onwards that preserves traditions that reach back one thousand years earlier to the Lord Buddha's three sojourns on the island. Subsequent additions (translated as the Culavamsa) were composed in the twelfth, fourteenth, and eighteenth centuries. The Mahavamsa constitutes the oldest historical literature in South Asia. It is also the only ancient chronicle that has been updated and brought down to the present. In 1977, the Prime Minister of Sri Lanka, J.R. Jayewardene, extended the chronicle to the beginning of his administration and "great emphasis has been placed throughout the history of Buddhism in Sri Lanka on the idea that the connection between past and present must be unbroken, whether between a sacred place and the historical events that created its importance or between a group of monks and the historical origins that guarantee the authenticity of their teachings" (Kemper 33). Not only are past and present unified through the chronicles, but according to nationalists, the heart of the chronicles attests to the unity of nation and religion (see Little 26–32).

Since the British conquest of the Sri Lankan state (Ceylon then) in Kandy in 1815, the Mahavamsa has been at the centre of nationalist debates centred on notions of unity, serving as "the warrant for the interlocked beliefs that the island and its government have traditionally been Sinhala and Buddhist, and that a person cannot be Buddhist without being Sinhala" (Kemper 2). By the 1980s, newspaper writers began to characterize Sinhalese ethnic chauvinism by calling it "the Mahavamsa mentality" (Kapferer 105). The problem is, as critics points out, that the past and the present are "not nearly as much alike as some scholarly and popular representations would have people believe" (Kemper 13). The understanding of communal conflict in Sri Lanka has been hindered by the "unwarranted and anachronistic imposition of the dominant political identities of the present day on to the past" (Nissan and Stirrat 19). Present day Sinhalese and Tamils are not likely to be descendants of those mentioned in the chronicles for a host of reasons (see Nissan and Stirrat 22–24). For one, wave after wave of immigration followed the chronicle's first compilation, "a complication scarcely noticed in the popular understanding of the past"; nor is it recognized that "many of today's Sinhalas are yesterday's Tamils" (Kemper 13). Attempts to link past to present seamlessly, as many critics insist, have become an important and dangerous tool of political legitimation. In Ondaatje's novel the blending of fact and fiction in Palipana's translations of the inscriptions, not to mention the blending of fact and fiction in the novel as a whole, highlights the predicament in Sri Lanka where "myth has become historical reality and history myth" (Kapferer 34).

In addition to underscoring the ongoing controversy over the truth value of the chronicles, Ondaatje reinforces further in his novel the connection between Buddhism and earthly politics by fashioning striking parallels between its portrait of Palipana and the real-life eminent Sri Lankan epigraphist Senerat Paranavitana, the first Sinhala commissioner of archaeology. In the 1920s, Paranavitana published an interpretation of inscriptional evidence that was used to legitimate the claim that the first Sinhalese king Vijaya, celebrated in the Mahavamsa for repeating the unification of the island first enacted by the Buddha, was not simply a hero, but a member of the Aryan race. To borrow Paranavitana's own words, "the evidence is overwhelming that the original Sinhalese came to Ceylon from the Western regions of the Aravarta [the land of the Aryans]" (Paranavitana I, 93). As the medieval historian R.A.L.H. Gunawardana suggests, one of the most significant products of Orientalist scholarship in the nineteenth century was the invention of the Aryan; this invention, he argues, was followed not long after by the invention of Dravidian (see Gunawardana 1990, 70–79). As Steven Kemper observes, Wilhelm Geiger, who first visited the island in 1895 and analysed the Mahavamsa at the turn of the nineteenth century, used the tools of comparative linguistics to analyse the morphology of Sinhala. His study led him to the conclusion that Sinhala was, in fact, an Indo-Aryan language. For Geiger, categorizing the language was "simply a matter of scientific taxonomy; for Sinhalese nationalists, it became a fundamental element in the twentieth-century claim that Sinhalese sprang from a distinct and elevated bloodline" (Kemper 90; see also Little 16; Nissan and Stirrat 22–24). A host of respected scholars have refuted the claims made by Paranavitana, including Gananath Obeyesekere, who in a letter to the *New York Times* declares: "This racist nonsense is part of the current mythology of middle-class Sinhalese" (Obeyesekere qtd. in Tambiah

1986, 183–84). Obeyesekere goes on to characterize Paranavitana's and others' references to Aryan pedigree as "a hypothesis no longer acceptable to serious historians" (Obeyesekere qtd. in Tambiah 1986, 183–84).

The parallels drawn in the novel between Palipana and Paranavitana are even more striking when one considers that in 1939 Paranavitana discovered and translated the gold foil Vallipuram inscription, offering a highly controversial reading of the text (see Gunawardana 1995, 10–16). Ironically, groups "on either sides of the barricades" found Paranavitana's 1939 view useful for their purposes; one group has seen in the reading of the inscription justification for Sinhalese domination over the Jaffna Peninsula (Gunawardana 1995, 15). In keeping with the novel, at one stage in the controversy on the Vallipuram inscription, it was noted that the gold foil in question was not traceable. According to Gunawardana, this gave rise to the claim that the inscription had been a clever forgery. More recently, the well-known monk and scholar Walpola Rahula came forward to announce that "he had safe-guarded the gold foil. It was presented to the President of the Republic on February 3, 1991, at a dramatic ceremony which was given wide publicity in the media. The inscription is now being kept at the National Museum in Colombo" (Gunawardana 1995, 15). However, as Ranjini Obeyesekere (Princeton University) informed me, controversy still rages over Paranavitana's reading and translation of "interlinear writing," which he claims to have deciphered on existing rock inscriptions. As Obeyesekere explains, "no other scholars or epigraphists could see such an interlinear inscription; hence the controversy over what they saw as 'fanciful imaginings' at best" (Obeyesekere, personal communication).

By drawing such close connections between Palipana and the real-life figure of Paranavitana, Ondaatje underscores how myths of racial superiority and national unity and purity developed in Europe in the nineteenth century, along with other "gifts" of the colonizers, influenced readings of Buddhist sacred chronicles and became intertwined with notions of religious and political identity in Sri Lanka. In fact, critics have suggested that, to a great extent, the current obsession with unity can be traced to the influence of the colonizers. In 1902, for instance, a Buddhist monk explained that, to influence the English, Buddhists had to learn their secrets: "We must now learn from them, whom we mistake to imitate more in dress and drink than in their ennobling qualities, the secret of their power of unity which makes them a great people, brings them out of a comparatively savage state in a few generations, and makes for them now a consolidated and mighty empire . . . and enables them to conquer and govern us who are morally weakened by superstitious barriers. Grasp this mighty power of unity, then, true to our creed as followers of our Lord of Wisdom, use it peaceably to gain our rightful end" (qtd. in Kemper 199). As well, the leaders of the Theosophical Society founded in the US in 1875, Colonel Henry Steele Olcott (a former Union officer in the American Civil War) and Madame Helena Blavatsky played a key role in Sri Lanka's Buddhist revivalism of the 1880s. As Little explains: "Olcott quickly published The Buddhist Catechism, which claimed to capture the essence of Buddhism in popular form and thereby provide a rallying point for mobilizing and unifying the Sinhala. Soon thereafter, he founded the Buddhist Theosophical Society (BTS), and by 1890 he had established a hundred or so BTS schools. The schools mostly mimicked the missionary model, and many of them became highly successful in disseminating "the basic religious ideology of the educated Buddhist bourgeoisie" (23).

Olcott and Blavatsky also fostered the education of Don David Hewavitarne, later known as Anagarika Dharmapala. Originally a student in the Christian school system, Dharmapala was encouraged Olcott and Blavatsky to learn Pali, the language of classical Buddhism, and to immerse himself in the study of Buddhist doctrine. In the end, Dharmapala became the most influential figure in Buddhist revivalism, which rested on "an appeal to the past glories of Buddhism and Sinhalese civilization celebrated in the Mahavamsa and other chronicles as a way of infusing the Sinhalese with a new nationalist identity and self-respect in the face of humiliation and restrictions suffered under British rule and Christian missionary influence" (Tambiah 1992, 6). Dharmapala championed what has been called the Sinhala obsession with the past in speeches that referred to the sacred Sinhala legacy in terms of a glorious "colony of Aryans" or "sons of the soil" that extended well back before the second century B.C. (see Little 19–36).

In Ondaatje's novel, Palipana, modelled after Senerat Paranavitana, who inherited Dharmapala's ethnonationalist beliefs, refuses to give up "the unprovable truth" he claimed to have discovered, choosing instead to retreat to the Grove of Ascetics, the remains of an ancient forest monastery or "leaf hall." This, we are told, was "in keeping with the sixth-century sect of monks who lived under such strict principles that they rejected any religious decoration" (84). Palipana spends the remainder of his life with his young niece, Lakma, educating her and journeying together to sacred Buddhist sites. Once again, the description of their innocent pilgrimages might seem to shore up an image of a transcendent Buddhist faith that fuses past and present, and thereby transcends history: "We are, and I was, formed by history," Palipana tells his niece, "but the three places I love escaped it. Arankale. Kaludiya Pokuna. Ritigala" (105).

However, as the legend that Palipana relates about the king's dismemberment of the monks in the sacred grove reminds us, there are no places of absolute refuge. Despite Palipana's desires, there is also no escape from history and politics. Within the novel, the danger associated with blurring the difference between past and present is perhaps best illustrated by the contemporary practice of burying victims of late-twentieth century ethnic warfare in ancient graves located in sacred sites. Indeed, the entire narrative follows Anil and Sarath's desperate attempts to distinguish past from present in their search for the identity of a skeleton, nicknamed Sailor, "buried no more than four to six years ago" in a sixth-century graveyard for monks. Anil anticipates that she can deduce from the facts of his death—the broken forearm, partial burning, damage to vertebrae in the neck, and the bullet wound—the "permanent truths" of how he died. Furthermore, she believes that these truths combined with the place where he was found—caves located within government-protected archaeological preserves—are enough to prove that the government was responsible, and to point to an organized campaign of murder. The focus in the novel on sacred places dating back to the sixth century, in keeping with its emphasis on the highly politicized nature of the ancient chronicles also composed during the sixth century, can thus be understood in terms of the current overarching religious and nationalist agenda to portray a fusion of temporal and spatial horizons. Remarking on the artificial, yet incredibly powerful impact of this "fusion of horizons," Kemper notes that although renovation "saves the past," it does so, at a cost "because the process usually makes the past more like the present" (136). He goes on to recall the words of the monk who restored the relic mound words that highlight the political implications of this fusion of past and present: "'at certain times during the nights I heard *pirit* being chanted from the side of the *dagaba*. The great forest was spreading to a never-ending distance. I pondered the unbroken association of the Sinhala nation and Buddhism from beginning to end, and again from end to the beginning'" (qtd. in Kemper 136).

Indeed, what is perhaps most noteworthy in the controversy surrounding Senerat Paranavitana's discovery and translation of the Vallipuram inscription, according to Gunawardana, is the fact that rival parties "were unanimous in their acceptance of the premise that conditions prevalent eighteen centuries ago were germane to the political issue of their own times" (1995, 16). As critics observe, the war which has been fought between the armed Tamil separatists and the Sinhala-dominated government has been "accompanied by rhetorical wars fought over archaeological sites, place-name etymologies, and the interpretation of ancient inscriptions" (Little 3). A speaker at a gathering of archaeologists and historians compared the role of the archaeologist in the field to that of the soldier in the ongoing war in the North, commenting that the "contribution of the latter was no less important" (Gunawardana 1995, 16).

Palipana's work as an archaeologist and his nostalgic religious pilgrimages are therefore situated in this overarching, political context. In Sri Lanka, the government has opened archeological sites continuously to the public and these have become popular areas of Buddhist pilgrimage. According to Steven Kemper, where the "looming presence of Anaradhapura and Polunnaruva justifies Sinhalese reoccupation of these core areas, less-known sacred places serve the same function in peripheral parts of the Northern and Eastern Provinces, especially areas that have a majority of Tamil inhabitants" (Kemper 145). Charting how maps of sacred sites and Buddhist monasteries have altered, Kemper notes the steadily increasing number of ancient places from a modest count below 100 in 1979 to 276 in 1981.

Not coincidentally, the final episode in Ondaatje's novel draws our attention to the process of renovating sacred sites, featuring the artisan Ananda's attempt to rebuild a giant statue of the Buddha. According to the Pali canon, Ananda was the Buddha's constant attendant; after the latter's death, Ananda recited the entire Sutra Pitaka from memory. In a similarly elegiac gesture, Ondaatje's Ananda labours to restore a statue whose face has been broken into more than "one hundred chips and splinters of stone" (303). Although Ananda completes the statue and participates in the Buddhist tradition of the ritual of the eyes, the wounded statue of the Buddha, whose "eyes would always look north," (306) serves as a haunting reminder of the outcome of the bloody conflicts in the northern provinces. These conflicts among the Buddhist Sinhalese-dominated government, the anti-government factions, including the JVP, and the Liberation Tigers of Tamil Eelam have all but shattered the ideals of Buddhism. Read in the context of the ongoing historical connection between Buddhism and the ethnic violence in Sri Lanka, *Anil's Ghost* does not promote a transcendent, unified vision of Buddhism free from the fetters of politics. Moreover, in a country, where symbols of temporal and racial unity and fragmentation are historically embedded and politically charged, it is significant that, as Ondaatje's narrator explains, "up close the [sculpture of the newly restored Buddha's] face looked quilted" (302). Rather than "homogenize the stone" and "blend the face into a unit," Ananda decides to "leave it as it was" (302). The novel thus registers a shift from the unifying and protecting image of the thread of the *pirit* ceremony to the image of quilting, a form of stitching that likewise unifies yet, at the same time, acknowledges separation and difference. In portraying Buddhism, Ondaatje gestures toward the ideals of transcendence, wholeness, and unity. Ultimately, these are ideals that Ananda, one of the country's finest artisans, and Ondaatje refuses to reinscribe. Instead, we are left pondering "the fields where Buddhism and its values met the harsh political events of the twentieth century" (300).

WORKS CITED

Coomaraswamy, Ananda Kentish. *Elements of Buddhist Iconography*. Cambridge: Harvard UP, 1935.

Goonewardena, Kanishka. *"Anil's Ghost*: History/Politics/Ideology." Paper presentation, Congress of the Humanities and Social Sciences, Université Laval, Québec, Canada, 24–26 May 2001.

Gunawardana, R.A.L.H. *Historiography in a Time of Ethnic Conflict: Construction of the Past in Contemporary Sri Lanka*. Colombo: Social Scientists' Association, 1995.

Gunawardana, R.A.L.H. "The People of the Lion: The Sinhalese Identity and Ideology in History and Historiography." *Sri Lanka: History and the Roots of Conflict*. Ed. Jonathan Spencer. London: Routledge, 1990. 45–86.

Ismail, Qadri. "A Flippant Gesture Towards Sri Lanka: A Review of Michael Ondaatje's *Anil's Ghost*." *Pravada* 6.9 (2000): 24–29.

Kanaganayakam, Chelva. "A Trick with a Glass: Michael Ondaatje's South Asian Connection." *Canadian Literature* 132 (1992): 33–42.

Kapferer, Bruce. *Legends of People, Myths of State: Violence, Intolerance, and Political Culture in Sri Lanka and Australia*. Washington: The Smithsonian Institute P, 1988.

Kemper, Steven. *The Presence of the Past: Chronicles, Politics, and Culture in Sinhala Life*. Ithaca: Cornell UP, 1991.

Little, David. *Sri Lanka: The Invention of Enmity*. Washington: United States Institute of Peace P, 1994.

MacIntyre, Ernest. "Outside of Time: Running in the Family." *Spider Blues: Essays on Michael Ondaatje*. Ed. Sam Solecki. Montréal: Véhicule P, 1985. 315–19.

Murkherjee, Arun. "The Sri Lankan Poets in Canada: An Alternative View." *Toronto South Asian Review* 3.2 (1984): 32–45.

Nissan, Elizabeth, and R.L. Stirrat. "The Generation of Communal Identities." *Sri Lanka: History and the Roots of Conflict*. Ed. R.L. Stirrat. London: Routledge, 1990. 19–44.

Obeyesekere, Gananath. *The Cult of the Goddess Pattini*. Chicago: Chicago UP, 1984.

Obeyesekere, Gananath, Frank Reynolds, and Bardwell L. Smith. *The Two Wheels of Dhamma: Essays on the Theravada Tradition in India and Ceylon*. Chambersburg: American Academy of Religion, 1972.

Paranavitana, Senerat. *Sinhalayo*. Colombo: Lake House, 1967.

"Pirit." *The Pirit Ceremony* (2002): <http://www.accesstoinsight.org/lib/bps/wheels/wheel402.html>.

Smith, Bardwell. "The Ideal Social Order as Portrayed in the Chronicles of Ceylon." *The Two Wheels of Dhamma: Essays on the Theravada Tradition in India and Ceylon*. By Gananath Obeyesekere, Frank Reynolds, and Bardwell L. Smith. Chambersburg: American Academy of Religion, 1972. 31–57.

Spencer, Jonathan, ed. *Sri Lanka: History and the Roots of Conflict*. London: Routledge, 1990.

Sugunasiri, Suwananda, H.J. "'Sri Lankan' Canadian Poets: The Bourgeoisie That Fled the Revolution." *Canadian Literature* 132 (1992): 60–79.

Tambiah, S. *Buddhism Betrayed*. Chicago: U of Chicago P, 1992.

Tambiah, S. *Sri Lanka: Ethnic Fratricide and the Dismantling of Democracy*. Chicago: U of Chicago P, 1986.

Tambiah, S. *World Conqueror and World Renouncer*. Cambridge: Cambridge UP, 1976.

Ondaatje's *The English Patient* and Rewriting History

Stephanie M. Hilger

Ondaatje's "English" patient starts his frequently interrupted and mediated I-narration with an acknowledgment of the influence and the power of the writing of history. He tells Hana, his devoted Canadian nurse, that "I am a person who if left alone in someone's home walks to the bookcase, pulls down a volume and inhales it. So history enters us" (18). That he inhaled the dusty smell of Herodotus's writings becomes clear when Hana looks at the book which came with him through the plane crash and the fire. It is "a copy of *The Histories* by Herodotus that he has added to, cutting and gluing in pages from other books or writing in his own observations—so they all are cradled within the text of Herodotus" (16). The "English" patient's palimpsestic creation of history and identity appears as an acknowledgment of Herodotus's claim that "this history of mine . . . has from the beginning sought out the supplementary to the main argument" (119; see also Tötösy 2005). The "English" patient's supplementary exploration endeavors to complete Herodotus's project of "piecing together a mirage" (119). This desire to explore further and map in greater detail locates the "English" patient and Herodotus within a long-standing tradition of writing about the Other. The "English" patient acknowledges this tradition: "I knew . . . charts painted on skin that contain the various routes of the Crusades . . . So I knew their place before I crashed among them, knew when Alexander had traversed it in an earlier age, for this cause or that greed" (18). In evoking this tradition, Ondaatje blurs the thin line between history and fiction in order to complicate both the perception of the Other and the Self and his blurring occurs in a narrative in which fragments become centrally important in dealing with questions of identity.

The novel thematizes the concern with fragments on a formal level. *The English Patient* is—as the title of the second part suggests—"In Near Ruins" (25). The formal fragmentation parallels the reality that the characters have to face. In the present of the narration—at the end of World War II—they have taken refuge from reality in a bombed Italian monastery that is "in ruins." Although their stay in the Villa San Girolamo could appear as a flight from the outside world, the fact that each character attempts to remember the past in order to get a grip on his/her identity stresses the importance of the larger context. As a result, the novel consists of flashbacks, which are often vague and provide the reader only with a fragmentary account of both history and each character's story. In an attempt to redefine their identity, the characters turn to books, themselves partly destroyed by the war, that thematize the representation of the cultural Other: Herodotus's writings, Cooper's *The Last of the Mohicans*, Tacitus's *Annals*, passages from the Bible, Kipling's *Kim*, Stendhal's *The Charterhouse of Parma*, song lyrics, and accounts from the London Geographical Society. These fragmented accounts of the Other become mirrors of the characters' mutilated identity, inscribed with history's debris and its ruins.

The first scenes in the novel present the reader with the mutilated body of the "English"—as he is believed to be throughout most of the novel—patient. His mutilation is mirrored by the destruction around him, be it that of the Villa or of the partly destroyed books in which there are "gaps of plot" (7), including his own story. A plane crash has melted his body into a paralyzed lump of aubergine-colored human flesh. The "English" patient's body represents the ambiguity of the term "history" metonymically; it contains both the effects of history and his story. In *The Writing of History*, Michel de Certeau describes history as "*a text* organizing units of meaning and subjecting them to transformations whose rules can be determined" (41). The "English" patient becomes the battlefield for different historical meanings which his body—the text—establishes for those who read it and attempt to understand its rules. Each character transforms the text's meaning in different ways by establishing his or her own relationship to the "English" patient. As Certeau points out, "*intelligibility is established through a relation with the other*; it moves (or 'progresses') by changing what it makes of its 'other'—the Indian, the past, the people, the mad, the child, the Third World" (*The Writing of History* 3). The characters' attempt to make the "English" patient intelligible, to fit him into a category, is at the same time an indirect endeavor to come to terms with their own relation to a changed and changing reality, in which the question of who the "Other" is, cannot clearly be answered.

Incited by Hana's curiosity, the "English" patient attempts to overcome his amnesia. He starts his narration by defining himself in relation to the "Other," the Bedouins who rescue him after the plane crash. He describes these nomads as "water people" and observes that "even today caravans look like a river" (19).The Bedouins are nomads; they escape definition because they are not contained within one place. Ondaatje continues a tradition of associating the indefinable "Other" with nomads that goes back to Herodotus. In his history, Herodotus describes "wandering Scythians, who neither plow nor sow" (211) and who disappear from those places where the Persian army wants to capture them. Significantly, Herodotus's focus on the Scythians appears in the same book—Book Four of his history—as his wish to map the world the way it "really" is. Herodotus tries to define the Scythians, but he acknowledges that this topic is difficult to map: "additions being what [his] work always from the very first affected" (213), Herodotus does not give his readers a straightforward history, but, rather, points out that there are different accounts. There is "the account which the Scythians themselves give" (206), but the "Greeks who dwell about the Pontus tell a different story" (207) and finally there "is also a different story . . . in which [he] [is] more inclined to put faith than in any other" (208). Despite his own preference for a specific account, Herodotus does not conceal the other versions, but instead points at the gaps in his knowledge. In Herodotus's description, the Scythians "are not to be found where they are sought. They are never *there*. Nomadism is not an attribute of the Scythian or the Cannibal: it is their very definition. What is foreign is that which escapes from a place" (Certeau, *Heterolo-*

gies 70). Herodotus's Scythians continue to be the ungraspable Other, as do Ondaatje's Bedouins whom the "English" patient remembers on his journey into the past.

Although the "English" patient speaks the language of the tribe which rescues him, he can never locate it exactly. The nomads keep escaping the cartographer's eye. The closest the "English" patient comes to locating them is as "one of the northwest desert tribes" (Ondaatje 9). As a consequence it remains the "—— tribe" (95) for the "English" patient and his readers. This blank parallels that of the "——, the secret wind of the desert" (16), the wind that accompanies the unnamable tribe, the Other. The ungraspable Other is—like the Scythian—"a figure on the fringe who leaves the premises, and in doing so jolts the entire topographical order of language" (Certeau, *Heterologies* 70–71). There is no term for a signified that cannot be mapped. The nomads' wandering subverts the colonizer's language by exposing the uselessness of his linguistic signifiers and by projecting a gap unto the mutilated body of someone who, it seems, had been in charge of colonizing their terrain. The tribe also undermines colonial power more directly by appropriating the "English" patient's colonial knowledge to its own ends: "For some he draws maps that go beyond their own boundaries and for other tribes too he explains the mechanics of guns" (22). The "English" patient yields the knowledge of those instruments which made colonization largely possible in the first place, maps and weapons.

In 1944, approximately two years after his crash, the tribe members bring their patient to the British base at Siwa. There he "was one more enigma, with no identification, unrecognizable" (95) because—as is indirectly conjectured later in the novel—the tribesmen took away his identification plate. The removal of this sign opens up a blank in his identity, which could also have made him into the "——" patient. But by deciding to bring "their" patient to the British base, the —— tribe establishes his identity as British. He becomes the "English" patient, but the adjective is always used with implicit quotation marks. His physical signifiers do not refer to a stable signified; the nomadic quality and the mysterious identity of the —— tribe is reflected mirror-like upon the "English" patient. He appears as Herodotus's "Scythian," totally Other, elusive and mysterious. At the same time that Herodotus focuses on the indefinable nature of the Scythian, he also hints at the possibility that the Scythian might be a barbarian, an intimation which can be transposed to Ondaatje's title character. Herodotus reports to have come across androphagi on the "inland boundaries of Scythia" (235): "The manners of the androphagi are more savage than those of any other race. They neither observe justice, nor are governed by any laws. They are nomads, and their dress is Scythian; but the language which they speak is peculiar to themselves. Unlike any other nations in these parts, they are cannibals" (236). The figure on the fringe becomes the absolute manifestation of the "uncivilized" Other. All marks of civilization are absent: there is no judicial system, their language is not intelligible and they are cannibals and thereby possess the ultimate marker of barbarity. Herodotus's description poses the question of what establishes identity. Language manifests itself as one of the markers of identity. Yet the "English" patient speaks various languages—English, German, and the tribe's dialect—rather than only one. He crosses linguistic as well as national boundaries and therefore remains an unidentified alien figure with his "black body" (Ondaatje 3) and his "dark face" (4). There is always something we do not know about the "English" patient. Is he a "barbarian"? Has he profited from the death of others in the context of the war? Is he a traitor? Is he the equivalent of Herodotus's cannibals in twentieth-century history? These questions hover over the novel and remain unanswered. The mysteriousness that surrounds the title character raises the suspicion that he himself might have behaved in savage ways, inconsistent with justice or laws. Even though different characters attempt to fill the gaps in his story and darn the holes that history has torn in the tissue of the Self, the "English" patient's identity remains fluid and therefore suspicious. He is the unsettling presence at the end of colonialism and the war because history writes the problems of a "period of adjustment" (54) upon his body.

The "English" patient hovers on the dividing line between the civilized and the barbarian. His presence undermines any rigidly established barrier between these two terms. In creating the character of the "English" patient, Ondaatje continues Michel de Montaigne's sixteenth-century questioning of this barrier. Certeau observes that Montaigne examines the possible transition of terms traditionally associated with the "uncivilized" Other to the side of the colonizer, the "civilized": "The name comes undone. It functions as an adjective in relation to places that have the value of undefined nouns. It bursts into pieces disseminated throughout space. It becomes dispersed in contradictory meanings, which are indifferently assignable to cases that used to be kept carefully separate: for example, "savage" remains over where it was, but with an inverted meaning, and "barbarian" comes our way, assigned to the very place from which it had been excluded. In this way, the place of the Cannibals is emptied—it becomes vacant and distant. Where are they?" (Certeau, *Heterologies* 73).

Certeau's comment relates to Montaigne's way of identifying the "place of the other" (67) in the specific historical context of the sixteenth-century discovery of the "New World." Montaigne was one of the first thinkers to deconstruct many of the tropes within the tradition of writing about the Other. He interrogates the order of center and margins by positing polarities which he establishes only in order to show how they collapse into each other. Montaigne's observation about the dissemination of the name and the inversion of the savage/civilized binary is enacted by Ondaatje's construction of the "English" patient, who no longer has a name. The figure of the "English" patient causes this binary to collapse in the context of the twentieth century. The term "barbarian" now becomes applied to the colonizing powers who claim to be the "civilized." The barbarity of the "civilized" is less deniable and more visible—through the media—than ever before in history. After the fascist mass destruction of all kinds of Others, after the Allies' dropping of the atomic bomb on Hiroshima and Nagasaki and the use of colonies and dependencies as battlefields, the term "barbarian" has shifted to the "civilized" and has become disseminated throughout space. The novel refers to World War II as the "last mediaeval war" (Ondaatje 69) and to the fighting in the desert as "The

Barbarians versus the Barbarians" (257), thereby highlighting the cruelty of twentieth-century history.

The "English" patient's charred body becomes a metonymic representation of the new dark age into which humanity has entered. His body dramatizes the conflict between a historiographical and a psychoanalytical conception of time and memory. These two disciplines conceive of the relationship between the past and the present in different terms because "psychoanalysis recognizes the past *in* the present; [whereas] historiography places them one *beside* the other" (Certeau, *Heterologies* 4). After the plane crash, the "English" patient is different from who he was before. He has been propelled into the elusive space of the nomadic Other. In this sense the past is different from the present and stands beside it, as a result of which the past can be studied from a historiographical point of view. There is a difference, a distance which creates the impression of objectivity, but at the same time there is also a *différance* which complicates the relationship between the present and the past by foregrounding the fact that they are intimately connected by the psychoanalytic concept of the "mnemic trace, the return of what was forgotten" (3–4). From this perspective a purely historiographical approach cannot maintain the illusion of two separate time periods because the "gap that had placed between them an urgency inspiring scientific investigation (and the origin of its 'objectivity') begins to waver. It is thrown topsy-turvy, it is displaced, it moves forward. This movement is precisely due to the fact that this gap was posited, *and* that now it cannot be maintained" (Certeau, *The Writing of History* 37). The power of memory displaces the constructed gap between the activity of inquiry and the object that is being studied. The present and the past are intimately connected. The return of what was forgotten and repressed creates an ambivalent space for knowledge, not only for the "English" patient who tries to recall his past, but also for those who want to fill the gaps in his identity in order to make sense of their own lives.

The plane crash has made the "English" patient forget his national origins. It appears that this amnesia has brought his earlier wish to "erase [his] name and the place [he] had come from" (139) to full realization. He has become a signifier without a signified. Yet, the novel teases the reader with the possibility of knowing who the "English" patient really is by mentioning the name "Almásy" (142).The name appears without any direct reference to its bearer. The reader establishes the link between "Almásy" and the "English" patient him/herself when he/she realizes that "Almásy" is the only name without a clear referent and must therefore designate the unnamed and unnamable character in the novel. In his acknowledgments at the end of the novel, Ondaatje refers to his sources, among them "R. A. Bagnold's review of Almásy's monograph on his explorations in the desert" (303). Steven Tötösy de Zepetnek identifies the historical Almásy, an aristocratic Hungarian explorer, as a model for the "English" patient (see Tötösy 1994, 2005). Yet, as Tötösy concludes from his overview of a variety of German and Hungarian historical sources, there is a "signification of questionable identity" (Tötösy 1994, 144) regarding the historical Almásy as well. For Tötösy, "the interesting factor here is the question about Almásy's slippery identity, an analogue to the 'English' patient's in the novel" (145). In the novel, the "English" patient establishes his slipperiness when he mentions that, "after ten years in the desert, it was easy for [him] to slip across borders, not to belong to anyone, to any nation" (139). The idea of elusive identity in this "postmodern text" parallels the complexity in the identity formation of the Hungarian nation (Tötösy 1994, 141). By hinting at the fact that his title character is based on the Hungarian Almásy, Ondaatje teases his readers with the possibility of solving the mystery of identity. Yet, a closer look at the fictional construct of Almásy's identity reveals that Ondaatje propels us into yet another realm of fragmentation, questioning, imagination, and ambivalence.

The association of the "English" patient with the Hungarian Almásy undermines the idea of monolithic identity because Hungarian national identity is highly complex and ambivalent to begin with. As Benedict Anderson has pointed out, Hungary is a forceful example of the fact that nations are "imagined communities ... cultural artefacts of a particular kind" (Anderson 4) based on the "need for a narrative of identity" (205). The readers' and the characters' attempt to reconstruct a narrative of identity for the "English" patient becomes an act of communal imagination, informed by the search for decisive clues. When he acknowledges his ability to speak German upon his arrival at the Allies' hospital, the "English" patient seems to provide the reader with a clue to his cultural identity by implicitly referring to the Habsburg empire's Germanic center, Vienna. But at the same time he knows everything not only about Britain—"ask me about Don Bradman [an Australian cricket player who was knighted in 1949 by Britain]. Ask me about Marmite [*the* British yeast spread], the great Gertrude Jekyll [a twentieth-century British garden designer]" (95)—but also "where every Giotto was in Europe" (95). The "English" patient's reference to his knowledge about Britain could be an attempt at averting the suspicion of having collaborated with Nazi Germany, yet it might also suggest that he was a German spy while at the same time referencing the stereotype of the cultivated Central European. But then, can the audience expect a definite answer from a character who declares that "[he] came to hate nations" and argues that "we are deformed by nation-states" (138)?

The other characters in the novel, themselves hurt and their identity mutilated, gather around the "English" patient in their attempt to come to terms with history. He becomes, as Stephen Scobie points out, their "screen" (99), because "[e]ach character deflects his or her true desire through the image of another" (99). The "English" patient provides those surrounding him with the ultimate image of the Other; he absorbs their own quest for identity. The "English" patient's cathartic quality in this framework of "deferral or substitution" (99) becomes clear in his interactions with Caravaggio. Caravaggio wants to know what the "English" patient's political involvement was during the war; he attempts to prompt the return of what was forgotten and repressed. He urges the "English" patient to speak and hopes that the morphine which Hana regularly administers will help. Caravaggio's need to reassemble the "English" patient's splinters is fueled by a feeling that they are the clues to coming to terms with his own fragmented postwar identity: "Caravaggio watches the pink in the man's mouth as he talks. The gums perhaps the light iodine color of the rock paintings discovered in Uweinat. There is more to discover, to divine out of this body on the bed, nonexistent except for a mouth, a vein in the arm, wolf-grey eyes. He is still amazed at the clarity of discipline in the man, who speaks sometimes in the first person, sometimes in the third person, who still does not admit that he is Almásy" (247). Caravaggio assigns the "English" patient to the place of the nomadic and unidentifiable Other that needs to be controlled and circumscribed. The "English" patient acquires characteristics of a "wolf," a threatening and concealed presence in the wilderness. Yet, at the same time he also appears as a saint whom the members of a specific community visit for their own edification. He is explicitly referred to as a "despairing saint" (Ondaatje 3) and an "effigy" (161) at certain points in the narrative. Caravaggio's insistence on the "English" patient's mouth and his eyes parallels Certeau's observation about hagiographical accounts, which stress the importance of "the language of the body, a topography of holes and valleys: orifices (the mouth, the eye) and internal cavities" (Certeau, *The Writing of History* 279). Understanding the language of the orifices in this completely mutilated body is the purpose of all those who come and visit the "English" patient, but especially for Caravaggio who believes him to be the reason for his own physical and emotional mutilation.

The conversations—with the "English" patient lying on the "couch" and Caravaggio sitting or walking around—acquire the aura of Freudian psychoanalytic discourse. The frequency of these "sessions" and the process of "transference"—in which the analysed thinks through his own issues and transfers them to the analyst— and "counter transference" (by the analyst) establishes a psychoanalytic setting. But this setting is reversed because the analyst's—Caravaggio's—primary aim is his own healing—rather than that of his patient—which he can only reach by trying to put the fragments of his patient's body into place. In his attempt to make the "patient" speak, Caravaggio shares Freud's approach and his "assurance of finding in any discourse 'small fragments of the truth' ('stükchen [sic] Wahrheit')—splinters and debris relative to those decisive moments—the forgetting of which organizes itself into psychosociological systems and the remembrance of which creates possibilities of change for the present state" (Certeau, *Heterologies* 6). Despite Caravaggio's attempts to extract a continuous narrative from the "English" patient's mouth, he only receives fragments, which he tries to assemble into a picture of the past in order to make life in the present possible. Immersing himself into the historical debris of the Other is Caravaggio's method of attempting to heal his own wounds.

Focusing on the fragmented nature of consciousness is a method of dealing with the feeling of disintegration of the postwar and the postcolonial period as Theodor Adorno has shown in his 1951 *Minima Moralia. Reflexionen aus dem beschädigten Leben.* These "reflections from a damaged life" are a collage of seemingly random thoughts on the postwar existence. The structure of Adorno's thoughts parallels what Douglas Barbour calls the "labyrinthine" (207) character of *The English Patient,* which he further characterizes as "Ondaatje's carefully casual *bricolage* of disassociated moments, the accumulation of narrative fragments" (209). The narrative fragments reflect the mutilation of the different characters. Adorno's figure of the mutilated man is not only enacted by the "English" patient but also by Caravaggio. Caravaggio, the former thief, has been robbed of the use of that body part which previously constituted the most "essential" part of his identity, his hand. During the war Nazi officers cut off his thumbs. He now is the "man with bandaged hands" (27). Caravaggio holds the "English" patient responsible for his loss of identity because he suspects him of having been a German spy. But his pain is tinted with the pleasure associated with the focus on fragments. At the same time that the bandages act as protective "gloves" (53), they also highlight Caravaggio's fetishized parts and thereby provide him with the narcissistic focus on the fact that he is not "whole" anymore: "The narcissism, which has been robbed of its libidinal object by the disintegration of the I, is replaced by the masochist pleasure of not being an I anymore; and the growing generation guards her absence of the I so jealously as few of her possessions as a communal and permanent property" (Adorno 79; my translation).

The masochistic pleasure of the postcolonial/postwar subject's focus not only on his own fragments but also on those of others turns into a narcissism of disintegration. By highlighting absence, the subject defends itself against the lack of identity by establishing this "hole" as his individuality. By displacing the attention onto the fragmentation of others, the subject attempts to come to terms with its own disintegration. Yet, at the same time that Caravaggio tries to heal himself, he also desires revenge. He feels most comfortable in the presence of "the headless statue of a count" (34), which acts as a substitute for the punishment he wants to see inflicted on Almásy. Caravaggio's bandaged hands awaken Hana's desire to care for the man to whom they belong. She not only takes care of the "English" patient, but also of Caravaggio in an attempt to halt a process of self-destruction that had started during the war. Her maternal quality as a nurse is deeply entwined with a deliberate act of self-mutilation, an act prompted by the presence of "destroyed bodies [which] were fed back to the field hospitals like mud passed back by tunnellers in the dark" (49). She cuts off her hair, "the irritation of its presence during the previous days still in her mind—when she had bent forward and her hair had touched blood in a wound" (49–50). She breaks with her past by acknowledging her miscarriage and the deaths of her lover and father. She feels drawn to the Villa San Girolamo which "had the look of a besieged fortress, the limbs of most of the statues blown off during the first days of the shelling" (43). Not only do these statues represent the physical destruction, but they also mirror the characters' continuing fear of destruction and cruelty.

The danger of destruction hovers over everyone in the Villa San Girolamo, but especially over Kirpal Singh, the Indian sapper who defuses bombs for the British army. The danger the sapper faces daily is displaced unto his desire to "aim his rifle and fire and hit some target precisely. Again and again he aims at a nose on a statue or one of the brown hawks veering across the sky of the valley" (73). By targeting the statue, he wants to mutilate that part of himself which—figuratively—enables him to detect bombs, his nose. He can literally "smell" the danger in the air when he comes near a hidden bomb. But this "nose" is not mere intuition because Kip has been taught by the British army. He is the product of the English colonial power in India and exemplifies the domesticated Other who, being a "not quite/not white" (Bhabha 92) subject, is never granted full equality. His teacher, Lord Suffolk, represents the colonial "desire for a reformed, recognizable Other, as a subject of a difference that is almost the same but not quite" (Bhabha 86). Kip is one of the "authorized versions of otherness" (88), as the mutilation of his name indicates. His name is Kirpal Singh but the British gave him the nickname Kip when some officers interpreted the butter stain on one of his reports as kipper grease. A kipper is "a salty English fish" (87), usually smoked or dried. Kip's identity has been "smoked out" so to speak, and "within a week his real name, Kirpal Singh, had been forgotten" (88). On an intertextual level, the mutilated name Kip evokes Rudyard Kipling and his titular "hero," Kim. In his own mutilation, Kip turns to the "English" patient. The relationship between Kip and the "English" patient "seemed to her [Hana] a reversal of *Kim*" (111). Yet it is more than a simple reversal of Kipling's narrative into "the young student was now Indian, the wise old teacher was English" (111) because "English" as applied to the "patient" and "Indian" as applied to Kip are classifications of nationality that do not acknowledge the new sense of identity in the postcolonial and postwar context.

As a defense against this mutilation and appropriation, Kip clings to his carefully layered turban and his long hair, the only markers distinguishing him from the British soldiers. Yet he knows that his attempt to establish a "whole" and monolithic identity is doomed to fail because in many respects he is the most "British" among his fellow soldiers: "I grew up with traditions from my country, but later, more often, from *your* country . . . I knew if I lifted a teacup with the wrong finger I'd be banished. If I tied the wrong kind of knot in a tie I was out" (283). He resents this appropriation and channels his anger toward the man whom he assigns to the place of those who forced their culture upon him. He directs his rifle away from the statue and instead "points at the Englishman" (283), the "English" patient. He wants to kill what he sees in himself. This decisive moment occurs when Kip puts the earphones of his radio set on the "English" patient's head and forces him to listen to the account of "One bomb. Then another. Hiroshima. Nagasaki" (284). He wants to rid himself of the guilt he feels because he helps defusing those bombs the colonizers throw on each other's countries instead of using his part of the "tremor of Western wisdom" (284) to prevent the "bombing [of] the brown races of the world" (286) by the "contract makers. The map drawers" (284). He resents and acknowledges his complicity with the colonizer "the moment the "eyes of the sapper and the patient meet in this half-dark room crowded now with the world" (285). He realizes the paradox of "cutting away, defusing, limbs of evil" (285) for those who are bombing the "brown races," with whom he has consciously started to identify after the crucial event of the dropping of the atomic bomb.

But the novel does not stop at this point. Rather than celebrating the characters' hybridity, the reference to the atomic bomb establishes a new binary in which the characters are trapped at the end of the novel. It does not matter to Kip whether the "English" patient was on the side of the Germans or the British; what prompts Kip to return to India as a doctor is his inclusion of the "English" patient into the category of those who dropped the atomic bomb: "American, French, I don't care. When you start bombing the brown races of the world, you're an Englishman" (286). Kip realizes that "they would never have dropped such a bomb on a white nation" (286). In this sense, the atomic bomb forcefully reconstructs the binary which the characters have gradually and painfully deconstructed in an attempt to emerge from their solipsism. The world of the Villa San Girolamo is destroyed as the outside world breaks in. The glances the reader gets at Kip and Hana at the very end of the novel when they are both back in their "native" countries show a new kind of imprisonment and make Caravaggio's earlier statement that "the trouble with all of us is we are where we shouldn't be" (122) appear as a dark prophecy. While Ondaatje's novel might, at first sight, appear more pessimistic than many other postcolonial theorists' and authors' celebration of hybridity, it provides the reader with the possibility to participate in the writing of history and therefore also in the shaping of the future. The "reader, who must take a place in the communal act, must stay awake to keep the teller company and finally tell his own version of the story" (Cooke 208). The reader, instead of reciting historical lessons, has to look at the "stone of history skipping over the surface" (299) and come to his or her own conclusions about how to gauge the binary opposition on which the novel ends. Yet the implications of a novel which focuses on the unavoidable reality of fragmented identities are not neutral in this respect. Binaries establish oppositions which eventually give way to the ambivalence of the historical process, thereby undermining any rigidly established barrier between those who are "barbarian" and those who are "civilized." After all, the "English" patient remains a mystery, as do most events in history.

WORKS CITED

Adorno, Theodor. *Minima Moralia. Reflexionen aus dem beschädigten Leben.* Frankfurt: Suhrkamp, 1951.

Anderson, Benedict. *Imagined Communities: Reflections on the Origin and Spread of Nationalism.* New York: Verso, 1983.

Barbour, Douglas. *Michael Ondaatje.* New York: Twayne Publishers, 1993.

Bhabha, Homi K. *The Location of Culture.* London: Routledge, 1994.

Certeau, Michel de. *Heterologies: Discourse on the Other.* Trans. Brian Massumi. Minneapolis: U of Minnesota P, 1986.

Certeau, Michel de. *The Writing of History.* Trans. Tom Conley. New York: U of Columbia P, 1988.

Cooke, John. *The Influence of Paintings on Five Canadian Writers: Alice Munro, Timothy Findley, Margaret Atwood and Michael Ondaatje.* Lewiston: Edwin Mellen, 1996.

Herodotus. *The History of Herodotus*. Trans. George Rawlinson. Ed. Manuel Komroff. New York: Tudor Publishing, 1928.

Ondaatje, Michael. *The English Patient*. New York: Vintage International, 1992.

Scobie, Stephen. "The Reading Lesson: Michael Ondaatje and the Patients of Desire." *Essays on Canadian Writing* 53 (1994): 92–106.

Tötösy de Zepetnek, Steven. "Ondaatje's *The English Patient* and Questions of History." *Comparative Cultural Studies and Michael Ondaatje's Writing*. Ed. Steven Tötösy de Zepetnek. West Lafayette: Purdue UP, 2005. 115–131.

Tötösy de Zepetnek, Steven. "*The English Patient*: 'Truth Is Stranger than Fiction'." *Essays on Canadian Writing* 53 (1994): 141–53.

Post-Nationalism and the Cinematic Apparatus in Minghella's Adaptation of Ondaatje's *The English Patient*

Hsuan Hsu

Theories of the cinematic gaze, strongly influenced by the work of Lacan and Althusser, often denigrate visual pleasure as a politically compromised response. Christian Metz, for example, links film spectatorship to the pathological practices like fetishism, disavowal, and voyeurism; Laura Mulvey, agreeing that films are fundamentally voyeuristic, calls for the "destruction of pleasure as a radical weapon." Jean-Louis Baudry suggests that ideological manipulations are inherent in the cinematographic apparatus itself: it feeds empty simulacra to mute, immobilized spectators, just as the apparatus composed of flames and silhouettes in Plato's allegorical cave supplies illusory images that dissuade prisoners from pursuing Truth. In this paper, I discuss the notion that that such confining models of spectatorship fail to do justice to a particular "mainstream" film such as Anthony Minghella's adaptation of Michael Ondaatje's *The English Patient* (1996). Minghella's film is, simultaneously, pleasurable and politically productive: indeed, it embodies a radical politics of pleasure, an adulteration of vision that undermines nationalist ideology by creating a post-national audience tied together by suppressed flows of "adulterous" desire.

In her study of Latin American national romances, Doris Sommer draws a suggestive connection between marital and national desire. While moving their readers to desire the union of a central pair of lovers, national romances produced simultaneously in them a yearning for the sort of nation in which such a union could be realized: "The unrequited passion of the love story produces a surplus of energy . . . a surplus that can hope to overcome the political interference between the lovers. At the same time, the enormity of the social abuse, the unethical power of the obstacle, invests the love story with an almost sublime sense of transcendent purpose. As the story progresses, the pitch of sentiment rises along with the cry of commitment, so that the din makes it ever more difficult to distinguish between our erotic and political fantasies for an ideal ending" (Sommer 48). Sommer implies that, in the case of these "foundational fictions," the ideological strategy of blurring the distinction between erotic and political desires was a means justified by their end: the creation of communities of readers, and hence the establishment of self-determining nations, in Latin America. *The English Patient,* however, takes place in Europe during World War II, when nations themselves initiate and justify enormous abuses of power: its plot hinges on the political interferences that nationalism throws in the way of the illicit lovers, Count László de Almásy and Katharine Clifton. When Almásy walks from the Cave of Swimmers to El Taj to fetch help for the injured Katharine, British soldiers detain him as a German spy, and Katharine dies alone. Afterwards, as he is flying her body back to civilization, German machine gunners shoot down his British plane. The lovers, it seems, could only have been united on the "earth without maps" that Katharine imagines in her dying moments. In the Latin American colonies described by Sommer, marriage provided a means of bourgeois consolidation that "filled the 'relative vacuum of social structures' to construct a social organization preliminary to public institutions including the state itself"; it also channeled eroticism into reproductive relationships which would populate newly consolidated nations (Sommer 19). *The English Patient,* however, derives its libidinal force from adultery rather than marriage. If marriage represented alliances between cultures, classes, and races in national romances, Ondaatje and Minghella's filmic post-national romance employ extra-marital bonds as metaphors for *inter*national alliances. Geoffrey Clifton's statement that he and Katharine "were practically brother and sister before we were man and wife" (Minghella, *The English Patient*; all quotations are from the film) links intra-national marriage to incest implicitly and suggests an introverted form of society that precludes external ties. Almásy, Katharine, Hana, and Kip embody and enact desires that transgress both national and familial boundaries.

The English Patient dramatizes the way in which foundational fictions, while producing national desire by means of libidinal and geographical mapping, give rise to various marginalizations and exclusions or foundational "frictions" simultaneously. Marriage, with its insistence on productive and sanctioned eroticism, suppresses adultery, along with homosexuality and other unmapped forms of sexual satisfaction. In addition to frustrated adulterous and homosexual relationships, *The English Patient* also includes several instances of non-genital eroticism, such as a close-up of the Patient's mouth receiving a plum from Hana and the surrogate "love scene" in which Kip swings Hana, suspended in a harness, around the upper walls of a church. The film's governing metaphor for all these unsanctioned pleasures is adultery, perhaps the most common form of extra-marital love. Whereas marriage is public and official, adultery is by definition private and illicit, a violation not just of societal laws, but of vows voluntarily undertaken. Moreover, adultery, unlike marriage, is ideally unproductive: this contrast is evoked when, after Katharine swoons at the Christmas party in order to be alone with Almásy, a solicitous English woman responds by assuming that she must be pregnant. Nevertheless, the film appropriates adultery as a productive figure for freedom from marital and national constraints, from the imperative to produce children for the sake of an arbitrarily imagined national community. Adultery—whose etymological derivation from *ad-alter* connotes a tendency "towards an Other"—comes to embody an ethical imperative to resist the restrictive boundaries of marriages and the nations they help to build.

Perhaps the film's most extreme form of nationalism is carried out, ironically, by members of the *International* Sand Club, a group of desert explorers with ties to Britain's Royal Geographic Society. Although Almásy considers his exploration to be an apolitical scientific pursuit, the maps he makes of the desert become powerful political weapons when war breaks out in Northern Africa. The film exposes the ways continuously in which cartography contributes nationalist and imperialist projects of territorial partitioning and appropriation. These geographical partitionings, in turn, inform several metaphorical acts of "mappings," including not only the maiming and appropriation of human bodies, but also the "cuts" and framings of the camera itself. Several sequences implicate not only Almásy, but the camera and cinematic audience as well, in the colonial violence carried out by means of the cartographic gaze.

Almásy views cartography as a science that has nothing to do with politics: when his partner, Madox, tells him the British government has ordered "all international expeditions to be aborted by May 1939," Almásy is both baffled and annoyed: "What do they care about our maps?" Even when Madox explains that "In a war, if you own the desert, you own North Africa," he responds with scornful incredulity, "Own the desert!"; elsewhere, he tells Katharine that the thing he hates most is "ownership." Yet his maps become crucially involved in the battle between Britain and Germany for power over North Africa. Moreover, a closer look at both the dynamics of the cartographic gaze and his behaviour toward Katharine suggests that Almásy's pursuit of geographical knowledge is deeply implicated in imperialism's visual practice of cutting up, appropriating, and dominating landscapes.

Aerial cartography involves a distanced, panoramic gaze that levels off the landscape in order to quantify and plot its features. This process of quantifying requires a grid or screen that mediates between the eye and the terrain. This model—omniscient eye, mediating screen, and object of vision—incorporates the structure of the disembodied, transcendental "gaze" which Jacques Lacan distinguishes from the "look" (81–135). In *The Threshold of the Visible World,* Kaja Silverman gives the following account of a diagram which Lacan uses to represent the field of vision: "In it, the subject is shown looking at an object from the position marked "geometrical point." He or she seemingly surveys the world from an invisible, and hence transcendental, position. However, the intervening 'image,' which coincides with the 'screen' in diagram 2, immediately troubles this apparent mastery; the viewer is shown to survey the object not through Alberti's transparent pane of glass, but through the mediation of a third term. He or she can only see the object in the guise of the 'image,' and can consequently lay claim to none of the epistemological authority implicit in the perspectival model" (Silverman, *Threshold* 132).

The "image" or screen that intervenes between viewer and object occupies the position of the cartographic grid, which mediates between the aerial eye and the land being "surveyed." *The English Patient,* however, dramatizes Lacan's point that the purely objective gaze represents an ultimately untenable position: ocular mastery is always only apparent, and Almásy employs the cartographic grid not so much to claim epistemological authority as to lay claim to landscapes and bodyscapes. The eye may aspire toward the gaze, but its striving for transcendence is always tainted, or adulterated, by the fact that the look is "always finite, always embodied, and always within spectacle, although it does not always acknowledge itself as such" (Silverman, *Male Subjectivity* 134).

Despite his professed antipathy toward "ownership" and his pursuit of visual objectivity, it becomes clear that even Almásy's map-making is tainted by desire. Minghella draws several visual connections between landscape and bodyscape early in the film: the opening credits depict a brush painting shadowy bodies on a flesh-colored parchment, then make a smooth transition into an aerial shot of the desert, which also resembles a body; the first flashback sequence shows Almásy interrogating someone in Arabic about "a mountain the shape of a woman's back." This image recurs later when, staring at Katharine's back, be begins to see her body as an object of possession as well as desire: "I claim this shoulder blade—no, wait—I want—turn over [he indicates the indentation of her throat, which he later learns is called the "supersternal notch"] I want this! This place—I love this place—what's it called? This is mine! I'm going to ask the king permission to call it the Almásy Bosphorous." When Katherine temporarily stops sleeping with him, he tells her that "I want to touch you. I want the things which are mine, which belong to me." Almásy's urge to name and possess parts of Katharine's body combines fetishistic and colonial desire, both of which involve violent processes of partitioning. Both at the farewell dinner and at the earlier Christmas party, Almásy watches Katharine through gridded screens—analogues of those of the map maker's. His room, where the two first make love, has similar windows which cast shadowy grids on their bodies, transforming them into erotic complements to the maps hanging from Almásy's walls. These cartographic grids are transferred ironically onto Katharine's body itself when she dies after the cuckolded Geoffrey tries to kill her, Almásy, and himself in a plane crash: she is wearing a grid-patterned dress. Also, a subjective shot at the beginning of the movie shows Almásy's view of the world through the grid of a reed mask that the Bedouins who rescue him have placed over his charred and disfigured face. When he is brought to a hospital in Italy, a British officer immediately attempts to determine his nationality: when the officer labels Almásy (who we know is neither English nor patient) an "English patient," the map maker ends up being all but mapped to death himself.

Cartographic violence is even more intense in the case of David Caravaggio, a Canadian agent working with Geoffrey in Tobruk. After Rommel's troops have taken the city with the help of maps acquired from Almásy, a German interrogator has Caravaggio's thumbs amputated in the film's most gruesome scene, ostensibly in order to punish him for committing adultery. Since the sequence begins with an overhead shot of the interrogation scene mediated by a gridded screen, the metaphorical violence of both the cartographic gaze, with its aerial partitioning of space, and the cinematic gaze, organized as it is by framings and "cuts," is literalized in the cutting off of Caravaggio's thumbs. Cartographic boundaries and cinematic frames alike regularly cut bodies into pieces precisely by seeing them through a mediating screen or grid: "cinema represents itself as a twentieth-century continuation of the cartographic science" (Shohat 46). The technology of film is also implicated in the photographs which enable the Germans to identify him: Caravaggio tells Almásy later that, before tracking down the man who handed the maps to the Germans, he found and killed both the interrogator and "the man who took my photograph." Yet the amputation scene, with its excessive violence, its close-up of Caravaggio's fingers, and a scream that continues beyond the visual cut-away from the hand, also incites viewers to identify with the subject of torture, and thereby bypass the cartographic grid. Caravaggio's pain, coupled perhaps with the spectators' guilt at their own complicity in it, enables an identification which traverses the mediating screen: after seeing the razor sink into his thumb, one checks to make sure one's own thumbs are still there. While the cartographic gaze is an instance of the human eye attempting to attain the position of the transcendental gaze, *The English Patient* recalls constantly vision to the body by means of eroticism and pain. If cartography, by drawing the boundaries of nations, also inscribes marriage as a set of boundaries for desire, adultery represents one way of escaping, or reconfigurating, the organizational grid. But for the most part, the film depicts only failed attempts and unfulfilled desires to transgress social and national boundaries: only the "frame story"— which consists of the nurse Hana's relationships to the dying Almásy on the one hand, and the Sikh explosives expert Kip on the other—results in an escape from the national and marital grids.

Colonialism's cartographic gaze involves a dialectical deployment of the activity of transgressive, international map-makers. On the one hand, their work is prerequisite to the production of maps; on the other hand, those very maps depict nomadic travelers as subversive to their totalizing project. Michel de Certeau claims that the totalizing map excludes tour describers and "the operations of which it is the result or the necessary condition" (121). *The English Patient* dramatizes this process by which the itineraries which cross and connect different geographical places are systematically effaced. The map forms "states" of erotic as well as geographic knowledge and renders ground-level desires illegitimate, if not illegible. "Beneath the discourses that ideologize the city, the ruses and combinations of powers that have no readable identity proliferate; without points where one can take hold of them, without rational transparency, they are impossible to administer" (Certeau 95). Adulterous, homosexual, and other ungraspable desires proliferate in both the flashback and the frame narratives of the film, until most of them are frustrated or incorporated by the cartographic gaze.

Although both he and Geoffrey Clifton are geographers, Almásy insists that aerial maps are too far removed from their objects: "You can't explore from the air," he tells his friend Madox: "if you could explore from the air, life would be very simple." The next thing he says, while priming the propeller of his plane, is "Contact." As in the torture scene, where Caravaggio's pain evokes a bodily identification across the cinematic screen, this scene implicitly prefers intimate "contact" to the aerial map-maker's distanced gaze. Ironically, Almásy advocates ground-level exploration only in order to produce more accurate maps. This replicates the contradiction in his love life: his adulterous affair with Katharine undermines the boundaries drawn by marriage, but only so that he can reinscribe a fetishistic and quasi-imperialistic claim to the "place" at the base of her throat. Lying in Almásy's bed, Katharine also reinscribes the very discursive terms she is trying to escape, musing that "here I am a different *wife.*"

In addition to the literally adulterous affair between Almásy and Katharine, *The English Patient* includes several other instances of adulteration more loosely conceived.

"To adulterate" is to move toward the other, to "corrupt, debase, or make impure by the addition of a foreign or inferior substance" (*Webster's* 30). When Almásy pastes notes, and journal entries, and Katharine's paintings into his volume of Herodotus, and when, dying alone in the Cave of Swimmers, Katharine writes in the same book about the dissolution of boundaries between bodies and countries alike—they are literally adulterating the *Histories*. Similarly, international romances—whether between Katharine (British) and Almásy (Hungarian), Hana (Canadian) and Kip (Sikh), Gioia (Italian), and Caravaggio (Canadian), or Bermann (German) and Kamal (Egyptian)—are relationships of mutual adulteration. Bermann, describing his homosexual relationship with Kamal, wonders, "How do you explain, to someone who's never been here, feelings which seem quite normal?" The deictic, "here," likens his emotional state to a geographical locale, a place that's indescribable because it falls outside of conventional boundaries. When a drunken and frustrated Almásy toasts the International Sand Club as "Misfits, buggers, fascists and fools," he suggests that homosexuals, presumably because their relations are seen as "unnatural" or "unproductive"—comprise one of the stereotypes against which British nationalism defines itself. Continuing his toast—"His Majesty! Der Führer! Il Duce!," Almásy blurs the boundary that justifies the war in the first place, intimating that the British are no less despotic than the fascists they are fighting. Finally, he observes that "The Egyptians are desperate to get rid of the Colonials": the insertion of "buggers" into a political polemic links the demarcation of sexual boundaries with the "fascist" project of colonialism.

Gilles Deleuze and Felix Guattari argue in *Anti-Oedipus* that "by boxing the life of the child up within the Oedipus complex, by making family relations the universal mediation of childhood, we cannot help but fail to understand the production of the unconscious itself, and the collective mechanisms that have an immediate bearing on the unconscious" (48–49). In other words, Freud's Oedipal family romance is an "iron collar," a mediating grid which limits and disfigures the very desires it purports to map. They propose two alternatives to this "molar" map of heterosexuality: "We are statistically or molarly heterosexual, but personally homosexual, without knowing it or being fully aware of it, and finally we are transsexual in an elemental, molecular sense" (70). Their rendering of these molecular desires thus echoes the sentiments of Almásy's perverse political outcry: "the outcry of desiring production: we are all schizos! We are all perverts! We are all libidos that are too viscous and too fluid" (67). The family romance prescribes heterosexual marriage, instituting a morality of morality which denigrates adultery, homosexuality, and molecular, transsexual desires as "immoral." Silverman calls this prescription "the ideology of the family," the dominant fiction of sexuality and society that "not only offers the representational system by means of which the subject typically assumes a sexual identity, and takes on the desires commensurate with that identity, but forms the stable core around which a nation's and a period's 'reality' coheres" (Silverman, *Male Subjectivity* 41). *The English Patient* includes several instances of unmappable sexuality: an eroticized opening shot of the smooth, flesh-like desert; a close-up of Almásy's ruined lips receiving a skinned plum from Hana; Hana's affection for the dying Almásy, which Caravaggio calls "love"; and Kip's feelings for his friend Hardy (trying to describe them, he realizes that "I don't even know what I'm talking about"), which Hana calls "love." Madox even seems to love the molecular sand of the desert, scooping a handful into his pocket when he leaves for Britain. But once again, most of these trajectories of desire are either frustrated (Hardy and Almásy die) or complicit in colonialism (Madox appropriating a pocketful of sand, Hana using Almásy to recover from her own emotional "war wounds"; even Bermann's homosexual love for the young Kamal, mentioned earlier, can be interpreted as metaphor for invasion).

Perhaps the only "lines of flight" which escape sexual and geographical maps entirely are those followed by the extra-marital lovers, Kip and Hana. Kip, who discharges German mines for the Allies, removes potentially violent traces of imperialism. A mine, after all, is the most intense and paradoxical of proprietary claims: like Almásy, who demands the parts of Katharine that are "mine" after he has lost her, mines keep on asserting that land is "mine" long after those who planted them have left. Practical only in the planter's absence—only for a retreating army—mines (again like Almásy's utterances of the word, "mine") are mechanisms of disavowal which claim ownership of always already lost objects, and, if successful, destroy the very objects that they claim. By defusing these—more specifically, by "clearing the *roads* of mines" (my emphasis)—Kip reopens the way for both civilian and libidinal traffic, for desires that do not impose cartographic grids or "the names of powerful men." His undoing of identity is even more explicit in the bomb he defuses in one of the film's tensest scenes: he does not realize when he reads off the serial number—*KIP*2600—that the bomb literally has his name on it. This defusing also suggests Kip's swerve away from his namesake, Rudyard Kipling, whose colonial sympathies he criticized incisively earlier in the film. Hana's line of flight from the cartographic gaze is even more complex than Kip's, and requires a detour through recent theorizations of the cinematic apparatus.

In 1945, André Bazin celebrated the disembodied status of the photographic gaze, drawing attention to the French word for the photographic lens, *objectif:* "originality in photography as distinct from originality in painting lies in the essentially objective character of photography. For the first time an image of the world is formed automatically, without the creative intervention of man" (Bazin 13). The camera, that is, effaces the subjectivity of vision, calling for what Christian Metz terms "primary identification"—the spectator's identification with the camera's gaze, "with himself as a pure act of perception" (Metz 49). It follows that films portray a "hermetically sealed world" wherein "the extreme contrast between the darkness in the auditorium (which also isolates the spectators from one another) and the brilliance of the shifting patterns of light and shade on the screen helps to promote the illusion of voyeuristic separation" (Mulvey 201). Organized largely by the cartographic gaze, *The English Patient* seems to confirm such models of cinema as an experience structured by an un-crossable boundary separating audience from screen.

Jean-Louis Baudry, in an influential essay entitled "The Apparatus," compares the cinematic apparatus to the allegorical cave described in book VII of Plato's *Repub-*

lic. Plato's prisoners, immobilized both by actual chains and by their internalized need for illusion, passively submit to the spectacle projected before them: "It is true they are chained, but, freed, they would still refuse to leave the place where they are" (Baudry 302). The apparatus—a fire placed behind and above the spectators which projects the silhouettes of sculpted puppets—prevents the captive audience from moving, from even wanting to move: "it is their motor paralysis, their inability to move that, making the reality test impractical for them, reinforces their error and makes them inclined to take for real that which takes its place, perhaps its figuration or its projection onto the wall/ screen of the cavern in front of them and from which they cannot detach their eyes and turn away. They are bound, shackled to the screen, tied and related—relation, extension between it and them due to their inability to move in relation to it, the last sight before falling asleep" (Baudry 303). Katharine's death in the Cave of Swimmers involves a strikingly similar apparatus: immobilized by her broken ankle and ribs, she watches painted silhouettes of swimmers illuminated by the fire; though "horribly cold," she refuses to move toward the light: "I really ought to drag myself outside, but then there'd be the sun"; earlier, injured in the plane crash, Katharine begs Almásy, "please don't move me." While she is dying, Katharine writes in Almásy's "scrapbook" (his volume of Herodotus's *Histories*) the lyrical passage that represents the film's thematic and melodramatic climax:

> My darling, I'm waiting for you. How long is a day in the dark? Or a week? The fire is gone now and I'm horribly cold. I really ought to drag myself outside, but then there'd be the sun. . . . I'm afraid I waste the light on the paintings and on writing these words. We die, we die rich with lovers and tribes, tastes we have swallowed, bodies we have entered and swum up like rivers, fears we have hidden in like this wretched cave. I want all this [the saffron she wears in a thimble] marked on my body. We are the real countries, not the boundaries drawn on maps with the names of powerful men. I know you'll come and carry me out into the palace of winds—that's all I've wanted, to walk in such a place with you, with friends: an earth without maps. The lamp has gone out, and I'm writing in the darkness.

The light by which Katharine looks at the paintings is analogous to the light projected on the screen: as it fades—as the film's illusion ends—Katharine experiences the blurring of temporal ("how long is a day in the dark?") as well as geographical boundaries. Completely dependent on light, she dies simultaneously imagining a world without maps and reinscribing "countries" by requesting that her body be "marked." Katharine's death allegorizes the frustration of adulterous desire, the process by which the cartographic gaze has killed her, projecting its grid of molar morals—literalized in the grid pattern on her dress—upon her body.

But Almásy—ho stands generally at the other end of the cartographic gaze, looking at Katharine through grids—fares no better. Caught in the networks of voyeurism (watching her without being seen) and "fetishistic scopophilia" (laying claim to her supersternal notch), he also ends up immobilized and afraid of light and movement. He declines a position in the window because "I can't bear the light, anyways"; and Hana settles with him in the monastery until his death because he "hates to be moved"—one might add, emotionally as well as physically. Instead of sunlight, he prefers to observe his own dreams: "I can already see. . . . I can see all the way to the desert. Before the war. Making maps. . . . I can see my wife in that view." Almásy's dreams recall his map making faithfully, but distort his adulterous affair so that he believes he was married. In addition to Plato's cave, Baudry also links cinema with dreams as theorized by Freud: like Plato's subterranean prisoners, dreamers undergo a regression to a state of immobility, a state in which real perceptions cannot be distinguished from fantasy (309). Almásy's dreams express his identification with nationalist ideology, his occupancy of a prescribed position: in them he is both the map-maker he really was and the husband he never became. As Silverman puts it, the cinematic illusion—the "given-to-be-seen"—"depends for its hegemonic effects on the slotting of the eye into a particular spectatorial position—into a metaphoric geometral point. The latter can then best be defined "as the position from which we apprehend and affirm those elements of the screen which are synonymous with the dominant fiction" (Silverman, *Threshold* 179).

In addition to Baudry's models of spectatorial regression, the film of *The English Patient* dramatizes also Metz's voyeuristic model of cinema. Metz argues that "cinematic voyeurism, *unauthorized* scopophilia," is much more voyeuristic than theatrical drama as a result of "the spectator's solitude in the cinema" and the "*segregation of spaces*" that renders the filmic space "utterly heterogeneous" to the audience, with which it cannot communicate (63–64). Completely alone, seeing without being seen, Almásy as both stalker (following Katharine to the Cairo marketplace, secretly watching her at parties and dances) and map-maker indulges in unauthorized scopophilia. Indeed, the film frames adultery itself in voyeuristic terms, since the earliest exchange of gazes between Katharine and Almásy occurs when Katharine retells the following story from Herodotus: "The king insisted he would find some way to prove beyond dispute that his wife was fairest of all women. "I will hide you in the room where we sleep," says [Candaules]. Candaules tells Gyges that the queen has the same practice every night. She takes off her clothes and puts them on the chair by the door to her room—"and from where you stand you will be able to gaze on her at your leisure." And that evening it's exactly as the king told him: she goes to the chair and removes her clothes one by one until she's standing naked in full view of Gyges, and indeed she was more lovely than he could have imagined." So far, the story matches every detail of cinematic scopophilia as decribed by Metz and Mulvey: the woman is mute, passive, and objectified, while Gyges wields his secret gaze in an act of spectatorial rape. But then the story's conclusion suggests that the "segregation of spaces" stressed by Metz and the "hermetically sealed world" described by Mulvey do not adequately describe spectatorship in, and of, *The English Patient*: "But then the queen looked up and saw Gyges concealed in the shadows, and although she said nothing, she shuddered. . . . And the next day she sent for Gyges and challenged him. And hearing his story, this is what she said—[Geoffrey interrupts banteringly, 'Off with his head!']—she said, 'either you must submit to death for gazing on that which you should not, or else kill my husband who shamed me and become king in his place'." So Gyges kills the king and marries the queen, and becomes ruler of Lydia for twenty-eight years.

When the spectacle returns the voyeur's gaze, the expected decapitation/ castration is not the only option. The alternative is to cross over the "threshold of the visible world," engage the spectacle erotically, and produce, in this case, a political transformation leading to an unusually stable twenty-eight-year regime. As a politically productive alternative to voyeuristic models of the apparatus, *The English Patient* offers a cinema of radical movement and heteropathic contact.

In Baudry's "Apparatus" essay, dreams are not as hopeless a cinematic model as Plato's cave. Baudry argues that dream-perceptions, and perhaps film as well, may produce not merely second-hand simulacra, but a more-than-real: waking from his first dreams of the desert, Almásy asks "Is there sand in my eyes? Are you cleaning sand from my ears?" The inability to distinguish hallucinations from reality informs "the specific mode in which the dreamer identifies with his dream, a mode which is anterior to the mirror stage, to the formation of the self, and therefore founded on a permeability, a fusion of the interior with the exterior" (Baudry 311). *The English Patient* moves towards just such a permeability, a mode of identification either anterior or posterior to the mirror stage, unfastened from the formation of the self. Baudry's notion of passing through the screen offers an alternative to the sedentary spectatorship imposed by Plato's cave, a cinema in which vision does not aspire towards the transcendental gaze, but instead affirms its basis in the body.

Commenting on the way in which Roland Barthes's look "irradiat[es] otherwise insignificant—or even culturally devalued—details" in *Camera Lucida,* Silverman describes "a wayward or eccentric look, one not easily stabilized or assigned to preexisting loci, and whose functioning is consequently resistant to visual standardization" (Silverman, *Threshold* 183). Vision, Silverman suggests, can be simultaneously embodied and nomadic: traveling along unpredictable itineraries, the wayward eye transports the body along with it. "The adulteration of vision," then, describes not only the adulteration that happens to vision when *more-than-real* objects impose themselves upon it, but also the adulteration of the body by heterogeneous memories and experiences that vision precipitates. Silverman goes on to imagine a visual text that "would displace me from my self, as well as from the geometral point. It would do so by enlisting me in an act of "heteropathic recollection." It would factor into my mnemic operations not only what resides outside the given-to-be-seen, but what my *moi* excludes—what must be denied in order for my self to exist as such" (Silverman, *Threshold* 185). Silverman's example of heteropathic recollection—a woman's voice reading from letters sent by the protagonist of *Sans Soleil,* "speak[ing] his memories" (Silverman, *Threshold* 186)— anticipates one of *The English Patient*'s many flashback devices: Hana reads texts that Katharine has already read or written into Almásy's book, their voices alternating as the film passes from one diegetic level to another. The entire film can be seen as a process of instilling Almásy's traumatic experiences (which at first even he cannot remember) into Hana's memory—and into the audience's as well, since Hana generally stands in as a sort of Ideal Spectator of the flashback scenes—by means of heteropathic identification.

In the midst of Metz's psychoanalytically inflected study of *The Imaginary Signifier*, a few seem out of place. One of these describes a form of identification that is neither primary (identification with the camera's gaze) nor secondary (identification with individual characters):

> What I have said about identification so far amounts to the statement that the spectator is absent from the screen *as perceived*, but also (the two things inevitably go together) present there and even "all-present" as *perceiver*. At every moment I am in the film by my look's caress. This presence often remains diffuse, geographically undifferentiated, evenly distributed over the whole surface of the screen; or more precisely *hovering*, like the psychoanalyst's listening, ready to catch on preferentially to some motif in the film, according to the force of that motif and according to my own phantasies as a spectator, without the cinematic code itself intervening to govern this anchorage and impose it on the whole audience. (54)

"My look's caress," a geographically undifferentiated spectatorial presence, describes an alternative to the gaze, which originates from a fixed, transcendental point. (Incidentally, the phrase resonates with one reviewer's enthusiasm about the way in which Minghella's "cameras caress the landscape" [Hobson 6]). Metz sketches a theory of individual cinematic response, an alternative to his usual implicit model of passive and impersonal cinematic subjection to the governance of primary and secondary identifications. In the second anomalous passage, Metz crosses the boundary of gender in order to describe his *presence* at a film: "Like the midwife attending a birth who, simply by her presence, assists the woman in labour, I am present for the film in a double capacity (though they are really one and the same) as witness and as assistant: I watch, and I help. By watching the film I help it to be born" (Metz 93). With their emphasis on an embodied spectatorial presence, these two passages indicate a potential line of flight leading out of Metz's voyeuristic model of spectatorship.

In one of *The English Patient*'s most memorable sequences, Hana and Kip make love without so much as touching one another. The sequence—in which Hana swings from wall to wall in a church, looking at their frescoes, on a rope counterweighted by Kip—stands in for a love scene, placed as it is between a courtship by candlelight and a naked conversation in bed. Hana's spectatorship provides an optimistic contrast to Katharine's death in Plato's cave: far from immobile, she literally moves from picture to picture; far from passive, she actively contributes to the spectacle, illuminating each image as she approaches it with her flare. Hana is *hovering* swinging to whichever painting she and Kip prefer, bringing (like a midwife) each one to light by her very presence. The sequence involves erotic as well as physical "transport": Hana calls out Kip's name as she rises into the air, then thanks him enthusiastically when she alights.

Giuliana Bruno, describing a cinema based on transport rather than an oppressive apparatus writes: "If we believe that 'whatever its particular fiction, the film produces a pleasure akin to that of the travelogue,' we can go further and assert that cinematic pleasure is more than the unique product of a textuality produced in the enclosed darkness of the apparatus—Plato's cave; it literally belongs to a wider territory. Breaking out of the cave, film theory should acknowledge that forms of *transito* lie at the root of cinematic pleasures, and place these pleasures in the context of journeys of the gaze through topographies" (Bruno 56). Instead of colonialist travelogues, which gaze unseen upon foreign geographies in order to gain knowledge and power over them, a transitorial cinema caresses and illuminates its objects without denying the embodied nature of its own look: it travels through unmapped landscapes and leaves them unmapped. As the film shuttles through time and space, between northern Africa in 1939 and Italy in 1945, its spectators can cross boundaries not only vicariously, but actively and physically helping to produce the very images they experience on the screen. This erotic, embodied look effectively dissolves the boundaries between self and other: "And so looking has force: it tears, it is sharp, it is an acid. In the end, it corrodes the object and observer until they are lost in the field of vision. I once was solid, and now I am dissolved: that is the voice of seeing" (Elkins 45).

The English Patient concludes with a generalized dissolution of boundaries: Hana's voice blends with Katharine's as they read the letter, Hana's piano theme blends with Almásy's song in Hungarian, and Hana emerges from the monastery, riding in a truck, staring at the sun in tears. In the audience's tears, the film produces a physical and more or less collective and collaborative trace, and its images cross the boundary between the screen and viewers' eyes. The cinematic apparatus based a voyeuristic command of vision dissolves before—or within—our very eyes as they become filled not with visual pleasure but with emotions of love and grief, not with cartographic desire but with an awareness of their own blindnesses.

WORKS CITED

Baudry, Jean-Louis. "The Apparatus: Metapsychological Approaches to the Impression of Reality in the Cinema." Trans. Alan Williams. *Narrative, Apparatus, Ideology: A Film Theory Reader.* Ed. Philip Rosen. New York: Columbia UP, 1986. 299–318.

Bazin, André. "The Ontology of the Photographic Image." *What Is Cinema?* Ed. and Trans. Hugh Gray. Berkeley: U of California P, 1967. Vol. 1, 9–16.

Bruno, Giuliana. *Streetwalking on a Ruined Map: Cultural Theory and the City Films of Elvira Notari.* Princeton: Princeton UP, 1993.

Certeau, Michel de. *The Practice of Everyday Life.* Trans. Steven Rendall. Berkeley: U of California P, 1988.

Deleuze, Gilles, and Felix Guattari. *Anti-Oedipus: Capitalism and Schizophrenia.* Trans. Robert Hurley, Mark Seem, and Helen Lane. Minneapolis: U of Minnesota P, 1996.

Elkins, James. *The Object Stares Back: On the Nature of Seeing.* San Diego: Harcourt Brace & Co., 1996.

Hobson, Louis B. "English Patient Is a Romantic Masterpiece." *The Calgary Sun* (29 November 1996): 6.

Lacan, Jacques. *The Four Fundamental Concepts of Psychoanalysis.* Ed. Jacques-Alain Miller. Trans. Alan Sheridan. New York: Norton, 1981.

Metz, Christian. *The Imaginary Signifier: Psychoanalysis and the Cinema.* Trans. Celia Britton Annwyl Williams, Ben Brewster, and Alfred Guzzetti. Bloomington: Indiana UP, 1982.

Minghella, Anthony. *The English Patient.* Prod. Saul Zaentz. Miramax, 1996.

Minghella, Anthony. *The English Patient: A Screenplay Based on the Novel by Michael Ondaatje.* New York: Hyperion, 1996.

Mulvey, Laura. "Visual Pleasure and Narrative Cinema." *Narrative, Apparatus, Ideology: A Film Theory Reader.* Ed. Philip Rosen. New York: Columbia UP, 1986. 198–209.

Ondaatje, Michael. *The English Patient.* Toronto: Random House of Canada, 1992.

Shohat, Ella. "Imagining Terra Incognita: The Disciplinary Gaze of Empire." *Public Culture* 3.2 (1991): 41–70.

Silverman, Kaja. *Male Subjectivity at the Margins.* New York: Routledge, 1992.

Silverman, Kaja. *The Threshold of the Visible World.* New York: Routledge, 1996.

Sommer, Doris. *Foundational Fictions: The National Romances of Latin America.* Berkeley: U of California P, 1993.

Webster's Third New International Dictionary of the English Language. Springfield: Merriam-Webster, 1993.

The Representation of "Race" in Ondaatje's *In the Skin of a Lion*

Glen Lowry

With a few notable exceptions, Ondaatje's depiction of racialized subjects has received only limited attention (see, e.g., Turcotte; Mukherjee; Rundle; Lowry). While his identity as a Singhalese emigrant or Canadian immigrant is often noted (see, e.g., Kamboureli; Richler; Wachtel; Young), critics tend to ignore the political implications of Ondaatje's work in relation to that of other writers of colour, effectively eliding "race" as an element of his writing. The elision has meant that the difficult questions of critical positioning, or what I, following Judith Butler, would term the "performative" aspect of his texts *qua* "racialized" writing, have fallen from view. Within the dominant postmodern discourse, i.e., a discourse focused on formalist readings of his texts, Ondaatje's writing becomes abstracted from the colonial and post-colonial contexts with which it engages. In an examination of Ondaatje's writing, up to and including *Running in the Family*, Arun Mukherjee has criticized an apparent lack of "cultural baggage... brought with him when he came to Canada" (114); she argues that because Ondaatje "does not write about his otherness" and his writing shows "no trauma of uprooting" (114), critics have been allowed to oversimplify the issue of Ondaatje's identity. Although it has become dated by Ondaatje's later writing, particularly his overt engagements in the issues of "trauma" and "otherness" at the heart of *The English Patient* and *Anil's Ghost*, both of which deal with (neo)colonialism and complex questions of social justice, Mukherjee's concern about the critical reception of his work is still relevant. Prioritizing social realism and intentionality, her contention that Ondaatje has "simply refused to address himself to the particular needs of his community" (132) is problematic; however, it does locate the matter of "race" blindness in responses to Ondaatje's writing: "The question, then, is whether Ondaatje's work contains more than 'the heat and the mountains and the jungle' of Sri Lanka that the white critics are unable to see in their ethnocentrism. For surely, Sri Lanka has more to it than the three things mentioned above. It consists of seven million human beings who ostensibly must have a world view unique to them" (Mukherjee 114).

Inasmuch as a dearth of "third world" (Mukherjee's term) references in the writing, wariness around giving interviews (Fagan 115; Finkle 90), and lack of public identification with writers of color, all seem to be instrumental in the continued construction of Ondaatje as an un-hyphenated—i.e., non-"racialized"—Canadian writer by predominantly "white" readers, Mukherjee's question remains vital. In raising the issue of representing "racialized" alterity, which is very different from marginality, Mukherjee's critique foregrounds an aporia in the critical discourse that I hope to address with this paper. Although it is, perhaps, less obviously so in this novel than in the two most recent novels, "race" is, nevertheless, a central concern in *In the Skin of a Lion*. Instead of taking issue with an apparent lack of "racialized" subjects (as Mukherjee might do) or assuming that the absence of non-"white" subjects is tantamount to a lack of interest in "race" (as the majority of critics seem to have done), I contend that Ondaatje's writing, from *In the Skin of a Lion* on, represents "race" as a complex problem of representation that not only puts into play the interpolated identities of so-called "racialized" subjects but of "white" subjects as well. Rather than fixating on Ondaatje's actual identity and becoming caught in a trap of racial positivism, we might think through the way his "passing" as a "white" writer, not to mention the appropriation of "racialized" difference upon which it depends, performs and undoes the dominant "race" codes of CanLit ("Canadian literature," here with reference to the field of scholarly discipline). Reading *In the Skin of a Lion* as a statement on the problematic construction of "whiteness" rather than "color," enables us to re-situate Ondaatje's work, and/or our interpretative performances of it, within a much more contradictory and contentious conception of CanLit as a space of "race." I propose, therefore, to return to this novel to help develop thinking about Ondaatje's writing as writing about "race." Focusing on his depiction of Toronto in terms of a complex history of shifting social spaces and the ethnic and racial identities of the novel's two central characters, Patrick and Caravaggio, this paper looks forward to a more thorough discussion of Ondaatje's critique of nationalism and multiculturalism. Focusing on the issue of "race" *In the Skin of a Lion*, I am arguing that this novel is a precursor to *The English Patient* and *Anil's Ghost* and, as such, that it offers insight into a multivalent development of racialized writing, both in terms of Ondaatje's work and CanLit as a whole.

I begin with a quote from *In the Skin of a Lion*: "Patrick Lewis arrived in the city of Toronto as if it were land after years at sea. . . . at twenty-one, he had been drawn out from that small town like a piece of metal dropped under the vast arches of Union Station to begin his life once more. . . . He was an immigrant to the city" (53). For Patrick, "the searcher," whose life and actions knit together the characters and plot of the novel, entering the city means arriving in modernity, in a space of contradiction, alienation and possibility: "Now, in the city, he was new even to himself. . . . He saw his image in the glass of telephone booths. He ran his hands over the smooth pink marble pillars that reached into the rotunda. The train station was a palace, its riches and caverns an intimate city. He could be shaved, eat a meal, or have his shoes coloured" (54). In the station, Patrick notices "a man well-dressed with three suitcases, shouting out in another language" (54). Two days later, "He saw the man again, still unable to move from his safe zone, in a different suit, as if one step away was the quicksand of the new world" (54). The juxtaposition of these two migrants suggests both Patrick's reluctance to move into this spectacular "new world" and the importance of the city in his reconstruction of self. Sitting on a nearby bench and watching the "tides of movement," Patrick feels the powerful "reverberations of trade" (54). When he speaks out his name," however, it becomes "lost in the high air of Union Station. No one turned. They were in the belly of a whale" (54). The use of the third person plural articulates an affinity between the Canadian-born Patrick and this figure of the well-dressed "foreigner," both of whom transform and are transformed by the city.

Ondaatje's narrative blurs the recognized order of originary identities. Overlapping the trauma of immigration with the alienation of urbanization, it refigures the expansion of Toronto, the modern industrial core of an emergent nation state, within an international flow of bodies and cultures. Imagining voices for marginalized individuals and/or their forgotten communities, *In the Skin of a Lion* re-maps Toronto in terms of class struggle; in so doing, it depicts a city under construction, returning readers to key sites in the social development of the nation. Ondaatje's representation of the building of the Viaduct and the Waterworks spatializes the city's historic development; these key sites become representations of complex, contradictory drives to control not only physical spaces but also their conception. Symbolically, the novel reminds readers that the monuments of the modern city bear traces of divergent social meanings and purposes. Thus, *In the Skin of a Lion* destabilizes a linear historical view of Canadian society as a top down initiative orchestrated by a predominantly Anglo ruling, or managerial class. The city Patrick enters is a space of linguistic and cultural diversity beyond the purview of Franco-Anglo biculturalism or Anglo-imperialism, but coterminous with it. If metaphorically, Patrick "begins his life once more" (53) searching for the lost millionaire, Ambrose Small, a heroic figure of prosperity in this depressed city, he ultimately establishes himself in the nexus of Toronto's working-class communities. His identity develops in relation to a host of other, not quite "white" subjects—Greek, Macedonian, Russian, and Italian. His actions and the kindness of others, rather than his name or his country birth, become the determining factors in his self development.

While this idealized conception of social being coincides with the ideological precepts of official multiculturalism, Ondaatje's engagement with the historical elision of class difference offers an important point of entrance into critiques of what has been referred to as "song and dance" Multiculturalism. Spatializing and historicizing ethnic development within an urban setting, this novel helps to reframe government policy and the ideology of its utopic pluralism. Put another way, Ondaatje's exploration of Patrick's working-class experience challenges notions of Canadian identity as a racially neutral basis upon which a "just" multicultural society is built. Patrick's cultural displacement is negotiated rather than static. At times, his cultural background allows him access to spaces of privilege—the Muskoka Hotel, Harris's office; however, in general Patrick moves through a complex social network in which cultural differences between any us (Canadian) and them (foreign) are seen in terms of class us (the labourers) and them (the rich):

> "I'll tell you about the rich," Alice would say, "the rich are always laughing. They keep saying the same things on their boats and lawns: *Isn't this grand! We're having a good time!* And whenever the rich get drunk and maudlin about humanity you have to listen for hours. But they keep you in the tunnels and stockyards. They do not toil or spin. Remember that . . . understand what they will always refuse to let go of. There are a hundred

fences and lawns between the rich and you. You've got to know these
things, Patrick, before you ever go near them—the way a dog before bat-
tling cows rolls in the shit of the enemy." (132)

Patrick is happiest amongst people with whom he shares little ethnic affinity. His personal growth is predicated on movement away from his Anglo-Irish roots; rather than
the inculcation of a kind of parochial Englishness, it points toward a more extensive
sense of cultural awareness and identity. Significantly, Cato's letters teach Patrick the
identity of the Finnish loggers with whom he shared his childhood landscape. In the
city, as a worker, he learns that the separation between himself and the itinerant loggers
is more apparent than real. Listening to Alice and reading Hana's archive, he deciphers
the unacknowledged social networks, and fundamental material relations, that have, in
part, structured his life.

When Patrick learns *gooshter*, the Macedonian word for *iguana,* he bridges the
divide between himself and those around him, and he is suddenly overwhelmed by their
"friendship, concern." Crying openly in their midst, exposing his loneliness, Patrick
draws an invitation to "The waterworks at eight, Sunday night. A gathering." This
breakthrough leads to a remarkable scene in which Ondaatje depicts the Waterworks,
not as an empty Mausoleum or new high-tech sanitized filtration plant, but as an inhabited space in which the workers perform and create their own counter-histories. Re-in-
scribing the monumental site of the R.C. Harris Filtration Plant—Toronto's official
tribute to its own Boulevard Haussmann—as a social space, re-imagining it as a zone
class conflict, the novel challenges us to revisit the official history and rethink our con-
ceptions of the city's spaces.

In an essay examining the archival basis for *In the Skin of the Lion*, Dennis Duffy
unearths documentary evidence for the kind of cultural linguistic conflicts depicted in
the novel. In terms of this scene at the Waterworks, Duffy's discovery of a pamphlet
protesting the intrusion of "foreign," non-English speaking workers into the Beach (the
neighbourhood housing the plant) provides an interesting example of historical archive
with which Ondaatje engages. Duffy feels that Ondaatje's novel might have included an
episode in which "local strollers" take issue with a security guard who blocks them
from entering the Waterworks. In fact, the apparent discrepancy between the archival
record of the conflict and the events depicted by Ondaatje presents readers with an important impasse. However, Ondaatje's choice to represent imagined events realistically
allows the novel to resist the primacy of the archival fact and to refigure agency in a
complex manner. In final analysis, the assumed similitude between historical fact and
the fiction upon which Duffy's conception of the novel's political potential rests is
grounded in a problematic reading of power relations. To put it simply, this assumption
relies on a conception of class conflict in which the aggressor is all powerful and the
victim completely disenfranchised. Ondaatje's text, on the other hand, presents readers
with the problem of having to construct a historical narrative against which to read the
fictional one: the event does not appear in the novel because it oversimplifies the com-

plexity of linguistic, cultural, and political relations represented, and therefore contradicts the story Ondaatje is telling.

Read from the perspective of counter-hegemonic historiography—Marxist, feminist, queer, and postcolonial—Ondaatje's "fictional history" provides more than a positivist attempt to add the stories of the disenfranchised to the history. More than simply expanding the parameters of Canadian literature to include writing about the working class and ethnic minorities forgotten in the "Official histories and news stories" of Toronto's metropolitan expansion, the novel challenges a dominant discourse which is "always as soft as rhetoric, like that of a politician making a speech after a bridge is built, a man who does not even cut the grass on his own lawn" (145). As others have pointed out, Ondaatje's writing crosses the line between fact and fiction, history and literature (see Bowering). However, rather than attacking the one (fact/history) from within the bounds of the other (fiction/literature), this novel performs a critical intervention within the emergence of the postmodern or multicultural canon/s to which it is ascribed—an intervention that draws attention to the historical function of CanLit as cultural praxis, rather than cultural expression. The forgotten stories from the building of Toronto, which have caught most critics' attention, are offset by quotations from popular song, art criticism, and Canadian literature. In his acknowledgments, Ondaatje specifies that he has had permission to print lyrics for "Up Jumped You with Love" and "I Can't Get Started," lines from the *Epic of Gilgamesh*, sentences from Judith Mara Gutman's essay "Lewis Hine and the American Social Conscience," two sentences from the journals of Anne Wilkinson, and lines from Martha Ostenso's novel *Wild Geese*. In addition to these few re-cycled fragments of text, Ondaatje's text gestures toward a young Al Purdy, Anne Wilkinson, and Judge Sheard of *Judge Sheard's Jokes* (grandfather of Sarah Sheard, to whom the novel is dedicated). The novel's revision of the historical account of Toronto's modern development embroils itself in a fanciful depiction of CanLit as social space or geography through which Caravaggio, the name itself an allusion to one notorious Renaissance painter, steals his way back to the city.

To this end, Ondaatje borrows "two sentences" from Wilkinson's journals: "Let me now re-emphasize the extreme looseness of the structure of things" (163) and "Demarcation. . . . That is all we need to remember" (179). Paradoxically, the text does not attribute either of the sentences to Wilkinson or her character, but rather ascribes the former to Alice and the latter to Caravaggio. Without an intimate knowledge of Wilkinson's writing one might pass over the sentences; only the *demarcation* of the text, the fact both sentences are in italics, draws attention to the gesture. In both cases, however, the stolen sentence function thematically. Alice's utterance of "Let me now re-emphasize the extreme looseness of the structure of things" is powerfully ironic. Coming to Patrick as a memory after her untimely death, it functions as a reminder of Patrick's shattered dream of their growing old together: "There was always, he thought, this pleasure ahead of him, an ace up his sleeve so he could say you can do anything to me, take everything away, put me in prison, but I will know Alice Gull when we are old" (164). The sentence also conjures up the chain of loosely related, seemingly coincidental events that brought Alice and Patrick together: her spectacular fall from the Bridge, Temelcoff's miraculous catch, an ensuing friendship with Clara, and Patrick's decision to abandon pursuit of Ambrose Small. As a counter-point to Patrick's searching, Alice's death is a thread which ties together key elements of the plot. The explosion that wrenches her from Patrick solidifies his connection with Temelcoff, Caravaggio, Hana, and in the end R.C. Harris while cementing his fate.

The second sentence—"Demarcation, that is what we all need to remember"— functions like a refrain in the last section of the novel and, as such, is crucial to the unfolding of its final episode. Much as the character of Alice becomes a realization of the first sentence, the figure of Caravaggio is firmly connected to this second one. Again, Patrick recalls this statement; he remembers Caravaggio uttering it while he and Patrick were painting of the penitentiary roof, just prior to Caravaggio's escape. Again, the statement is ironic. On the surface, it is a comment on the problem of painting an "intentional blue roof," which made "the three men working on it [become] uncertain of the clear boundaries" between roof and sky. It also speaks to Caravaggio's genius. We might say that in fooling the guards by painting himself into the scene, i.e., painting himself blue, Caravaggio flaunts the line between himself and his environment. Furthermore, the notion of "demarcation" resonates with Caravaggio's somewhat tenuous identity; it is connected with both colonial history and class politics. Historically, the demarcation line of 1496 was the historical line dividing the New World between Spanish and Portuguese interests or lands. The word is inflected with issues of ownership and proprietary relations between competing economic units. This particular term, particularly in the context of the phrase in which it surfaces, functions to further establish Caravaggio as a "racialized" figure.

A conventional reading of this indirect quotation might suggest that, through the voice of Caravaggio, Ondaatje has appropriated Wilkinson's writing. As literary scholars, we ascribe ownership to the individual from whose journal the words appear to be lifted; however, within the logic of the novel itself, the reverse might also be said to be true: Wilkinson has stolen Caravaggio's language. In fact, this phrase is ascribed to Caravaggio and it has provided the abstract basis for his plan. Realizing as he does that demarcation makes visible, he realizes also that it can be used to render himself invisible. In having himself painted the conspicuous blue of the prison roof, Caravaggio escapes by vanishing from sight. This is the story Caravaggio tells Anne when he meets her. We are told that "She sits across from him laughing at the story of his escape, not fully believing it" (201). We might extrapolate from this that Caravaggio has repeated this phrase—after all, it is the cornerstone of his masterly plan—and that later it comes to appear in Wilkinson's journal. We are lead to imagine that Wilkinson has picked this story up from the escaped thief. Again, Ondaatje undermines the originary moment of the very material; his novel appropriates and rewrites literary history within the frame of fiction.

To develop the significance of this meeting with Wilkinson, it is useful to consider Caravaggio's encounter with another figure of Canadian literature. During his escape, Caravaggio turns up in Trenton, where he meets a young boy who helps him to remove the blue paint. As Caravaggio is preparing to leave, the boy gives him a note with his name, Alfred, written on it. When Caravaggio apologizes for having nothing to give the boy in return, "The kid grinned, very happy. 'I know,' he said. 'Remember my name'" (182). This puzzling exchange does not appear to have a direct bearing on the plot itself: while the young Al is helpful in cleaning the paint off Caravaggio, he recedes into the fabric of the novel after Caravaggio goes on his way. For readers versed in the localism of Canadian poetry, the boy's name and that he is in Trenton suggest homage to Al Purdy. This fits with the Anne Wilkinson scene discussed above to establish a kind of literary map of his escape root. From Trenton to Bobcaygen, Purdy to Wilkinson, Caravaggio moves through a geography of literary reference. As a counterpoint to the historical archive out of which the urban events of the novel are collected, Caravaggio's escape takes place within the sanctified spaces of an agrarian literary tradition.

At the risk of undervaluing the complexity of Ondaatje's literary sleight of hand, one might argue that this figure of the thief moving through the landscapes of Canadian literature can be read as an imaginative reflection of Ondaatje's own presence within the centralist tradition of Canadian letters. The fact that Caravaggio speaks Ondaatje's re-appropriation of Wilkinson's journal entries and shares Purdy's slightly skewed sense of landscape suggests an affinity between writer and character. This affinity is heightened by Ondaatje's description of Caravaggio's gentle teachers, "the company of thieves ... who looked refined and wore half-moon glasses" (191). This passage depicts Caravaggio as an acolyte or devoted craftsman rather than as a common criminal: "Caravaggio was welcomed into their midst and lectured with great conservatism on the art of robbery.... They were protective of their style and area of interest. They tried to persuade the young man that what *they* did was the most significant but at the same time they did not wish to encourage competition.... He was in awe of them, wanted to be all of them in their moments of extreme crisis. He hung around them not so much to learn their craft but to study the way they lived when they stepped back into the world of order ... he was fascinated only by character" (191). Thus, he learns his way into the art of thievery by shadowing these men "in order to watch their performances." He learns to be comfortable in other people's houses, at home in their absence, "high up on the bookcases ... as still as a gargoyle against Trollope and H.G. Wells" (198). Like Patrick who is "always comfortable in someone else's landscape" and who enjoys "being taught the customs of a place" (138), Caravaggio learns to inhabit a space to which he makes no claim of ownership.

The racialization of Caravaggio is a much more explicit enactment of the ambivalence underlying Patrick identity. His escape through the imaginary landscape of Canadian literature on his way back to the city follows Ondaatje's description of his attack at the hands of the bigots, "smug without race." Within the thematic tropology of 1970s Canadian literature, Caravaggio's escape fits the Atwoodian model. On one level, Caravaggio's "survival" is based on his ability to escape through the wilds. His borrowing of a paragraph from Martha Ostenso's *Wild Geese*, with which the description of the prison attack begins, further suggests Ondaatje's indebtedness to this tradition. However, in reading Caravaggio's journey in terms of this more mainstream sense of Canadian literature, there is a danger of losing sight of the "racism" that precipitates it. The discursive layering, in fact the highly allusive nature of this section of the novel, points to a kind of double inscription—by which the character of Caravaggio both articulates and disavows the hegemonic subject of literary nationalism.

Rehearsing a common theme in the critical discourse, Smaro Kamboureli's introduction to Ondaatje in her recent anthology of multicultural writing in Canada, *Making a Difference: Canadian Multicultural Literature,* foregrounds the writer's identity as an immigrant of Ceylonese or Sri Lankan descent, without explicitly mentioning the subject of "race" or identifying Ondaatje with other writers of colour. Kamboureli does note Ondaatje's identification with "a generation of writers that "was the first real migrant tradition . . . of writers of our time—Rushdie, Ishiguro, Ben Okri, Rohinton Mistry" (Kamboureli 194), which, in the context of this anthology and its somewhat problematic mixture of white and non-white writers under a generalized rubric of difference and immigration, suggests an important shift in the discourse. While there is no suggestion how the excerpted fragment from *In the Skin of a Lion* speaks to this tradition of Asian writers Ondaatje sees himself fitting into, it fore grounds the question at the centre of my paper. How do we begin to read this novelistic depiction of class struggle amongst various European ethnic communities in relation to Ondaatje's implicit self-identification with this particular group of writers? How do we read the construction of a "white" identity in relation to the various interpelated, racialized subjectivities, against which it is constructed and over which it asserts power? In the context of contemporary CanLit and/or the emergence of multiculturalism in general, how does the appearance of a "white" subject presuppose an elision of particular class differences or the re-appropriation of racialized histories and experiences

In resisting the essential binaries of identity by which much of the critical understanding of Canadian literature is figured, centre/margin, "white"/non-"white," immigrant/"native," *In the Skin of a Lion* offers readers a highly complex site by which to theorize the function of "race" in the development of a "white" subjectivity as it is figured against the backdrop of European ethnic communities. One might say that Ondaatje's novel "reverses the gaze" and throws the question of "race" back on the readers. If working backwards, contemporary critics tend to think of "whiteness" (when it is thought about at all) in terms of a kind of homogenous Western or European subjectivity, this novel points towards the history of this emergent racial identity. As a number of postcolonial critics have suggested the assumption that "whiteness" signifies some kind of neutral position in opposition to various "racialized" identities is itself one of the master tropes of modern "racist" thought. As "race" theorists have made clear, the tendency to assume that racism is solely concerned with the construction of others, people of color and First Nations, obfuscates or again naturalizes the fact that "whiteness" is itself a construct. In "returning the gaze," cultural theorists have argued that the formation of a "white subject" and the attendant system of social value to which it is connected is dependent on a series of differences in which "race" functions. As such, "whiteness" is part of the complex and violent history of Western racism; it is a social construct with which divisions of labour and social values are controlled (on this, see Stoler; Razack). A common suggestion made within the circles of anti-racist activism and pedagogy is that more work needs to be done understanding this historical fact. The argument that "race" is only an issue in texts that deal specifically with a "racialized" subject or character or conversely which articulate overt racism depends on the facile conflation of "whiteness" with an absence of "racial" significance, or mores precisely recognizable signifiers of "race" or "racialized" identity.

If, as George Eliot Clarke argues, "The general incoherence of color-based identity in Canada permits Canadian whiteness to exist . . . as an ethereal force . . . a kind of ideal whiteness, ready for export" (100), then the question left open is how does this floating identity, the ethereal force of whiteness, come to depend on the hegemonic control of "race" discourse? By what means does the assumption of "whiteness" as a neutral position, something that simply is rather than something that comes into being (in place and time), effect that construction of a "racialized" other. According to Clarke, the popular conception of Canada as a nation that has developed free from a US-style history of "race" conflict is in itself a particular kind of racism. The oft rehearsed notion that Canada is or has been a predominantly "white country" that came to be peopled by the descendants of European settlers is but part of a recurrent struggle for self-creation, which pits a national identity off against various non-European immigrants and First Nations people ("First Nations" is the Canadian term for the Indigenous Indian population). With the emergence of state-sponsored Canadian Multiculturalism and a revamped notion of citizen articulated in the new Charter of Rights and Freedoms, which provide the historical context into which this novel is published, "racial" difference comes to be re-conceived in terms of immigration and arrival. In the dominant discourses of cultural production, "racialized" identities are taken to be extrinsic to the emerging multi-ethnic "Canadian," a residue of histories and conflicts beyond the borders of this (post) modern nation-state. Thus, in the popular histories Canada's multicultural literature, "race" continues to have a silent function. *In the Skin of a Lion*, in focusing on European immigrants and the social struggle of the working classes, does more than legitimize the notion of Toronto as a "white" city. It brings to light a complex set of discourses and identity formations that continue to shape the development of multiculturalism in Toronto specifically and Canada in general. In spite of the fact, that both geographically and historically the city comes into being through the expropriation of First Nations land and culture, that it is illegal for people of Chinese ancestry to vote, that there are restrictions placed on the hiring of "white" women in "Chinese businesses," that neighbourhoods and a number of high profile institutions—the University of Toronto, the Granite Club, the Royal Canadian Yacht Club—have by-laws barring "Jews" and "Catholics," that night clubs were paying different rates for Black performers, there is a complacency amongst readers of Ondaatje's novel in acknowledging the ethnic and racial reality of Toronto during the 1930s.

As I have suggested elsewhere (Lowry 2001), the space or neighbourhood in which much of the action in the novel takes place is the spawning ground for a group of fascist sympathizers who walked the streets wearing black arm bands and who were to instigate the Christie Pits riot of 1933. In reading *In the Skin of a Lion* as a novel about the working class without paying some heed to the manner in which labour politics and ethnic identity are connected, without acknowledging the racism rampant within the closed social circles of the ruling class but also in various labour movements, critics perpetuate the idea that Toronto, like the nation of which it would come to be the social and economic centre, developed outside racism. The question that needs to be addressed in the discussion of this novel is how it is that critics have come to see discontinuity, rather than continuity, between the ethnic divisions depicted in it and the systematic creation of "race"-based privilege that we now recognize as the downside of national politics. In adding the figures of Patrick and Caravaggio to the writing of the city, Ondaatje's novel does more than simply expand the scope and texture of what has become Toronto. The struggle these two characters undergo suggests a re-conception of the multicultural citizen that has been emerging in and through the development of Canadian cultural politics during the 1970s and 1980s. The question that I have attempted to open in my reading of this novel is the relationship between the development of "racialized" subject positions and the emergence of "whiteness" as a historically contingent position of privilege—the invisible identity in the cultural mosaic of a new Canadian Multiculturalism.

WORKS CITED

Bowering, George, and Michael Ondaatje, eds. *An H in the Heart: A Reader.* Toronto: McClelland and Stewart, 1994.

Clarke, George Elliott. "White Like Canada." *Transition: An International Review* 73.1 (1998): 98–109.

Duffy, Dennis. "A Wrench in Time: A Sub-Sub-Librarian Looks beneath the *Skin of a Lion.*" *Essays on Canadian Writing* 53 (1994): 125–40.

Fagan, Cary. "Where the Personal and Historical Meet: Michael Ondaatje." *The Power to Bend Spoons: Interviews with Canadian Novelists.* Ed. Beverley Daurio. Toronto: The Mercury P, 1998. 115–21.

Finkle, Derek. "Vow of Silence: Michael Ondaatje..." *Saturday Night* 3.9 (November 1999): 90–94, 96.

Kamboureli, Smaro. "Introduction." *Making a Difference: Canadian Multicultural Literature.* Ed. Smaro Kamboureli. Toronto: Oxford UP, 1996. 1–16.

Lowry, Glen. *After the End/s: CanLit and the Unravelling of Nation, "Race," and Space in the Writing of Michael Ondaatje, Daphne Marlatt, and Roy Kiyooka.* Ph.D. Dissertation. Burnaby: Simon Fraser U, 2001.

Lowry, Glen. "Between *The English Patient*s: 'Race' and the Cultural Politics of Adapting CanLit." *Essays on Canadian Writing* 76 (2002): 216–46.

Mukherjee, Arun. "The Poetry of Michael Ondaatje and Cyril Dabydeen: Two Responses to Otherness." 1985. *Oppositional Aesthetic: Readings from a Hyphenated Space*. By Arun Mukherjee. Toronto: TSAR Books, 1994. 112–32.

Ondaatje, Michael. *Anil's Ghost*. New York: Knopf, 2000.

Ondaatje, Michael. *The English Patient*. Toronto: Random House of Canada, 1992.

Ondaatje, Michael. *In the Skin of a Lion*. Toronto: McClelland and Stewart, 1987.

Ondaatje, Michael, ed. *The Long Poem Anthology*. Toronto: Coach House Press, 1979.

Ondaatje, Michael, ed. *From Ink Lake: An Anthology of Canadian Short Stories*. 1990. Toronto: Vintage Canada, 1995.

McClintock, Anne. *Imperial Leather: Race, Gender, and Sexuality in Colonial Contest*. New York: Routledge, 1995.

Razack, Sherene H. *Looking White People in the Eye: Gender, Race and Culture in Courtrooms and Classrooms*. Toronto: U of Toronto P, 1998.

Richler, Noah. "Ondaatje on Writing." Review of Michael Ondaatje, *Anil's Ghost*. *National Post* (1 April 2000): B1, B2–B3.

Rundle, Lisa. "From Novel to Film: *The English Patient* Distorted." *Border/lines* 43 (1997): 9–13.

Stoler, Ann Laura. *Race and the Education of Desire: Foucault's History of Sexuality and the Colonial Order of Things*. Durham: Duke UP, 1995.

Tötösy de Zepetnek, Steven. "Social Discourse and Cultural Participation in a Multicultural Society." *Canadian Culture and Literatures*. Ed. Steven Tötösy de Zepetnek and Yiu-nam Leung. Edmonton: Research Institute for Comparative Literature, U of Alberta, 1998. 57–69.

Turcotte, Gerry. "'Fears of Primitive Otherness': 'Race' in Michael Ondaatje's *The Man with Seven Toes*." *Constructions of Colonialism: Perspectives on Eliza Fraser's Shipwreck*. Ed. Ian McNiven, L. Russell, and K. Schaffer. London: Leicester UP, 1998. vi, 192.

Wachtel, Eleanor. "An Interview with Michael Ondaatje." *Canadian Literature* 53 (1994): 250–61.

Young, David. "An Ondaatje for the Ages." Rev. of Michael Ondaatje's *Anil's Ghost*. *The Globe and Mail* (1 April 2000): D2, D16.

The Motif of the Collector and Implications of Historical Appropriation in Ondaatje's Novels

Jon Saklofske

Unlike his more recent publications, such as *In the Skin of a Lion, The English Patient,* and *Anil's Ghost,* Michael Ondaatje's early novels *Coming Through Slaughter* and *The Collected Works of Billy the Kid* are texts that collect and interrelate fragments of prose narrative and poetic images in hybridized arrangements that resemble disorganised scrapbooks. Despite their slipshod appearance, these books challenge traditional literary forms and maintain a consistent tension between narrative fragmentation and cohesion. The content of these unconventional experiments with form is no less unorthodox. Ondaatje focuses his creative authority on actual people that have been neglected or over-whelmed by history, that have been "silenced by either too much documentation . . . or far too little" (Barbour 7). His activity of collecting and transforming particular seeds and scraps of the past in a fragmented and fictional form enables Ondaatje to avoid the limitation of historical tradition and expectation of historical validity. Covered by his fin-gerprints, these privately recovered and restored fragments are retold and reintroduced into public circulation. In *Coming Through Slaughter,* Ondaatje contaminates and re-plenishes Buddy Bolden's forgotten history with a self-conscious synthesis of memory and imagination, both of which corrode the supposed objectivity of history with indi-vidual perspective and shatter the silence of a nearly-forgotten figure. Rather than be-coming a historical treatise, argument or unifying and limiting paradigm, the text resur-rects Bolden as a dynamic presence that actively confronts history. *Coming Through Slaughter,* composed from partial accounts, bits of official records, multiple perspec-tives, and invented fictions, can thus be viewed as a private narrative collection that has been publicly produced in a non-traditional form, simultaneously challenging the past with its own forgotten fragments and affecting present expectations.

While Ondaatje does "rescue" the figure of Bolden from obscurity, elevating and complicating his memory, the liberties the author takes with his subject to achieve this re-presentation require further interrogation. Such an investigation, however, should avoid the temptation to define ethical limitations to creativity or to judge Ondaatje's ac-curacy in handling his historical subject. Indeed, Ondaatje makes no pretence to truth, suggesting in a small disclaimer at the end of *Coming Through Slaughter* that "While I have used real names and characters and historical situations I have also used more per-sonal pieces of friends and fathers. There have been some date changes, some charac-ters brought together, and some facts have been expanded or polished to suit the truth of fiction" (158). At the same time, in the same way that the impersonal machine of his-tory sometimes commits an injustice to such unique personalities as Billy the Kid or Buddy Bolden, so the intensely personal activity of the author's fictional use of these same figures may involve a similarly problematic appropriation.

To understand Ondaatje's "historical" activity and to establish a foundation upon which to evaluate his responsibility to the history and memory of Buddy Bolden, I consider the author as a "collector" figure, although I realise that in doing so I may be imposing the same fictions on the author that he does on his subjects. The motif of the "collector" I appeal to appears in Walter Benjamin's essay "Unpacking My Library": Benjamin's conception of the collector figure along with subsequent commentary by Ackbar Abbas allows many of the concerns that surround Ondaatje's encounters with and transfiguration of Bolden's sparse historical record to be understood. For Benjamin, the collector is one who acquires bits and pieces of history, "who gathers his fragments and scraps from the debris of the past," takes possession of them and owns them (Arendt 46). For a collector, "ownership is the most intimate relationship that one can have to objects" (Benjamin 67). In a sense, Ondaatje's publication of his fictionalised version of Bolden's story finalises his profitable copyright, his ownership of one of the few portraits of the man. Although achieving a similar ownership, his version of Billy the Kid is one of many, like buying stock in a well-known company within an already flourishing market. While such business metaphors might appear troublesome when applied to the lives and histories of human beings, Benjamin makes an even more troubling suggestion that pieces of history can be rescued and freed through the ownership practised by collectors. Indeed, Benjamin claims that "one of the finest moments of a collector is the moment when he [rescues] a book [... and gives] it its freedom—the way a prince [buys] a beautiful slave girl in the *Arabian Nights*. To a book collector ... the true freedom of all books is somewhere on his shelves" (64). To generalize beyond the collecting of mere books, a collector's attitude toward his possessions "stems from an owner's feeling of responsibility towards his property" (66). The ownership of property is nothing unique or particularly troublesome to the contemporary reader, but the above statement, which likens books to slaves, which includes, metaphorically, humans or human history in the collector's view of property, lends a sinister, amoral quality to the collector figure. This slave metaphor also lends a disturbing resonance to Ondaatje's authoritative possession of Bolden's character in *Coming Through Slaughter* that overshadows even the best authorial intentions.

Benjamin's collector figure and Ondaatje's embodiment of that motif appear to be nothing more than selfish and amoral petty thieves, like Caravaggio, who is described in *The English Patient* as "a man who slips away, in the way lovers leave chaos, the way thieves leave reduced houses" (117). Ondaatje's and Benjamin's collectors are not so simply characterized, however. While the whimsical collector does present a danger to the present public sphere by turning away from it and establishing himself in a private past, he also resists the authority and the tradition of history by seeking strange, valueless (or personally valuable) things. Tradition discriminates, separating and selecting the relevant from the irrelevant, but the passionate, unsystematic collector levels all differences and works against systematic classification (Arendt 43). By sheltering and exalting unique objects loyally, by destroying "the context in which the object once was only a part of a greater ... entity," the collector "the heir and preserver ... turns into a destroyer" (Arendt 45) of exclusive history and accurate portraiture by voicing his own selective agency. Enacting a subversive protest against the typical, against social tradition and cultural history (Arendt 45), Ondaatje, in *Coming Through Slaughter* bases his central figure on an actual person who has nearly slipped through the cracks of official history into obscurity. In contrast to the earlier claim that the "ownership" practised by the collector figure calls into question Ondaatje's relationship with and responsibility to his historical subject, the suggestion here is that without Ondaatje's admittedly fictional efforts, the already obscure memories and records of Bolden's existence would fade even further.

More, I argue that Ondaatje's project remains paradoxical, however, for Ondaatje, like an authorial Dr. Frankenstein, brings a patchwork Bolden back to life, but uses this life to fuel a self-centred exploration of his own creativity. Bolden, recreated through Ondaatje's awareness, is a figure who, "in the public parade" goes "mad into silence" (Ondaatje 108), who suicides his public presence in the midst of a growing fame to avoid becoming "a remnant, a ladder for others" (Ondaatje 102). This fictional rationalisation of Bolden's madness potentially clarifies the mystery of his historical dead end, but also complicates Ondaatje's involvement, for Bolden has, indeed, become a remnant for Ondaatje to build on, a ladder upon which the author can climb on his own route to fame. In a confessional passage later in the book that appears opposite a page of impersonal facts about Bolden's life, a voice that can be easily perceived as Ondaatje's own recollects a contemporary encounter with spaces that the musician historically occupied. Finding only "the complete absence of him," this voice alternatively locates Bolden through identification, recognition and the "shock of memory" (Ondaatje 133). Stating that he does "not want to pose in [Bolden's] accent, but think in his brain and body" and add colour and depth to the "black and white" classifications found in history books, Ondaatje defends implicitly his "possession" of the musician (Ondaatje 134). Yet through this self-identification and recreation of Bolden as a recognisable mirror image of his own self-perception, Ondaatje not only associates himself with a virtually unknown creative legend but also reveals lingering anxieties about the appropriateness of his own project. Like Ondaatje's written output, Bolden's musical output is "tormented by order," for he tears "apart the plot," describes "something in 27 ways" and moves "so fast it [is] unimportant to finish and clear everything" (Ondaatje 37). Similarly, as editor of *The Cricket*, Bolden, like his creator, respects "stray facts, manic theories, and well-told lies," taking "all the thick facts and [dropping] them into his pail of sub-history" (24), his collection of subjective perspectives. Bolden, speaking through Ondaatje, calls *The Cricket* "my diary ... and everybody else's" (Ondaatje 113). The chatter that makes up *Coming Through Slaughter* bears some resemblance to *The Cricket*'s gossip pages, suggesting that Ondaatje, as the collector and inventor of this self-reflexive collage is aware of the damage that can be done through his practice of creative and sometimes inaccurate portraiture.

Similarly, as seen through the figure of Bellocq, the photographer, the danger that the collector figure is merely a "cultural barbarian" (Abbas 223), a destructive, postmodern threat to past, public and present spheres is a distinct possibility. However, Abbas, in "Walter Benjamin's Collector: The Fate of the Modern Experience," points out that that the collector is in a paradoxical social space (216). He arrives at this through an examination of Nietzsche's view of the collector. Nietzsche, in *Untimely Meditations*, defines the collector as an antiquarian collage maker, a pathological and irresponsible figure who, through creative and careless consumption, abstracts bits and pieces of the past from historical reality and validity (75). Nietzsche's collector, like Bellocq, is a pathetic figure, a "traumatized, privatized and impotent individual, the *etui* man of the interior" (Abbas 226). This use of the word *etui* suggests not only a container for miscellany, but also a container for surgical instruments. Abbas's implicit suggestion, then, is that the collector figure may not necessarily be as reduced in creative disposition as Nietzsche conceives him to be. The collector may, indeed, be a figure that has the power to operate on the world by skilfully using the elements of his collection. Abbas later states this point explicitly, claiming that the activity of collecting, which Nietzsche sees as demonstrating a deficiency in "discrimination of value" and "sense of proportion," actually *deforms* and, in essence *reforms* history (223). In other words, not only does the passionate collector preserve the "dead past," he also recovers "all of the objects and values that have failed to 'make it' historically" (223), just as Ondaatje overcomes historical exclusions and biases by collecting characters like Bolden who have been left behind. Indeed, while the destructive Bellocq, who resembles a hunter more than a collector, privately tortures his collection, Ondaatje, displaying the recreative urges of the writer-collector, exhumes the historical, transforms and recycles it, makes it "novel," sends his altered images out into the public sphere and takes responsibility for their presence. Inherent in collector's antagonistic relationship with selective history, then, is a constructive and creative opportunity for reform, for a creative reconsideration of exclusive and traditional historical paradigms. Still, like Bellocq's private violence against the images of the women he photographs, the result of this surgical activity may "add a three-dimensional quality to each work" (Ondaatje 55), but it can also leave scars on its subject, on the image of the person that is used as a vehicle to realise such change. Observing the "making and destroying coming from the same source, same lust, same surgery his brain was capable of" (55), Ondaatje recognises the inherent complexity in Bellocq's creative vandalism as well as the similarity to his own actions.

To understand more fully the collector's position it is useful to turn briefly to the "postmodern," a term that is often inserted into critical analyses as carelessly as defamatory exclamations are published in *The Cricket*. Abrams views the postmodern project as "not only a continuation, carried to an extreme, of the counter-traditional experiments of modernism, but also diverse attempts to break away from modernist forms which [have . . .] become . . . conventional" (Abrams 110). Further, postmodernism attempts to "subvert the foundations of our accepted modes of thought and experience so as to reveal the 'meaninglessness' of existence and the . . . 'abyss' . . . on which our . . . security is precariously suspended" (Abrams 110). In a general sense, the postmodern project and the collector motif contain the same potential for irresponsibility and destructiveness, for both resist exclusive alignment with either the present or the past and, perhaps in doing so, a future. Barbour describes Ondaatje as a "postmodern writer" (6) because his writing contains such qualities as "paradoxes, leaps of imagination and vocal gymnastics" (8). Further, Barbour describes Ondaatje's prose as a type of "carnivalized writing" (8), a "collage construction" that combines a diversity of individual voices with "documentary" and "novelistic" impulses to create "fictional worlds full of lively gaps" (7). Yet, given the radical possibility inherent in the above characterization of the postmodern, the playful sense of irresponsibility suggested by "lively gaps" questions the extent of Ondaatje's participation in a postmodern project. While *Coming Through Slaughter* does employ narrative techniques that challenge traditional preconceptions of novelistic form, to generalize and assume that this alone makes Ondaatje's project "postmodern" is erroneous.

Linda Hutcheon, in her book *The Politics of Postmodernism*, suggests that "the postmodern has no effective theory of agency that enables a move into political *action*" (3). Just as a turning away from the present places Ondaatje beyond the modernist project, then, the constructive and creative *action* of this collector-writer is much more than merely a "denaturalizing critique" (3), and places *Coming Through Slaughter* outside an exclusively postmodern classification. A possible objection can be raised, though, that Ondaatje's creative activity shares some modernist shortcomings, in that past collective tradition is merely replaced by an individualized perceptual paradigm. However, the form of *Coming Through Slaughter* avoids closure and evades any establishment of an organised presentation or the encouragement of a systematic perception, however individualized. It can be concluded, then, that Ondaatje's fictional recreation of Bolden both embraces and rejects traditional, modern, and postmodern characteristics and evades characterization by any one of these terms.

Despite the limitations of his association between the collector and modernism, Abbas does provide some valuable insights into the similarities between collector and *writer* that further enhances my notion of the collector motif. Abbas suggests that writers, like collectors, both try "to make something out of the rubbish heaps of history, turning compositions out of compost" (Abbas 222). The relation of the writer to the image, he claims, is like the collector's relation to the object (Abbas 229). Considering Benjamin's view that "ownership is the most intimate relationship that one can have to objects" (Benjamin 67), Abbas senses that "under certain conditions, the experience of possession could be transformed into the possession of experience" (Abbas 231). This, then, necessitates a "rethinking of the nature of ownership" (Abbas 231) such that possession becomes a matter not of contingency, but of strategy. Ownership is a strategic "interruption: not in the sense that the private owner takes objects out of circulation but in the sense that he takes objects that *are* out of circulation and confronts cultural history with them" (Abbas 231). Writer-collectors are like the figure of Baudelaire's ragpicker, who places collected fragments or overlooked "master-pieces" back into the "historical conditions...that make them possible" (Abbas 232). They remind culture "that it cannot afford to forget the underside of culture, though what is passed on as culture [and history] is established very much on the basis of such a forgetting" (Abbas 232). This type of writing turns the past into a "possession" (Abbas 232), a "material means by which this history is passed on" (Abbas 234), "and so [ensures] its transmissibility" (Abbas 232). Thus writing one's collection can be regarded "as a way of telling," a way of "transmitting experience through objects" by responding to those objects and opening them up to interpretation (Abbas 234). The relation between the collector-writer and his etui, then, is not one of exclusive mastery, but one of responsive transmissibility as well. Although the collector leaves his fingerprints on his objects, although Ondaatje alters the histories that he handles, the collector-writer preserves, presents and opens up interpretative possibilities without destroying the object's origin but also without completely ignoring or getting caught up in this context. The creativity inherent in this recycling project allows the collector to promote multiplicity and problematize repressive structures, to embrace some facets of the postmodern project while responsibly avoiding its nihilistic leanings. Collecting is an aesthetic strategy of transmissible excess, of communicative accumulation without repression, for the collector-writer is "always a reader, an interpreter" (Abbas 236), creatively and productively interacting with his collected objects. Transmissible interpretation is the fruitful result of the collector-writer's project, it is a "form of action in the world" (Abbas 237) that embraces, yet takes us beyond the postmodern apocalypse.

Although *Coming Through Slaughter* is an example of collection-writing that manages to avoid extremes of revolutionary idealism and apolitical nihilism in the treatment of its subject, a creative affectation and alteration of Bolden remains inevitable. Ondaatje, the writer-collector, despite his intense identification with the historical figure, "uses Bolden" (Solecki 264) and "remains in control of his material" (Solecki 265) in that he does not become completely consumed by his subject or consumed in the same way that Bolden is. He "temporarily submit[s] to [Bolden's anguish], without ever making a complete assimilation with that mode of being" (Solecki 264). In contrast, Bolden is overwhelmed by his musical material (Solecki 265). Thus, while both Bolden and Ondaatje attempt to resolve the "contradictory desires for privacy and fame" (Solecki 263), only Ondaatje comes through the slaughter by collecting and recreating history. *Coming Through Slaughter* presents and contains Ondaatje, for he becomes an essential part of the public collection, a nodal point in the constellation that represents Buddy Bolden. However, Ondaatje's book is also a veil that distances the writer from the reader and allows the private and public spheres to coexist. In doing so, Ondaatje maintains a private space of affinity between self and subject, but also publishes the story of such affinity, releasing Bolden back to the public as an affected but not consumed collection that includes Ondaatje as another voice in Bolden's portrait and as an invisible editor of the figure's collective history. Bolden's character cannot find a way to do this—nothing mediates between public and private for the unrecorded musician and, with "his own mind . . . helpless against every moment's headline" (Ondaatje 15) he moves chaotically through both extremes. Ondaatje shows this, forcing

Bolden to perform one final time and claiming identification with this puppetry, while, as puppeteer, hiding safely behind his ordered collection and escaping Bolden's fate. Michael Jarrett reinforces these claims by observing that Ondaatje "responds to Bolden's legend not as a pilgrim (idolatrous), but as a tourist (fascinated)" (Jarrett 38). Indeed, tourists often have a superficial understanding of provinces that they visit and make up for this lack of empathy by inaccurately distorting the foreign into something familiar. The tourist is also a selfish collector of souvenirs, of objects that are removed from their cultural context and transplanted to a private collection of memories. Ondaatje's finding a familiar image in Bolden, despite *Coming Through Slaughter*'s creative preservation of the jazz player's memory, still appears to reflect the superficiality of fascinated tourism and the ownership of souvenir collecting.

Ondaatje utilises Bolden as a departure point in the same way that Bolden plays his jazz (Jarrett 27) and uses the stories left behind in his barber shop as part of his performance (Ondaatje 43). Author and character continually mirror each other, suggesting that their overall relationship is one of co-dependence rather than a struggle for dominance. Further, through the use of stylistic techniques identified by Barbour (see above), Ondaatje's creative collection of fragmentary facts and fictions opens up Bolden's legend, preserves him as a dynamic experience and releases him from a tradition that largely overlooks him. Ondaatje's written communication of the creative collection is the release of that collection back to the public by a collector who admits to never being able to master his objects. It is an author opening up history to his readers by publishing an account that asserts itself not as truth, but as an affected collection, one that can be re-collected by readers, modified, multiplied and passed on. It is neither slavery nor oppression; it is transmissibility and storytelling. It is the use of art as a dynamic form of history-telling.

Ondaatje's other prose works display further experimentation with the spectrum of potential consequences that the privileging of personalized recollection over commonly accepted histories can produce. While he retreats further into fiction in the novels following *Coming Through Slaughter*, Ondaatje continues to explore the dynamics and consequences of collection and representation through new characters. In *In the Skin of a Lion*, which examines atypical social microcosms within the larger impersonal histories of a city, the character of Alice, in her early incarnation as a nun, is swept off a bridge in a gust of wind, but is saved by the solitary daredevil and builder, Temelcoff. Following this, this nameless nun, of habit, and symbolic of religious historical tradition and ritual, re-enters history in a different way, a more political way and following her rebirth becomes a challenge to such exclusive traditions. In *Coming Through Slaughter* Ondaatje, the collector-author tied to the structure of history who swings just beneath this structure, saves Bolden from plunging into the anonymity of excluded history. Like Temelcoff, Ondaatje allows Bolden to re-encounter history differently. And the activities of Patrick Lewis, another character in *In the Skin of a Lion*, can also be compared to the paradoxes inherent in Ondaatje's project. Lewis is an extremist, initially building the tunnel that leads to a water filtration plant, then trying to destroy it with a bomb. His extremity is as impotent as Bolden's, however, for Patrick partially constructs history, then is ignored by its lumbering progress. Yet Ondaatje, the curious collector-writer allows their fictions to re-enter the present as presence, to challenge history, to have a say in the future, but not to dominate in the manner of ideological prescription or history past.

Julie Beddoes, in "Which Side Is It On? Form, Class and Politics in *In the Skin of a Lion*," claims that this novel's commentary on ideology, its voicing of the struggles of the silent immigrant class, is overwhelmed and eventually subverted by its own aesthetics of form, its creative gaps and ambivalence (Beddoes 214). However, as I illustrate here, Ondaatje problematizes exclusive, formal historical tradition and ideological constraint with his ambivalent aesthetic. Linda Hutcheon asserts that the novelist has "the power to change how we read history and fiction, to change how we draw the lines" (Hutcheon 103). Ondaatje, the collector, asserts this power, but "power" wrongly recalls the menacing echoes of the exclusive historical machine and the capitalist seriousness of Ambrose Small. Ondaatje, rather, has the *ability* to undermine historical limitation through inclusion rather than exclusion. By promoting the public's encounter with inclusive multiplicity and ambivalence, while showcasing the experience of and reasserting the presence of the historical object, Ondaatje promotes an expansion of consideration rather than enforcing a new paradigm. The private project is collecting, the effect is resurrection and the aesthetics of public presentation are the key to transmissibility and survival. Indeed such a strategy is more successful than Beddoes claims, for she and I are both engaged with characters that, whether based on historical figures or representative of certain cultures or classes, were, until Ondaatje, falling off the bridge.

Moving even further away from the creative anxiety and uncertainty communicated by *Coming Through Slaughter*'s fragmentary construction, *The English Patient* is a text that embraces a more traditional narrative form while communicating Ondaatje's awareness of himself as a collector figure and his growing acceptance of his own unique approach to history. This richly layered and ambitious anthology of intersecting collections is one that further interrupts the boundaries of the bound book by resurrecting some of the characters from *In the Skin of a Lion* and placing them in the main collection of characters that occupy a bombed-out villa. This villa is a broken *etui*, standing partially destroyed, just as Ondaatje's prose is a ruptured container out from which his preserved yet altered collections spill. The war-torn landscape around them is a place in which Hana fears that "the personal will forever be at war with the public" (Ondaatje 292). Inside the villa, however, the characters are "shedding skins" (Ondaatje 117), transforming, much like Alice's opportunity to shed her old role, to actively reappear only after having disappeared in *In the Skin of a Lion*. The isolation and private space of the collected characters in *The English Patient* presents the opportunity for redefinition and preparation for survival in a new environment. "Out of the quicksand" of history they are "evolving" (Ondaatje 234).

Separately, their actions and conversations reveal continually the attitude towards history and the manner of writing that Ondaatje, as a collector, displays. Hana pulls books off shelves and adds fragments in the margins and on the flyleaves (61, 118). Kip interrupts circuits and currents. Caravaggio is a thief, an amoral collector. The English patient's sole possession is a copy of Herodotus's *The Histories* "that he has added to, cutting and gluing in pages from other books or writing in his own observations" (Ondaatje 16). Indeed Herodotus himself, recreated in a portrait by Almásy, is described as "one of those spare men of the desert who travel from oasis to oasis, trading legends as if it is the exchange of seeds, consuming everything without suspicion, piecing together a mirage" (Ondaatje 119). If the writer of *Coming Through Slaughter* can recognise and insert himself in the historical figure of Buddy Bolden, then he is most certainly reflected in the collective activities of these fictional characters as well. Ondaatje's collection-stories are at once margin and centre, destructive and creative. They are "private winds" (Ondaatje 17) that stir and circulate the dust of history; they are private oases in the shifting postmodern desert, a "desert [that can] not be claimed or owned" (Ondaatje 138).

The English Patient is full of descriptive passages and poetic images that are phrases without politics, unmapped aesthetic instances that interrupt a reader's search for coherence. Such images and fragments, like the characters of Ondaatje's novels, have "collective" importance, "the way a stone or found metal box or bone can become loved and turn eternal in a prayer" (*The English Patient* 261). Almásy thinks of himself as a collection of such fragments, as a "communal" history or book (261). Indeed, for most of the book, he is just that: a faceless, skinless, nameless figure whose identity or history can only be pasted together from recollected fragments, from stories told. Although he physically dies, his story is passed on. He is transformed and transmitted, and can now "walk on... an earth that [has] no maps" (261), having been privately collected by those who gather the pieces of his story. Like Almásy, Bolden becomes a communal history and is given back to the public unmapped desert as a published oasis of collected fragments. Just as oases and safe villas function to create hospitable space within the inhospitable deserts and mined terrain of *The English Patient, Coming Through Slaughter* enables the emergence and survival of Bolden's forgotten fragments within and beyond the shifting postmodern landscape.

Ondaatje's writing gives the objects of his collection a presence, a chance to re-enter the process of history. Certainly an interpretation of the object takes place, certainly there is a selfish component to this fictional resurrection that reflects commodification and fetishization. But the authority of Ondaatje's personal interpretations in *Coming Through Slaughter* are interrupted by his own writing style, just as his method of collecting interrupts the authority of the past. The fragmented presentation of this work, then, prevents its author from fully appropriating, assimilating, possessing or enslaving his subject and reintroduces the object into the present as a capable multiplicity, capable of survival through transmission and interpretation. Ondaatje's unique combination of the collector's self-centredness with a self-consciousness form of presentation in *Coming Through Slaughter* allows him to go beyond the inaction of the postmodern project without retreating into the structural limitations that postmodernism challenges. In the manner of Bolden, but in the medium of Almásy's commonplace book, Ondaatje communicates, through song and squawk, beauty and violence, dust and wind, the dynamic experience of collected history, inviting us to become reader-collectors, to continue to gather, interpret, revive, multiply and retransmit the pieces.

Note: The author acknowledges funding received from the Social Sciences and Humanities Research Council of Canada that made possible the research and writing of this paper.

WORKS CITED

Abbas, Ackbar. "Walter Benjamin's Collector: The Fate of the Modern Experience." *Modernity and the Text*. Ed. Andreas Huyssen and David Bathwick. New York: Columbia UP, 1989. 216–39.

Abrams, M.H. *A Glossary of Literary Terms*. 5th ed. Chicago: Holt, 1985.

Arendt, Hannah, ed. "Introduction." *Illuminations*. By Walter Benjamin. Trans. Harry Zohn. New York: Schocken, 1969. 1–55.

Barbour, Douglas. *Michael Ondaatje*. New York: Twayne, 1993.

Beddoes, Julie. "Which Side Is It On? Form, Class and Politics in *In the Skin of a Lion*." *Essays on Canadian Writing* 53 (1994): 204–15.

Benjamin, Walter. "Unpacking My Library." *Illuminations*. By Walter Benjamin. Ed. Hannah Arendt. Trans. Harry Zohn. New York: Schocken, 1969. 59–67.

Hutcheon, Linda. *The Politics of Postmodernism*. New York: Routledge, 1989.

Jarrett, Michael. "Writing Mystory: *Coming Through Slaughter*." *Essays On Canadian Writing* 53 (1994): 27–40.

Nietzsche, Friedrich. *Untimely Meditations*. Trans. R.J. Hollingdale. Cambridge: Cambridge UP, 1983.

Ondaatje, Michael. *The English Patient*. Toronto: Vintage, 1993.

Ondaatje, Michael. *In the Skin of a Lion*. Toronto: Penguin, 1988.

Ondaatje, Michael. *Coming Through Slaughter*. Concord: Anansi, 1976.

Solecki, Sam. "Making and Destroying: *Coming Through Slaughter* and Extremist Art." *Spider Blues: Essays on Michael Ondaatje*. Ed. Sam Solecki. Montréal: Véhicule, 1985. 246–67.

Touching the Language of Citizenship in Ondaatje's *Anil's Ghost*

Sandeep Sanghera

Sri Lanka is the "wife of many marriages" writes Ondaatje in his *Running in the Family* (64). An island that "seduced all of Europe," it has been courted by many conquerors who, over time, have "stepped ashore and claimed everything with the power of their sword or bible or language" (64). With each courting and conquering, its identity has changed. And names are important as we learn with Sarath and Anil's hunt to locate Sailor's. The island's name has gone from Serendip to Ratnapida, meaning the "island of gems" and then from Taprobane to Zeloan (*Running in the Family* 64). And then variations on the last, Zeloan, its spelling changing from Zeilan to Seyllan to Ceilon to Ceylon. All that coming to a full stop (for now) with its present day name of Sri Lanka, a "tear," a "pendant off the ear of India" (*Running in the Family* 147, 63). Each name marks a "marriage" and each "marriage" marks the arrival of ships that "spilled their nationalities" onto its shores (*Running in the Family* 64). And that marks the muddling up of identity politics for that spilling, over many generations, eventually leading to almost everyone on that island being "vaguely related" with "Sinhalese, Tamil, Dutch, British, Burgher blood in them" all (*Running in the Family* 41). Identity, here, gets layered and that continued layering undermines the notion of the national subject. Just who and what is a Sri Lankan? "God alone, knows, your Excellency," answers Emil Daniels when asked that very question by a visiting British governor in the 1920s (*Running in the Family* 41) and this sentiment is echoed in the 1990s by Ondaatje himself in an interview for the magazine *New Letters:* "It's pretty mixed," he says, "there was [this] sort of intermarrying—who knows what was going on" (Ondaatje qtd. in Presson 87).

Playing god then, Ondaatje tackles this confusion in a manner that Ajay Heble calls an inability to "articulate" one's own citizenship (190). And Ondaatje does the tackling in interesting ways; he does so via language. In *Anil's Ghost,* he presents Anil Tissera, who, after a fifteen-year absence, returns to the land of her birth, no longer able to speak the first language she learned. Ondaatje then posits the question, just who is Anil? Is she a foreigner? If so, is she American (for that is where she studied and lives "mostly"), or is she British (for that is the passport she carries) (*Anil's Ghost* 57)? Or as a representative of an international human rights centre based in Geneva, is she a mishmash citizen of all things Western? In that context then, how does Sri Lanka fit in, since, after all, that was her first home? That was the space where she first learned to walk and talk. So could she be hyphenated? But then is she a Sri Lankan-American or a Sri Lankan-Brit or is she just a generic Eastern-Western mix? Maybe she is a Sri Lankan returnee? Could she be just plain Sri Lankan? Or in having left and now no longer able to speak her mother tongue, does that make her no longer Sri Lankan as well? Again and again, Anil's citizenship is examined in ways in which it is coveted and relinquished, conferred and revoked. And, again and again, all that is looked at via the lens of language for language proves to be *the* thing that either invites people into or ousts them from national homes.

"The last Sinhala word I lost / was *vatura*," writes Ondaatje in "Wells": "The word for water./ Forest water. The water in a kiss. The tears / I gave to my ayah Rosalin on leaving/ the first home of my life. // More water for her than any other / that fled my eyes again / this year, remembering her,/ a lost almost-mother in those years / of thirsty love" (*Handwriting* 50). And in *Anil's Ghost*, her "last conversation in Sinhala," writes Anil, "was the distressed chat she'd had with [her ayah], Lalitha . . . that ended with her crying about missing egg *rulang* and curd with jaggery . . . [and Lalitha] weeping, it felt, at the far ends of the world" (*Anil's Ghost* 145, 142). This last, tear-filled talk in her mother tongue is a costly one. Anil spends seven days eating little to save up enough money to place this call to Colombo. A month later, she falls under the "spell" of her "future, and soon-to-be, and eventually ex-husband" who enters her life "in bangles and on stilts" and, in doing so, symbolizes Sri Lanka to Anil (142). It is into his accepting ears then, that she spills words of longing for that place. She "whisper[s] her desire for jaggery . . . [for] jakfruit . . . refers to a specific barber in Bambalapitiya" (141). And is "understood." And that—being understood—makes all the "difference" (141). With her man, Anil needs neither to explain nor justify her longing for Sri Lanka. Because it is a longing that is felt, just as much, by him as well. It is shared. And that sharing does more than just knit husband and wife. Through intimate talk of intimate Sri Lankan spots, the two citizen themselves to the land they have left. In Ondaatje's words, they take "their country with them to [the] new place" (Ondaatje qtd. in Bush 240). With words, they bring Sri Lanka to London and with words, they hold onto that island.

The problem arises, however, when the man who once entered Anil's life "in bangles and on stilts," leaves. Anil and her husband's talks, albeit intimate, did take place within the "smoke of one bad marriage" (142). And that marriage burns to an end. Once "good-bye[s]" are said, Anil "emerge[s] with no partner. Cloudless at last" (144, 145). But she emerges having let go of more than just her man. In divorcing him, Anil loses the only one with whom she could speak of Sri Lanka. In leaving, he takes with him that sort of intimate talk which had linked Anil to that island: "with his departure, there was no longer any need to remember favorite barbers and restaurants along the Galle Road" (145). So she stops doing so. While her ex returns to Colombo to pre-sumably walk along the very roads they once reminisced, Anil lets go of those same roads. He turns to Sri Lanka and she turns away. And that—her turning away from her motherland—is clearly tied up with letting go of her man. She never says his name out loud again, "she no longer [speaks] Sinhala to anyone" (145), and she no longer talks of Sri Lanka. All that is left is the sarong her parents send her every Christmas, the news clippings of swim meets, and her marginal missing of fans: "the island no longer [holds] her" (11). Citizenship is consciously let go.

Anil then turns "fully to the place she [finds] herself in" (145). And that place is the field, the classroom, and the lab where bodies are exhumed for and examined. She settles into her studies, drawing her books close to her. In doing so, she settles into other languages as well: "I know the name of several bones in Spanish," she tells her lover Cullis, happily tired and slurring her words, "*omoplato* is this. Shoulder blade"—the curve of shoulders, in fact, prove significant in locating language and, through that, securing for oneself citizenship; but more on that later—"*maxilar*—your upper jaw bone. *Occipital*—the bone at the back of the skull"; and so on. "*Cubito. Omoplato. Occipital*" (34). Anil stands, clearly now, "alongside the language of science," she "practically memoriz[es]" Spitz and Fisher (145). She speaks this new language while falling asleep and even once asleep, "deep in the white linen bed," her hand continues to "move constantly as if brushing earth away" ... as if, that is, still digging and searching for bones ... for the words for bone (34). And standing not just "alongside the language of science" Anil now stands clearly on the side of English as well (145). English and not Sinhalese is now the language that roots her. And that is evidenced by her taking to Sri Lanka—an island whose language she can no longer speak—her girlfriend Leaf's American postcard. Suspicious of Sarath's alliances—"her mind circling around" him—she spins the postcard "between her thumbs" and rereads it to make herself "feel better" (28). Having returned to the land of her birth, Anil now turns to the English words of an "American bird"—"some communication from the West"—to ground her (29, 28). Anil's choices and transformation now explain her earlier conscious shifting of citizenship where she "had courted foreignness" (54) and it spotlights it through language where feeling "completed abroad," Anil speaks "just English" now (54, 36).

After fifteen years, Anil returns to Sri Lanka as an outsider who now turns to the Western world—to its English words—to center her. But the island does not quite let go of Anil. Initially, she is conferred citizenship by those who overlook her now knowing only "a little" Sinhala and attempt, instead, to write her back into the land she has left (9). "You were born here, no?" says the official who accompanies Anil from Katunayake airport to Colombo (9). "You have friends here, no?" Finally, he crowns her the "prodigal" daughter who has returned after fifteen years. But Anil flatly refuses all that, stating she has no friends there—"not really"—and is "not a prodigal ... not at all" (10). Later, this link to the island is again brought up and again it is just as quickly dismissed by Anil: "*So—you are the swimmer!*" are Sarath's first words of greeting to her ... words that are later echoed by Dr. Perera (16). That early (watery) celebrity citizens Anil to Sri Lanka. Although she has long been gone, her name lives on and that—her name remembered—matters poignantly for it is remembered in a place where names routinely, tragically go missing. Even Palipana's own name is erased from the latest edition of the Sinhala encyclopaedia. Ultimately, that remembering points to her still belonging and although Anil acknowledges her Sri Lankan birth, she ignores this early celebrity and, in doing so, dismisses the citizenship that such celebrity affords her. "Not a swimmer," she tells Sarath, "right. Right," he answers backing off (17). Then as if to punctuate this fact, she later takes "two steps forward on the sharp stones and [dives into the river] with a belly flop" (48).

Others initially confer citizenship upon Anil who returns to the land of her birth no longer speaking Sinhalese. Soon, her citizenship—once granted by the people—is revoked by them as well. And this revoking is made public. Anil is asked to give a talk on poisoning and snakebite to an audience of local health professionals who could just as easily give the talk themselves and who, in fact, would be more fluent in it as it speaks of their space and not hers. After all, she left Sri Lanka fifteen years ago and now returns, dismissing the very things that root her to the island. And she does all that dismissing in the language of a "visiting journalist" speaking of "vainglorious government[s]" (27). Anil knows that the choice of subject for the talk is "intentional"; she knows it is an attempt to "level the playing field between the foreign-trained and the locally trained" and, in doing so, spotlight her status as a "foreign celebrity" who is no more knowledgeable or talented than the local experts (25). And all that serves to clearly place her outside of Sri Lanka. Anil's new citizenship—as a foreigner—is then neatly summed up by Chitra Abeysekera who greets her as that "woman from Geneva" (71).

This revoking of Anil's Sri Lankan citizenship takes place most poignantly, however, when she is ousted out of the most intimate of spaces and is ousted clearly via language, that is, via her inability to speak Sinhalese. Anil pays a visit to her ayah, Lalitha, with whom, fifteen years ago, she had her "last conversation" in the first language she learned (145). She returns able to speak only "a little" and to "write" only "some" Sinhala (9, 36). A language in which they once wept, standing at "far ends" of the earth, is now a language "lost" with the two standing face to face (142, 22). Initially, both Anil and Lalitha transcend that linguistic divide through touch. They reach for each other and, in that reaching, communicate their affection. The "old woman was weeping; she put her hands out and ran them over Anil's hair. Anil held her arms. . . . She kissed Lalitha on both cheeks, having to bend down to her because she was small and frail." The two then sit down and that "lost language" sits down between them. Anil holds her ayah's hand in silence. Lalitha, in turn, can only point at a picture of her granddaughter to explain to Anil her relation to the woman with the "stern eyes" who witnesses their "sentimental moment" (22). The granddaughter speaks to her grandmother "loudly" in Tamil but her speaking it "loudly" when Lalitha is only "whispering" hints, perhaps, at that linguistic move being deliberate. Speaking in Tamil, the granddaughter chooses to speak intentionally a language from which Anil is even further removed from than Sinhalese. And she makes no offer to translate for Anil. In doing both, she uses language and the withholding of language to write Anil out of Lalitha's home. And that—writing Anil out of the home of one "old woman"—translates into writing Anil off the island (22).

The loss of language surfaces as an "ache" inside Anil (22), an ache which no one can translate for it is an ache that the body simply feels and where "there are no words" (7). But translation, up to now, is precisely what Anil has relied on. Aware that she is moving around the island with "only one arm of language," she turns to Sarath who serves as her Sinhalese-speaking right hand (54). It is Sarath who explains that she is a doctor to the man the two of them find crucified to tarmac (111). Sarath says "something to [Gunesena] over his shoulder and the man tentatively [gives] her his left hand . . . Anil soak[s] a handkerchief in the saline solution and squeeze[s] it onto his palm, the bridge nail still in it" (112). Later, when she spots the same "markers of occupation" in a "squatting" Ananda as she had earlier in Sailor and wants to confirm that it is so, it is to Sarath she turns to translate her desire to touch the artist (166). "Sarath explain[s] . . . Anil [takes] hold of Ananda's ankle in both hands. She presse[s] her thumbs into the muscle and cartilage, move[s] them up a few inches above his ankle bone. There [is] a dry laugh from Ananda. Then down to the heel again." And finally, it is to Sarath that she must turn to communicate even the simplest of gratitude: "Please, will you thank him . . . [thank Ananda]" (179). Although Anil, here, relies on Sarath translating, there is a growing desire for her to move beyond such translation and to speak for herself. When she comes across Ananda carrying the skeleton of Sailor in his arms, she can only "nod imperceptibly [at him] to show there [is] no anger in her" (170). But she is unable to explain that her need to touch this unnamed man is a need shared by both of them. Like these thoughts, there is so much more that is left unsaid such as when Anil wished she could have told Ananda "what Sailor's bone measurements meant in terms of posture and size. And he—God knows what insights he had" (170).

But having "long forgotten" not only the words but the "subtleties of the language" the two once shared" (170), she cannot. Now, there is only a nod to signify the absence of anger and these forgotten subtleties could be *the* key. If remembered and reclaimed, they could take Anil beyond language—beyond the literal use of words—and into a space where, through such subtleties, she could, in fact, communicate. And so, ironically, Anil could speak without having to say any words. Finding those subtleties then is equivalent to finding a kind of new tongue and finding that tongue could just open up the door to Sri Lanka's national home. Subtleties then are crucial; by learning the Sri Lankan language of subtleties, Anil could re-citizen herself to the land she left. Before these subtleties can be learned, they must first be found. And found they are, in the body of the Sinhalese alphabet. In *Running in the Family*, Ondaatje writes of the subtlety and softness of written Sinhalese, "the most beautiful alphabet . . . the first alphabet" he—and presumably Anil—"ever copied" (83). Ondaatje draws the "self-portrait of language . . . How to write" (*Running in the Family* 83) where the "physicality of language" (Hutcheon 310) shows up quite clearly in *Anil's Ghost* as well (310). There, the curling softness of the Sinhalese alphabet translates itself onto the actual, *physical* body of the Sri Lankan as well, drawing, in effect, the "self-portrait" of a Sri Lankan citizen. Like the letters which curve to resemble a "sickle, spoon, eyelid, . . . a lover's spine," there is a curve to the way in which characters move (83). And that curve surfaces, most clearly, in the form of the "Asian nod" (*Anil's Ghost* 16). In the novel, this Asian nod appears again and again. For instance, Anil asks Gunesena if he lives near the place they are driving through. He answers by "roll[ing] his head slightly . . . a tactful yes and no" (113). At one point she enquires after Sarath's wife and the rest-house owner answers that she is very "nice," but with a "nod for proof, then a slight tilt of [the] head, a J stroke, to suggest possible hesitance in his own judgment" (57).

And later, on first meeting Sarath's teacher, Anil notes that Palipana's head "kept tilting as if trying to catch whatever was passing in the air around him" (85). Not just confined to the movement of the head, the "Asian nod" surfaces also in the ways in which words are said. Sarath's "Right . . . Right," spoken with a "drawl" and said "twice," is "like the . . . nod" (16). It is an "official and hesitant agreement for courtesy's sake but include[s] the suggestion that things [are] on hold" (16). In its curling movement then, the "Asian nod" gives a response that hints simultaneously at a "yes," a "no," and even a "maybe." Nothing is said directly and that is the Sri Lankan language of subtleties.

Against this backdrop—against the subtlety and softness of the Asian nod which echoes, in its circularity, written Sinhalese—stands a very taut Anil. She "nod[s] exaggeratedly" and, at the age of sixteen, refuses adamantly adding even the curl of the letter *e* to her name . . . a curl suggested by an "astrologer-soothsayer" (26, 136). The *e*, in *Anile*, would have allowed the "fury to curve away" and the masculine edge to ease. But Anil, in refusing it, insists on standing tall, "taut and furious" instead (136). From then on, she moves through life like the final letter *l* in her name. Anil is "governed by verticals . . . [by] the straight line" (*Running in the Family* 83). After all, "she'd hunted down [her] desired name like a specific lover she had seen and wanted, tempted by nothing else along the way" (*Anil's Ghost* 68). And she had gotten it, bargaining the name out of the hands of her brother. Likewise in Sri Lanka, Anil expects "clearly marked roads to the source of most mysteries" and so "obsessive[ly] tunnel[s] toward discovery" (69) where this is exemplified most by her search for absolutes—for Truth—on an island where "truth bounce[s] between gossip and vengeance. [Where] rumour slip[s] into every car and barbershop" (54). Where the search for truth involves "commissions and the favours of ministers . . . involve[s] waiting politely for hours in . . . office lobbies" (55). And where, when found, truth is not of any interest if "given directly, without . . . diversions and subtexts . . . without waltzing backwards," without that subtle, Asian nod of the head (55). And after all that, truth, in fact, may not even exist at all: "We have never had [it]. Not even with your work on bones," Palipana tells her, "Most of the time in our world, [it] is just opinion" (102). Still Anil, who cannot yet speak the language of subtleties, tunnels towards it, "banging through ancient concrete with a mallet" (66), trying to reach it. Believing stubbornly that once found, "truth shall set you free" while, all the while, Sarath tells her it is only "a flame against a sleeping lake of petrol" (102, 156). Anil's insistence on a Truth and her straight-line search for it in a place where there are no straight lines and maybe there is no truth ends up, again and again, writing her out of Sri Lanka's national home: "Doors that [she thinks] should be open, are closed" (44), Anil goes to "offices" and "can't get in" (44). She is not a citizen.

Finally, Anil begins to see that she is in a space where things constantly curl. Like the Sinhalese alphabet and the Asian nod, there is a curve to it all. And that becomes most pronounced and maybe most poignant when Anil's search for another absolute—an Enemy—circles back to her. Riding with Sarath and Ananda, "two hours before Ratnapura," the three are stopped by a roadblock. A "hand snake[s] into the jeep and snap[s] its fingers." Anil's identity card is handed over. It seems to give the soldiers "trouble," perhaps they are wondering just what country she is a citizen of.... Next, her shoulder bag is emptied out "noisily" and the battery is pulled out of the back of her alarm clock and her "packets of batteries still sealed in plastic" are collected as well. The soldier then "walk[s] away and signal[s] them on." And with that, Anil becomes, in a way, a provider of arms. "The batteries are essential for making homemade bombs," Sarath tells her (162–63). Anil knows that and so she knows as well that her earlier insistence on drawing a line—"I don't know which side you are on," she once said to Sarath—does not hold on an island where there are no lines (53). Here, there is "terror everywhere, from all sides ... like being in a room with three suitors, all of whom [have] blood on their hands" (154). Here, one does not know "who [is] killing who[m]" (48). Or, for that matter, who is healing whom.

While "dancing to a furious love song that can drum out loss" (182), Anil, herself, finally curls (182). She "throw[s] her head back, her hair a black plume, back almost to the level of her waist. Throws her arms too, to hold the ground ... backward into the air ... pivot[s] her hip ... send[s] her feet over her ... her loose skirt having no time to discover gravity and drop[s] before she is on the ground again" (181). This is a new Anil. Sarath "watches a person he has never seen. A girl insane, a druid in moonlight, a thief in oil. This is not the Anil he knows" (181). This Anil, who studies the bones of others, finally turns to her own body and locates a curve within her and in locating it, she becomes that curve. Dancing, she does a back flip: Anil, for the first time, echoes the place that she is in. The "way a person [takes] on and recognize[s] in himself the smile of a lover" (*Running in the Family* 54), Anil takes on and recognizes in herself the curve around her. She curls. And she curls in a place—a space—where the Sinhalese alphabet—"almost sickle, spoon, eyelid"—curls ... where that Asian nod slowly circles and Sarath's drawl, which is like that nod, slowly curves too ... where Truth circles and circles ... and where the search for an Enemy curves back to Anil (83). As Catherine Bush puts it, here is that point "where body and landscape merge" (245). The new Anil then turns to the bodies of others and locates, in them, that same curve as well. And in their curves, she finds language. And that—curves housing words—others have known all along: "Years ago [Sarath] and Palipana entered unknown rock darknesses, lit a match and saw hints of colour ... [saw] the rock carving from another century of [a] woman bending ... Palipana's arm follow[ed] the line of the mother's back bowed in affection or grief. An unseen child. All the gestures of motherhood harnessed. A muffled scream in her posture" (156, 157). Anil turns to the curve of shoulders and not backs but finds in those shoulders that same language as well, the language of loss and love. And that is a language Anil has known all along, has known long before her return to Sri Lanka. On an excavation, much earlier, in Guatemala, she saw: "a woman sitting within [a] grave ... on her haunches, her legs under her as if in formal prayer, elbows in her lap, looking down at the remains of two bodies ... a husband and a brother ... lost ... during an abduction a year earlier. Now it seemed as if the men were asleep beside each other on a mat in the afternoon.... There are no words

Anil knows that can describe, even for just herself, the woman's face. But the grief of love in that shoulder she will not forget, still remembers" (7).

In Sri Lanka, her memory of Guatemala re-surfaces. Shoulders are spotted again and again but now they are touched. And that touch communicates. In the Emergency Services, a nurse approaches Gamini and touches him on the shoulder; "when he [does not] move she [keeps] her hand there. Anil [is] to remember all this very well. He [gets] up then, pocket[s] the book, and touche[s] one of the other patients and disappear[s] with him" (38). In the rest-house at Bandarawela, Sarath touches Anil's shoulder, takes the earphones from her, places them on his head and listens to cello (59). And Anil touches his brother's. Sitting by the breakwater along Galle Face Green, Anil touches Gamini's shoulder. Gamini brings "his hand up for a moment and then his head slip[s] away and soon she [sees] he has fallen asleep. His skull, his uncombed hair, the weight of his tiredness on her lap" (133). Hands are repeatedly laid on the curve of the shoulders of others and through that sort of "sweet touch from [this] world," a softness is spoken without saying any words (307). And when Ananda finally touches Anil, this last touch is, perhaps, the most profound of all.

Ondaatje's fiction, writes Karen Smythe, provides a "linguistic density that evokes an almost physical response," it is "writing that can tingle the senses" (3). True, but in *Anil's Ghost*, with Ananda and Anil, the reverse is almost true. In this novel, a physical response—his hand on her shoulder—brings forth that linguistic density where his touch calls up her story. And that—the body housing a person's history—Ondaatje has written about before: "My body," he writes in *Running in the Family*, "must remember everything, this brief insect bite, smell of wet fruit, the slow snail light, rain, rain, and underneath the hint of colours a sound of furious wet birds . . . dark trees, the mildewed garden wall, the slow air pinned down by rain" (202). In *Anil's Ghost*, Ananda's touch exhumes and brings to the surface—brings to the pores—all the memory that has been buried deep in Anil's body. His touch curls her back into her past. It takes her back to "Lalitha . . . her mother, somewhere further back in her lost childhood" (187). The touch takes her back before the language of subtleties was lost and Sri Lankan citizenship and belonging was given up . . . back before her settling on English as her only tongue . . . before her putting a stop to talk of "favourite barbers and restaurants along the Galle Road," back before the "spell" of her unnamed ex-husband, before the entrance and exit of her lover Cullis, back before her life in America and her British passport, and finally way, way back before Anil's return to Sri Lanka as that "woman from Geneva" (145, 142, 71). Ananda kneads away Anil's tears and with his hand on the curve of her shoulder, "touche[s] her in a way" that curves her back to her childhood (187). That curve back deposits her in a time and a place when she spoke Sinhalese and was Sri Lankan.

It is not just a touch that takes Anil into the past, it also roots simultaneously her in the present. It citizens Anil clearly to the Sri Lanka she stands in now. And it does so, by taking her beyond the bounds of a single language so that Anil emerges able to speak every tongue: "when his hand had been on her shoulder . . . she felt she could speak in any language, he would understand the purpose of any gesture" (197). Ananda, then, "touches [her] into [all] words" (*Running in the Family* 22). And Ananda's touch then re-citizens Anil who later stands before an audience of military and police personnel and gives a "citizen's evidence" (272). "I think you murdered hundreds of us," she tells them. "*Hundreds of us,*" Sarath thinks to himself. "Fifteen years away and she is finally *us*" (272). Finally, there is no more running away from the place she belongs.

WORKS CITED

Bush, Catherine. "Michael Ondaatje: An Interview." *Essays on Canadian Writing: Michael Ondaatje Issue*. Ed. Karen E. Smythe. Toronto: ECW, 1994. 238–49.

Heble, Ajay. "'Rumours of Topography': The Cultural Politics of Michael Ondaatje's *Running in the Family*." *Essays on Canadian Writing: Michael Ondaatje Issue*. Ed. Karen E. Smythe. Toronto: ECW, 1994. 186–203.

Hutcheon, Linda. "*Running in the Family:* The Postmodernist Challenge." *Spider Blues: Essays on Michael Ondaatje*. Ed. Sam Solecki. Montréal: Véhicule, 1985. 301–14.

Ondaatje, Michael. *Anil's Ghost*. Toronto: McClelland & Stewart, 2000.

Ondaatje, Michael. *Handwriting*. Toronto: McClelland & Stewart, 1998.

Ondaatje, Michael. *Running in the Family*. Toronto: McClelland & Stewart, 1982.

Presson, Rebekah. "Fiction as Opposed to Fact: An Interview with Michael Ondaatje." *New Letters* 62 (1996): 81–90.

Smythe, Karen E. "Listen It: Responses to Ondaatje." *Essays on Canadian Writing: Michael Ondaatje Issue*. Ed. Karen E. Smythe. Toronto: ECW, 1994. 1–10.

Oral History and the Writing of the Other in Ondaatje's *In the Skin of a Lion*

Winfried Siemerling

In the Skin of a Lion, Michael Ondaatje deciphers and invents the signs of another world coexisting silently with Toronto's written history and the surface of its present-day reality. The novel defamiliarizes habitual perceptions of Toronto by superimposing a reconstructed and imagined new world. With the non-English-speaking immigrants of Toronto, Ondaatje follows a whole community that crosses boundaries and borders to another reality and a new language. As in so many of Ondaatje's texts, from *The Collected Works of Billy the Kid* to *Anil's Ghost*, a searching figure tries to decipher a disappearance. In *In the Skin of a Lion*, the emergence of the world of the other begins with a moment in the night. The as yet unnamed world of the immigrants that emerges in fragments of oral history, conversations, and passages closely related to dreams, is associated throughout the novel with lights in the night. They are thus perceived in the absence of historical daylight and in the interstices of historically known (and constructed) perception of reality. Ondaatje's stories about Toronto and Ontario in the 1920 and 1930s begin with a short framing vignette that introduces the written text we are about to read in a context of oral speech and story telling: "This is a story a young girl gathers in a car during the early hours of the morning. She listens and asks questions as the vehicle travels through darkness. Outside, the countryside is un-betrayed. The man who is driving could say, 'In that field is a castle,' and it would be possible for her to believe him" (1). Besides alluding to the traditional request for a suspension of disbelief, this passage joins the mode of un-finalized, fantastic possibility with the atmosphere of a conversation during the night. The identity of the two as yet unnamed participants we encounter in this conversation is still shrouded in darkness, like the world outside just before dawn and the story not yet revealed. Light is shed upon the situation as the conversation progresses.

Ondaatje shows time and again an awareness of the authority that usually makes the "evidence" of the visible carry the day, a power, however, that sets his own written text necessarily over against the oral memory culture it brings to light. When the narrative, in an account of its own genesis, both leads and returns to the car drive at the beginning, Ondaatje draws our attention simultaneously to the fact that the visual images of the literary creation and its world have now replaced the initial darkness—and maybe superseded some of its possibilities. Not only has this potential been filled with stories; we are made aware that our eyes have been "listening," in this light, to the simulation of an oral tale in writing. Writing, of course, is the medium also used by a city historiography that has largely left out and overwritten the stories we have just read. But his last words—"Lights, he said"—end the book with a *fiat lux* in the plural. As the text takes us thus back to the scene at the beginning, we are not only reminded that this "elucidation" has been mediated by the "light beams" of a mobile, composite subjectivity traversing, in conversation and conjecture, a landscape of the possible; we also hear a "pluralized" variation of the biblical phrase that associates creation with the spoken word— a perception of reality that for Hans Blumenberg is typical of the Old Testament, in which "seeing is always predetermined by hearing, questioned or overpowered by it" ("Sehen immer schon durch Hören vorbestimmt, in Frage gestellt oder überboten [ist]"; 442; my translation).

The narrator of the initial scene, it will be revealed later in the stories he relates, is Patrick Lewis, who deciphers, with his slowly growing cognizance of other, foreign cultures, a new knowledge of himself. The first encounter between two different worlds is set, like the opening vignette, in the darkness of the early morning hours. Like the first signs of a landscape outside expected to arise out of the night, the lights of a "collection of strangers" (7), of a "strange community" (7), appear in the darkness outside the window of a small boy's room: he "stands at the bedroom window and watches; he can see two or three lanterns" (7). The name and identity of the boy, Patrick, emerge for us gradually, as the world of the other appears for him out of the darkness. When Patrick moves to an immigrant neighborhood in Toronto, where he will eventually catch up with the unknown stories about the world of the loggers he has encountered as a child. Here he also discovers a whole world of the other, outside his familiar boundaries (and for us beyond the horizon of a Toronto history written predominantly in English). Most significantly, with the discovery of the (in terms of the English language) silent other, and his journey into a foreign language and culture, Patrick translates himself into a new reality as much as he his transformed by it. Leaving his own past, the "immigrant to the city" (53) is, like the immigrants from abroad, "new even to himself" (54).

When he works in the tunnels under Lake Ontario that are needed for the new waterworks, he moves into the neighborhood of the Macedonians and Bulgarians who are his colleagues, and begins to perceive similarities between the contrasting worlds of self and other. As English-speaking Canadian he becomes the foreign other of the foreigners in his own land, "their alien" (113). Simultaneously he recognizes his own position as an outsider in their image: "The people on the street, the Macedonians and Bulgarians, were his only mirror" (112). His knowledge of these other cultures is limited, however, to a formal awareness of a common experience of alienation. A mediation of horizons begins only with a knowledge that lies, with the foreign language, unelucidated in the dark, beyond the compass of immediate visibility. This lack of words pertains also to our own, present-day knowledge of the historical reality Patrick is shown to enter. The section of *In the Skin of a Lion* that introduces us to Patrick's work in the tunnels, "Palace of Purification," begins with the taking of a photograph, an act of transcription that imposes an eerie silence on the scene: "For a moment, while the film receives the image, everything is still, the other tunnel workers silent" (105). Ondaatje's description of these photographs invites our ears synaesthetically, again, to hear another word and world underneath the written "white lye" that indicates the site of the actual work—also in a different, double sense a work yet to be done: "In those photographs moisture in the tunnels appears white. There is a foreman's white shirt, there is white lye daubed onto rock to be dynamited. And all else is labour and darkness. Ashgrey faces. An unfinished world. The men work in the equivalent of the fallout of a candle" (111). Again, a small bright light is evoked as the illumination of a potential world that is "unfinished," and has not yet come to light. The darkness of labor, the dynamite to be blasted, and the workers silenced at the moment the picture is taken, are without sound or language in these pictures that give us an "unfinished" portrait of the reality they seek—or pretend—to convey. The code we need to decipher these scenes is absent. This potential process from silence into language is a journey similar to the one Patrick begins when we see him trying to understand the foreign world around him. At first, he is confronted with a lack of known words, with an exotic language, and with pictures separated from language and explanation. His first "breakthrough" (112) comes with his first word in the foreign language, the Macedonian word for "iguana" (an animal he has received from his and Ambrose Small's lover, Clara, who thus provides him indirectly, not with a key to find the disappeared impresario, but with a lead for another kind of discovery). After the first word is found, a whole group of Macedonians "then circled him trying desperately to leap over the code of language between them" (113).

In a similar way, Patrick faces a silent picture without a code when he tries, later, to decipher the life of Clara's friend Alice. The old newspaper picture of construction workers at the Bloor Street Viaduct, which he is shown by Clara's daughter, Hana, has been separated from its caption. The windows of the library where Patrick hopes to find more information, "let in oceans of light" (143); but in this light only the written knowledge is visible that has been captured by the English language, and by the perspective of those who used it in this case: "The articles and illustrations he found in the Riverdale Library depicted every detail about the soil, the wood, the weight of concrete, everything but information on those who actually built the bridge" (145). When Patrick is finally able to find the missing caption, the written language provides him with a date, and with the name of his Macedonian acquaintance, Nicholas Temelcoff. The texture behind these bare outlines of history, however, is woven only out of Temelcoff's memory and narrations when Patrick shows him the picture. Although these stories have potentially existed, they have remained in the dark. But not only for Patrick do they begin to come to light; for Temelcoff himself they have been uncreated: "Nicholas Temelcoff never looks back.... Patrick's gift, that arrow into the past, shows him the wealth in himself, how he has been sewn into history. Now he will begin to tell stories" (149). These stories will turn out to be some of those related by (an as yet unnamed) Patrick during the opening car ride—and superimpose two speakers. The simulated oral mode will thus be retroactively marked at least by a double accent, since we now know that Patrick's narration is inhabited by Temelcoff's voice. The character of Nicholas Temelcoff is based on the Macedonian immigrant by the same name (who died on Sept. 12, 1988 in Toronto), and in particular on the research and the interviews with Temelcoff by the historian Lillian Petroff. The historiographic invisibility, up to that point, of the Macedonian immigrant community in Canada begins with their immigration records;

these reflect, however, only the passport definitions that listed Macedonians as Turks, Greeks, Bulgarians, or Serbians (Petroff 10–11). These immigrants shunned visibility in official written documentation by their own informed choice: "Used to avoiding Turkish authorities, Macedonians tried to evade Canadian officialdom as well...As in the old country, Macedonians risked official non-existence in North America" (Petroff 11).

In the new country, this culture is characterized by an unequal distribution of languages. As Robert Harney points out in his introduction to the volume *Gathering Place: Peoples and Neighbourhoods of Toronto, 1834–1945*, ethnic group identity is often expressed at home in the familiar language of the old country, and barely surfaces in the English language, which dominates the professional lives of the immigrants outside their community in the city. This situation is one of the reasons responsible for the fact that certain group realities remain silent potentials in Toronto's multi-layered city history. With a quotation from Italo Calvino's *Invisible Cities*, Harney opens an attack upon a form of city history that reinforces this tendency by emphasizing British immigration, reducing a multiplicity of group-specific perceptions of the city to monochromatic history: "Beware of saying to them that sometimes different cities follow one another on the same site with the same name, born and dying without knowing one another, without communication among themselves" (Calvino qtd. in Harney 1–2).

Referring to Clifford Geertz's notion of thinking as a profoundly public activity that takes place in markets, squares, and courtyards, Harney shows that these forms of public life still survive inside ethnic groups; the city as a whole, however, has not functioned as a communicative space—as that "Gathering Place" which the city's Native name refers to. Harney therefore suggests Toronto history rely more on oral history and its methodology. Petroff understands her own work in this sense, as an inner history of Macedonian immigration, as "creation of oral history, of an understanding of the 'memory culture' of Macedonian Canadians" (Petroff 10). But this elucidation, this coming to light of oral culture is of interest for Ondaatje also because of its implicit original disappearance, the inherent transformation exemplifying the possible and the unknown in motion. The first images we "see" of Temelcoff in the text (who is, again, as yet unnamed) are thus set, like the initial vignette and the first images of Patrick and the group of strangers, in the darkness of the early morning. The "faint light of the speedometer" in the moving vehicle at the beginning, however, has been transformed, by now, into a fire—and the landscape outside has become Toronto: "A truck carries fire at five A.M. through central Toronto....Aboard the flatbed three men stare into passing darkness....But for now all that is visible is the fire on the flatbed" (25). As the number of people increases to "twenty, crowded and silent" (25) (like the "strange community" Patrick has witnessed earlier), "the light begins to come out of the earth. They see their hands, the texture on a coat" (25). These strangers appear, for us as for themselves, out of the darkness like the bridge they build, which "goes up in a dream" (26). Eventually, they will take over the bridge—which grows in the void of the valley like Ondaatje's fiction in an unwritten space—with their flickering lights in the middle of the night: "The previous midnight the workers had arrived and brushed away officials who guarded the bridge ... moved with their own flickering lights—their candles for the bridge dead—like a wave of civilization, a net of summer insects over the valley" (27). Ondaatje's Temelcoff, like the unnamed workers moving on the truck in darkness, appears initially to himself invisible and silent after having crossed the border, after having left behind his old language and the old images of himself: "He never realizes how often he is watched by others. He has no clue that his gestures are extreme. He has no portrait of himself. ... As with sight, because Nicholas does not listen to most conversations around him, he assumes no one hears him" (42–43).

Temelcoff's invisibility in the pictures of the bridge is "seen," in *In the Skin of a Lion*, as part of a potential in which humanity extends itself beyond given reality. John Berger, in his essay "The Moment of Cubism"—evoked discreetly in the novel (34)—describes an artistic confidence similarly in new constructions as part of a historical moment in which the relationship between human possibilities and reality changed (see 34). In the years 1907–14 (the period prior to construction of the Toronto bridge), Berger sees human productivity transcend its old limits by means of new techniques and materials, through steel, electricity, radio, and film. A certain secularization is completed: "But now man was able to extend *himself* indefinitely beyond the immediate: he took over the territory in space and time where God had been presumed to exist" (7). Berger finds this changed relationship between human being and reality in cubism as well (15); beyond the imitation of visible reality, but also beyond Romantic emphasis on subjective experience, cubism thinks subjective experience as part of, and continuous with, perceived reality (20–21). Berger ascribes the intimation of a new world to these pictures that model perception itself, and force the imagination of the observer to search and to test possibilities. Cubism, for Berger, is prophetic (9).

To Ondaatje's commissioner Roland Harris, the progress of the bridge occurs, by night, like the prophecy of a Toronto that is invisible as yet. The bridge by night that exists half-real, half-imagined by the eyes that see in the darkness of the night, disappears beyond the edge of the valley, and transcends Toronto's visible image by day. This extending and prophetic vision is significantly compared with oral forms of language that construct other worlds in excess of given reality—rumors and tall tales: "For Harris the night allowed scope. Night removed the limitations of detail and concentrated on form. ... before the real city could be seen it had to be imagined, the way rumours and tall tales were a kind of charting" (29). Nicholas Temelcoff goes in Ondaatje's novel even beyond this human-made structure pointing into the void. With the other workers he disappears time and again—although held by ropes—"over the edge of the bridge into the night" (30). When Ondaatje refers to Temelcoff, who floats invisibly between the two sides of the valley as he lives between languages, as a "spinner" linking everyone, he alludes, with the archaic meaning of the word, to the spider web as one of his preferred textual metaphors; but the word "spinner" evokes also a "teller of the yarn." With the character of Temelcoff, who appears to us mediated by several instances, Ondaatje offers also an image of language that exceeds reality, and proceeds from the gaps of a historical discourse seeking strictly factual representation. Similar to Temelcoff's life between the old and the new continent and their languages, and between the two ends of the bridge opening out into the empty valley, Ondaatje's novel grows in the gaps of the transcribed interviews with the historical Nicholas Temelcoff. Although the work on the bridge is mentioned here, we learn next to nothing about the daily work experience (see Petroff 143; Temelcoff 6–8).

With Temelcoff's emergence in the new language simultaneously, the new emerges in Ondaatje's language, an otherness beyond the factual knowledge asserted by recorded history. Like the workers who climb—secured by ropes and anchored in historical truth—day after day "over the edge of the bridge into the night" (30), the novel advances in its telling of history; but, in a parallel formulation that recalls and contrasts with this secured advance, the story steps beyond that limit. A nun falls "off the edge of the bridge. She disappeared into the night . . . into the long depth of air which held nothing" (31). This fall and disappearance into the undefined darkness of the night opens here the possibility of a metamorphosis, and offers the space for an untold story (not dissimilar to the "vehicle" that "travels through darkness" at the beginning). The fall of the nun is caught by a secularized *deus ex machina*, the stranger, the other, Nicholas Temelcoff. As so often in Ondaatje's texts, both participants in this encounter transcend the demarcations of their former spaces. On the one hand, after this meeting of historically certified figure with the purely fictional one, the nun will change her name and her life, translating religious aspirations into secular hope; on the other hand, Temelcoff's speech begins, in a conversation with the as-yet nameless nun, to mix the accents and words of the old language with those of the new: "He talked on, slipping into phrases from the radio songs which is how he learned his words and pronunciations" (37). Similar to Patrick's entrance into a double-voiced reality both in his discovery of Macedonian words, and in his telling of the stories of himself and others in the middle of the night, Temelcoff reveals himself, on the dividing line between wake and sleep, in a double language: "He talked about himself, tired, unaware his voice split now into two languages" (37–38).

Ondaatje draws—so often in some of his most fascinating passages—on the materiality of signs to stage the encounter of different languages and realities. Whereas the technical medium of the radio and thus the ear and the spoken voice function here already as a catalyst in the orchestration of realities, of languages, and of voices that are alien to each other, the eye will have to wait, significantly, for the "talkies" to "lighten" —to ease and bring light to—the immigrants' experience: "The event that will lighten the way for immigration in North America is the talking picture" (43). The silent movie is associated with the voiceless darkness and grotesque of a nightmare: "These comedies are nightmares. The audience emits horrified laughter as Chaplin, blindfolded, roller skates near the edge of the un-balconied mezzanine. No one shouts to warn him. He cannot talk or listen. North America is still without language, gestures and work and bloodlines are the only currency" (43). Ondaatje tells us about immigrants who learn English by parroting actors in the theatre, destroying the punch lines with their multiple echo. Slow ballads and blues, rich with repetition, accommodate the newcomers as

well. "Sojourners walked out of their accent into regional American voices" (47), Ondaatje writes, letting Temelcoff alter himself in the modulations of the jazz singer Fats
Waller: "His emphasis on usually unnoticed syllables and the throwaway lines made
him seem high-strung or dangerously anti-social or too loving" (47). But the acquisition
of the foreign language by immigrants does not guarantee their visibility in the written
history of the host culture. With the interwoven story of the searcher and narrator Patrick, who himself accepts the status of a stranger in the world of the immigrant strangers, Ondaatje's novel listens to this historical silence and "renders" unrecorded history
in written, often necessarily fictional words. Patrick intervenes in a puppet play that
stages, as a pantomime and *mise en abyme*, the immigrants' silent life in the English
language of the city during an illegal meeting of workers at the waterworks, an "illegal
gathering of various nationalities" where "many languages were being spoken" (115;
see Lemon 53). Patrick's interruption of this pantomime enacting silent history will
have been, at the end of the novel, one of his first steps as a mediator and eventually
narrator of that silence. The play's main figure, whose silent gesture of despair he ends,
has emerged from the play as human being among silent puppets. She turns out to be
Alice Gull, who is later revealed as the "flying" nun. If the nun has not spoken in the
earlier scenes (silently added to the historical record of the bridge), she now gains a
voice in the novel's story, in the fictional version of history. While Patrick has ended
her silent play within the novel, she will end his silent role in the story.

     When Patrick reflects on his own outsidedness, on the fact that he "has clung like
moss to strangers, to the nooks and fissures of their situations" (156), unable ever to
have "been the hero of one of these stories" (157), he remembers Alice's description of
a play in which the power of language is handed on among several heroines: "After half
an hour the powerful matriarch removed her large coat from which animal pelts dan-
gled and she passed it, along with her strength, to one of the minor characters. In this
way even a silent daughter could put on the cloak and be able to break through her
chrysalis into language. Each person had their moment when they assumed the skins of
wild animals, when they took responsibility for the story" (157). The passage evokes
the novel's title and its first epigraph, taken from the *Epic of Gilgamesh:* "I will let my
hair grow long for your sake, and I will wander through the wilderness in the skin of a
lion." (93) In the epos—the story of a double—Gilgamesh abandons his way of life after the death of his friend Enkidu, with whom he has transgressed the laws and the
boundaries determined by the gods, in order to immortalize his name. He leaves his city
and his friends in order to learn the secret of immortality from Utnapishtim, to whom
eternal life has been given by the gods. But after a long journey through darkness, and
over the waters of death, he cannot pass Utnapishtim's test: he cannot vanquish death-
like sleep for six days and seven nights. Patrick's friend Alice dies, not because she is
punished by the gods like Enkidu, but through the more modern violence of a time
bomb, meant to transgress the order of the city. Like Gilgamesh, Patrick leaves the city
after the death of his friend. Burning down a resort hotel of the rich, he adopts the pose
of a violent anarchist (Joseph Conrad's *The Secret Agent* might be one of the intertexts

here), both to take revenge on those Alice has taught him to oppose, and to transcend the limits of his former life (as Temelcoff and Alice have done before him). After his return from prison, Patrick aims more precisely at the demarcation line between the anonymous dead of history, and those who are granted immortality by its "monuments." He enters the waterworks through its intake pipe, after having made himself invisible with the help of Caravaggio—a thief who routinely transgresses the boundaries of buildings, and has eluded the confinement of Kingston Prison by letting himself be painted into the roof (Blumenberg mentions Caravaggio together with Rembrandt as one of the first painters who used light as a localized factor, rather than letting a homogeneous light guarantee an evenly accented scene [446]; see also Sarris).

The anti-climactic scene in which Patrick, after having crossed the dark Lake Ontario as Gilgamesh had traversed darkness and the waters of death, faces the city commissioner Harris at night inside the water works, takes on rich signification with the intertextual references to the epos. By entering the waterworks, Patrick has most certainly not "successfully overcome the danger of being obliterated by official histories" (Gamlin 69). His encounter and dialogue with Harris pose the question of death and survival, practically at this decisive moment of the novel, and symbolically with respect to historically recorded reality. Threatening to destroy the building that today still immortalizes Harris's name, Patrick demands to know how many suffered death in the construction of the building. "No record was kept" (236), Harris answers. Patrick now asks Harris (who has survived in the light of written history), to turn off the light, and face him in his—Patrick's—world of darkness. But Harris reveals himself as a visionary dreamer who can see potential worlds beyond the visible realities of daylight. His visions of the city that came to him in dreams, he tells Patrick, often turned out to be possibilities the city had dismissed. Such a possibility, Patrick is being told, is he himself: "These *were* real places. They could have existed. I mean the Bloor Street Viaduct and this building here are just a hint of what could have been done here. You must realize you are like these places, Patrick" (237–38).

Patrick does not accede to historical immortality by blowing up the water works, in this fictionalized version of Toronto's history. In a surprising turn of events, Patrick falls asleep while telling the story of Alice's death; we hear its end as part of a dream. While this solution hardly corresponds to the climactic expectations connected with the realistic novel, it is clearly motivated by the mythic theme of vanquishing sleep and death, a theme the novel transposes from the epos to the realities of historiography. In the early light of day, Harris wins over Patrick, and with him the written history we know. Like Gilgamesh, Patrick does not pass the test of conquering sleep. To take the skin of a lion, and accede to the language of historically recorded reality, remains a story between possibility and dream. This status between an uncertain power and prophecy distinguishes as well the narrative of an earlier stage in Gilgamesh's journey, which Ondaatje now quotes: "[Harris] stood over Patrick. 'He lay down to sleep, until he was woken from out of a dream. He saw lions around him glorying in life; then he took his axe in his hand, he drew his sword from his belt, and he fell upon them like an arrow from the string'" (242; *The Epic of Gilgamesh* 94).

Patrick is not awakened here from out of his dream. Only in Ondaatje's novel, the historical possibility (and probability) of another history of Toronto comes to life, and with it a multi-faceted mural of the city that its dominant historiography has left in the dark. Ondaatje's writing distinguishes itself from this form of visible knowledge by appealing to an oral history that again and again finds its beginnings, in *In the Skin of a Lion*, as a tale about and of the other told in darkness. Like the bridge, Ondaatje's fictive oral stories are imagined in a night that, for Harris, "removed the limitations of detail and concentrated on form" (29). And thus Patrick, who loses his reality with the beginning of daylight in the water works, is awakened and remains awake when he tells his tale—unleashing his "arrow into the past"—during the car ride at night when the novel returns to its beginning. But Patrick's tale has come about, in retrospect, as a structure in which many perspectives intersect. His narrative during the car ride is possible because, in this case, he is kept awake by Hana, the listener. "She stays awake to keep him company," we read at the beginning. At the end we learn, furthermore, that she has woken Patrick from his sleep (243), and made him talk by her questions—just as Patrick, earlier, has motivated Temelcoff to tell his stories. As we come to attribute certain passages in retrospect to both Temelcoff's *and* Patrick's discovered power of language, at the end the frame narrative similarly identifies, and thus overdetermines, the written novel we have read with the oral story being told at the beginning. And now, we learn also that Hana, the listener, has been sitting in "the driver's seat" (244) part of the way, and has "gathered" the slowly "betrayed," imagined landscape of the narrative from her own perspective, "adapting the rearview mirror to her height" (244). Throughout the novel, the searcher Patrick, who has set out to find the disappeared, wealthy Ambrose Small, ends up finding the perspectives of "ex-centrics" (Hutcheon 94) that history has neglected: besides the story of Nicholas Temelcoff, those of ethnic minority immigrants, and those of women.

These multiple possible perspectives and points of view often create an oscillating, hologrammatic simultaneity of different possible assumptions for the reader—concerning the identity of the speaker of a passage, of its point in time, and of its status with respect to reality (both in the novel and in historical reality). The novel uses, for instance, a non-linear structure in which chronologically later events of the plot are presented (frequently as memory from an even later point in time) prior to earlier events—he most extreme case being the final car scene presented at the beginning. Similarly, a prolepsis indirectly "announces" Alice's end as memory (147–48), long before the details of her death are finally revealed in Patrick's dream. Furthermore, this very dream and Patrick's adventure in the waterworks are framed by a chronologically later episode, in which Patrick lies down to sleep (219, 243). The sentence, "He felt his clothes wet with the sweat of sleep" (243), recalls the water imagery of Patrick's journey through the lake on the previous pages; only his actually broken arm seems to balance the possibility that his encounter with Harris might have occurred in a dream. Similarly,

Patrick wakes up wounded after his earlier encounter with Ambrose Small. Yet as if in a dream, Small "doesn't move as Patrick steps up to him and cuts him at the shoulder" (95). A few lines later, the text continues: "When Patrick woke" (95). After one of several dreams Patrick has earlier about Small, he is directly asked by Clara: "I said, were you dreaming?"—and answers: "I don't know. Why?" (68). These interconnected temporal and "ontological" oscillations remind us both of the double possible modes of dream and manuscript that Ondaatje discerns in *One Hundred Years of Solitude* (Ondaatje, "García Márquez" 31), which for him "*is* a dream, an instant" (29), and of the double time structure he observes in García Márquez's book: "About halfway through the book you begin to feel that while you are still moving forward to the end you are simultaneously moving from midpoint to the beginning. Your consciousness is sliding both ways. Time has been shattered by Melquíades's experiments to overcome death" (Ondaatje, "García Márquez" 30). He continues: "We have been reading the manuscript of Melquíades or witnessing the dream of the first Buendía" (31). Already in the opening pages, Patrick is referred to as the "boy who witnesses this procession [of strangers in the darkness], and who even dreams about it" (8).

The juxtapositions and mutual framings of moments perceived normally as isolated in time, or by the separations among dream, possibility, and reality, emphasize the simultaneity of different historical and subjectively accessible spaces and times in the novel. Ondaatje answers thus John Berger's call that serves as his second epigraph: "Never again will a single story be told as though it were the only one." *In the Skin of a Lion* interprets effectively some of the possible implications of this manifesto by interweaving different planes of reality and time, thus opening the space for another dimension that coexists with the realities of Toronto and Ontario that we may be aware of. Worlds meet in a fluid choreography of possibility and actuality, dream and prophecy, versions of the past, of the present, and possibly of the future. This openness towards the space of the other, however, is accompanied by a self-reflexive awareness of mediality on the part of the writing self, which both discovers and opens itself to the silences, and the oral history, of the other. On the one hand, oral history plays a very conspicuous role in *In the Skin of a Lion* (as in Ondaatje's two previous works of fiction), and Ondaatje may well be seen among those novelists who—"despite themselves," as Hutcheon has suspected—"are McLuhan's true spiritual heirs" (52). On the other hand, Ondaatje thematizes writing also very explicitly as an act of self-discovery. We see the thief Caravaggio, for instance, who "was invisible to all around him" (199) and "had never witnessed someone writing before," stand outside a window and observe a woman write, "trying to discover what she was or what she was capable of making" (198). In this scene, the figure in the darkness outside begins to intermingle liminally with the room in which the written self is created—but the stranger at the window remains unnamed himself: "He was anonymous" (199).

Ondaatje's novel stages both the potential violence and the fascinating possibilities inherent in the perception, history, and writing of the other that necessarily implies an act of self-mediation and mutual creation. If his writing is fictive memory, it creates an example—and adumbrates the outline—of a distinct necessity: the coexistence of "invisible" cities and existences, both in the past and in Toronto's present. We often know about these realities only that they exist, or must have existed—in silence. If invisibility and darkness are typically associated, in *In the Skin of a Lion*, with the rich potential of a collective oral history, the eye is made aware of its other through writing, a medium associated with light. *In the Skin of a Lion* overtly addresses this mediation; in its last plural, however, the text seeks both to evade the mono-perspectival limits of this process, and to multiply its possibilities: "Lights, he said" (244). These "lights" often reveal infinitely altering perspectives that often do not move toward resolution. In the "final" encounter between Patrick and Harris, for instance, Harris reveals his "other" side as a being of the night, thus becoming Patrick's equal. Because of this unsuspected partial identity between the two, the exclusion of the other—the expected arrest of Patrick—never occurs here. But if this scene in the night carries a few traces of a dream, it brings its own possibility and potentiality to light. If this moment may not have happened except as a dream—either in history or in the novel—scenes of similar otherness and intent could have happened—and probably did in some form. The decision whether to exclude this reality of fiction, or whether to perceive the constructed fictionality of our own familiar room, is left to us.

Note: The above paper is an updated version of a text on pages 153–72 in Winfried Siemerling, *Discoveries of the Other: Alterity in the Work of Leonard Cohen, Hubert Aquin, Michael Ondaatje, and Nicole Brossard.* Toronto: U of Toronto P, 1994.

WORKS CITED

Berger, John. "The Moment of Cubism." *The Moment of Cubism and Other Essays.* By John Berger. London: Weidenfeld & Nicolson, 1969. 1–32.

Blumenberg, Hans. "Licht als Metapher der Wahrheit. Im Vorfeld der philosophischen Begriffsbildung." *Studium Generale* 10.7 (1957): 432–47.

The Epic of Gilgamesh. Trans. N.K. Sandars. Harmondsworth: Penguin, 1960.

Gamlin, Gordon. "Michael Ondaatje's *In the Skin of a Lion* and the Oral Narrative." *Canadian Literature* 135 (1992): 68–77.

García Márquez, Gabriel. *One Hundred Years of Solitude.* Trans. Gregory Rabassa. New York: Harper & Row, 1970.

Harney, Robert F. "Ethnicity and Neighbourhoods." *Gathering Place: Peoples and Neighbourhoods of Toronto, 1834–1945.* Ed. Robert F. Harney. Toronto: Multicultural History Society of Ontario, 1985. 1–24.

Hutcheon, Linda. *The Canadian Postmodern: A Study of Contemporary English-Canadian Fiction.* Toronto: Oxford UP, 1988.

Lemon, James. *Toronto since 1918: An Illustrated History.* Toronto: Lorimer, 1985.

Mumford, Ted. "Michael Ondaatje's New World." *Now: Toronto's Weekly News and Entertainment Voice* 6.36 (14–20 May 1987): 17.

Ondaatje, Michael. *Anil's Ghost.* Toronto: McClelland and Stewart, 2000.

Ondaatje, Michael. *In the Skin of a Lion.* Toronto: McClelland and Stewart, 1987.

Ondaatje, Michael. *Running in the Family.* Toronto: McClelland and Stewart, 1982.

Ondaatje, Michael. "García Márquez and the Bus to Aracataca." *Figures in a Ground: Canadian Essays on Modern Literature.* Ed. Diane Bessai and David Jackel. Saskatoon: Western Producer Prairie Books, 1978. 19–31.

Ondaatje, Michael. *Coming Through Slaughter.* Toronto: Anansi, 1976.

Ondaatje, Michael. *The Collected Works of Billy the Kid: Left Handed Poems.* Toronto: Anansi, 1970.

Petroff, Lillian. *The Macedonian Community in Toronto to 1940.* Ph.D. Dissertation. Toronto: U of Toronto, 1983.

Sarris, Fotios. "*In the Skin of a Lion*: Michael Ondaatje's Tenebristic Narrative." *Essays on Canadian Writing* 44 (1991): 183–201.

Temelcoff, N.S. "Interview with Lillian Petroff." Unpublished manuscript. 8 July 1975.

Reading Ondaatje's Poetry

Eluned Summers-Bremner

In an interview with Sam Solecki in 1984, Michael Ondaatje responds to the inter-
viewer's reference to his caginess in interviews, and to a question about whether this
ever causes him regret, with the phrase: "Very few people want to talk about architecture" (Ondaatje qtd. in Solecki, "An Interview" 322). Ondaatje's desire to speak of architecture and change in the structure of the contemporary novel is timely. In the last
few decades transnational displacement has made the novel—always a kind of conversation with quotidian ways of inhabiting the world—into a text that must imagine
travel, if not in content, then in form, in order to speak to the contemporary. And not
only physical travel, but the entire (post)modern architecture of displacement from familial, national and linguistic myths of belonging that Ondaatje's books chart so well,
from *Billy the Kid* to *Running in the Family* to *Anil's Ghost*. But the engagement with
home as a mode of travel runs throughout Ondaatje's poetry too, which, as numerous
critics have observed (see Barbour; Glickman; Cooke) is dynamized by a dialogue with
nature, with walking the border between the natural and the human in all its promising—and, in the earlier work, sometimes horrifying—imperspicuity. As architecture is
a conversation with landscape, if not at the outset, then necessarily later as it succumbs
to the force of wind and weather, so Ondaatje's poetics is, in my reading, a continual re-
staging of the mobility of dwelling; a sustained re-encounter with nature's—and human
nature's—strangeness. As part of this endeavor, much of the poetry is also involved in
what I call the "search for a name," exemplified perhaps by these lines from "Escarp-
ment," the closing section of the volume *Secular Love*:

> He loves too, as she knows, the body of rivers. Provide him with a river or a
> creek and he will walk along it. Will step off and sink to his waist, the sound
> of water and rock encasing him in solitude. The noise around them insists on
> silence if they are more than five feet apart. It is only later when they sit in a
> pool legs against each other that they can talk, their conversation roaming to
> include relatives, books, best friends, the history of Lewis and Clark, frag-
> ments of the past which they piece together. But otherwise this river's noise
> encases them and now he walks alone with its spirits, the clack and splash, the
> twig break, hearing only an individual noise if it occurs less than an arm's
> length away. He is looking, now, for a name. (Ondaatje, *Secular Love* 125–
> 26)

The speaker seeks "not a name on a map," not something already laid down, but
"something temporary for their vocabulary. A code" (Ondaatje, *Secular Love* 126) or a
mnemonic, as Leslie Mundwiler, invoking Frances Yates, describes the creative ambu-
lation of Ondaatje's work: "where the poems give a sense of place, the place is often a

frame or architectonic background for image or images which are active, vivid, sensual"
(Yates qtd. in Mundwiler 52), images which escape their frame, calling the retrospective understanding of architecture—a building as structure, something stable—into
question. The search for a name here is akin to the way a building bears the traces of its
dialogue with its surroundings, in its lonesome nighttime creaks, its winter dreamings.
A fire in the hearth is nature become culture, the unknowable flame now a comfort, protection. And fire in the hearth is a homeopathy of weather: the variables of a state of
atmosphere "with respect to heat or cold, presence or absence of rain" (*OED*) reduced,
broken in. A house is made from a violent dialogue with nature that is then forgotten,
rendered tame, but which in the night can also, disturbingly, reawaken: "He lies in bed,
awake, holding her left forearm. It is 4 a.m. . . . Through the window he can hear the
creek—which has no name" (Ondaatje, *Secular Love* 125).

The function of the name in the above extract is performative and suitably mo-
mentary. The speaker "slips under the fallen tree holding the cedar root the way he
holds [his lover's] forearm," hanging for a moment before "being pulled by water going
down river. He holds it the same way and for the same reasons. Heart creek? Arm
river? he writes, he mutters to her in the darkness" (Ondaatje, *Secular Love* 126). The
river is a moving body like and unlike the body of the beloved. *Secular Love* closes
with the lines: "He has gone far enough to look for a bridge and has not found it. Turns
upriver. He holds onto the cedar root the way he holds her forearm" (Ondaatje, *Secular
Love* 126). The name is a bridge the speaker cannot find on which his love might walk:
something allowing nature to converse with human nature, as a man to cross a flowing
river; the name for what's common to yielding to the river and the 4 a.m. waking holding his lover's forearm—both of them somehow necessary and both of them unknown.
Yet the name eludes: "Sun lays its crossword, litters itself, along the whole turning
length of this river so he can step into heat or shadow" (Ondaatje, *Secular Love* 126).
The sun has human qualities, an excess of ambition or production (it litters itself, over-
produces), makes the river a conversation, like a house is, with the weather: a place in
which to step for winter warmth or summer shadow. But its form is a crossword—try to
capture or use or subdue it, it's gone. It's more like a game or a puzzle one is engaged
in. Nature at the volume's close is like the father figure at the volume's opening, who
also speaks with rivers: "Tentatively / he recalls / his drunk invitation to the river. / He
has steered the awesome car / past sugarbush to the blue night water / and steps out /
speaking to branches / and the gulp of toads. / Subtle applause of animals" (Ondaatje,
Secular Love 16).

The father startles up, too, at 4 a.m., as "the invited river flows through the
house" and "he awakens and moves within it": "He wishes to swim / to each of his family and gaze / at their underwater dreaming / . . . / Wife, son, household guests, all / comfortable in clean river water" (Ondaatje, *Secular Love* 18). *Secular Love* is poetry of
travel, as love is both a labor (a travail) and a journey that begins in the family. Secular-
ity is mortal, this-worldly, as love is, yet love is also the closest we get, while living, to
expansive dissolution. The two work against each other. In staging a physical conversa-

tion with the river—and in other poems in the book, with travel, departures, and memory—the volume explores what is tangible yet at the same uncontainable of love, as of family, what escapes the stories we tell of each, that which we recall and, in doing so, remember losing ("When you can move through a house blindfolded it belongs to you"; "Things we clung to / stay on the horizon / and we become the loon / on his journey / a lone tropical taxi / to confused depth and privacy" (Ondaatje, *Secular Love* 87, 102)).

As psychoanalyst Serge Leclaire, following Freud, reminds us, "consciousness and memory are mutually exclusive" (Leclaire 76). Machines—like computers—have been modeled on the belief that memory is "at the same time the inscription of traces and the capacity to summon them" (Leclaire 76), but this is inaccurate, the property rather of an Enlightenment dream. Properly speaking, memory is the name for the lostness of the past, its continued habitation of our lives beyond our knowing. What we are accustomed to call memory is a *trace:* an inscription "hardened . . . into the mute . . . nature of the screen, erected . . . like a limit" between the one who thinks back now and the past, whose life flows on in its underwater world (Leclaire 77). One's history remains beneath and beyond and is protected by the memories that come to mind, as is human and natural life by the surface of water. Freud called these surface regulators or transmitting stations "screen memories," because their function, as Ondaatje here shows, is to live as screen: they mask and reveal, as the past continues to underwrite the present, and as direct access to this night-time writing is denied (Freud 1995). Of course, the denial of direct access is what makes us able to make use of memory and dreaming, in allowing them to make creative use of us. Thus the father in his "drunk state wants the mesh of place," physical artifacts ("glass plants, iron parrots/ . . . tarpaulins of Himalaya"; Ondaatje, *Secular Love* 15), all man-made things that summon the unreachable by man; un-homely elements to strain and hold, protect and enable, as alcohol does, and memory: "from now on I will drink only landscapes/ —here, pour me a cup of Spain" (Ondaatje, *Secular Love* 15). And just as we cannot truly know memory, to our gain, so we can never truly know our parents or their original desires for us, that are somehow encoded in the choosing of our names. The need to figure out a screen version, though, is signaled by what Jacques Lacan calls the (big) Other, referring to our arrival in an alien country—that of the world—that must be second-guessed ("Why am I here?" "What do they [parents, teachers, lovers] want from me?" and so on), and partly elaborated by our responses to our names. As Linda Hutcheon observes, writing of her own nominal alteration in its Canadian contexts, the changing of a name can have a bridging or enabling function but is at the same time an encrypting: to assert belonging via a new name defamiliarizes the old one, reminding us of its strangeness, its prior life, a buried history of enculturation.

A father, unlike a mother, is knowable or unknowable not as body but as name: a figure for the secondary home or encryption that is language. A mother bears a child but a father's claim lies in his word; in language (or in that of scientific tests, somewhat behind the working truth of things as usual). Thus the code of belonging that is the father's name is of a different order from that of the child housed in its mother's belly.

What kind of home is the name of a father? "He wishes to swim/ to each of his family" yet "stands waiting, the sentinel, / shambling back and forth" (Ondaatje, *Secular Love* 18–19). Perhaps a father is this wish to comfort and communicate unmade, the miss lived out between a person and his name, the unhappy performance of division—someone has to do it, as the saying goes. In Lacanian terms a father is a name for the performance of division worked by language, and law, an act curiously lacking in substance that must, as a result, be perpetually redone. For what does it mean to be "on the side of law" if not to be repeatedly called to make a judgment? The father in the earlier "Letter & Other Worlds" sends letters to his family that communicate this missing substance, a miscommunication or a time lag as address: "His letters were a room he seldom lived in / In them the logic of his love could grow / . . . / He hid where he had been that we might lose him / His letters were a room his body scared / . . . / With the clarity of architects / he would write of the row of blue flowers / his new wife had planted, / the plans for electricity in the house, / . . . / his heart widening and widening and widening" (Ondaatje, *Rat Jelly* 44, 46) until he falls into "his own privacy," a "terrible acute hatred," "the empty reservoir of bones" of his death which brooks no metaphor beyond the fall, "a new equilibrium" that no one can measure and that language cannot say (Ondaatje, *Rat Jelly* 46, 44). In *Secular Love* the father's drunken river dialogue, like that of the speaker's 4 a.m. holding of the beloved's forearm and the river-searching for a bridge and code, "something temporary," are attempts to navigate the mystery that is the father's name, to discover what knits nature to culture, kin to kin, and what escapes this exploratory labor (like the sun, the river and the loved one, herself elsewhere naming), what might capture and free it at once.

A code has two languages, but each one cancels out the other, just as memory is incompatible with the memory screen, dream knowledge with waking, and the father of "Letters" with the room the letters are (one "he seldom lived in," always running instead from his body's "town of fear"; Ondaatje, *Rat Jelly* 44). And yet a code as a method of communication conveys at least three things: the surface message (say, a name), the encoded or secret message (the name's meaning which we guess at; in the case of our own names, all our lives), and the reason for sending a secret message from one to another at all. The reason might be love, or deceit, or war, or all of these, and cannot always be discovered: the context is implicit but not always clear from our reading of the code, the hidden message. All we can do is try to figure it, the crossword of sun on river, the unavoidable estrangement humans make of nature. In his reading of language as social code, Lacan called the proper name a "trait" (Lacan 1965, qtd. in Nobus 99). A subject's identification with her or his name is a reading as attempted uncoding of the place kept for the subject, augured by the subject's name, in the *socius*, a place that is perpetually moving. Our responses to our names—signs of the mystery of a desire which precedes us—are thus belated attempts to guess the reason for our sending. Lacan's view of human existence as the living out of such estranging codes augurs no unwarranted intrusions into the coded worlds so aptly limned by Ondaatje's resonant poetry. The unconscious makes proper names fail (Julien 132), yet poetry, arising from the mobile interface of body and language, sense and feeling, can bring us closer to its truth. "Grammatical language and images merely produce the illusion of a consistent universe. But the unconscious disrupts these illusions, by dissociating meaning that only seems full from our pretences that it functions smoothly" (Ragland-Sullivan 69). Thus while "the human tendency is to try to explain what *is* by things from the outside or by impersonal innate tendencies, rather than by deficiencies and dissymmetries in being and knowing" (Ragland-Sullivan 69), this is a retrospectively anxious endeavor (Solecki describes Ondaatje's poetry similarly, where "what is at issue," he claims, "is the existence not of an alternate reality but of different perceptions of one which the reader has always assumed to be clear, patterned, meaningful" (Solecki, "Nets and Chaos" 93). The speaker at the close of *Secular Love* wants "not a name for a map—he knows the arguments of imperialism" which tells us such names have all been used to other ends before, but "a name for them," for what the lovers are doing, something to both hold and keep the present from itself, and from its fading before the future (Ondaatje, *Secular Love* 126). But this name will not reveal itself, except in so far as the looking for it makes the river walking and the river writing a special kind of doing, a working code for something, maybe love: "Heart Creek? Arm River? he writes, he mutters to her in the darkness . . . He holds onto the cedar root the way he holds her forearm" (Ondaatje, *Secular Love* 126).

This formally careful yet topically uncertain quality, a waltz with transience—the eventual fate of communicative efforts—can be seen in Ondaatje's earlier poetry also, although there it is more tortured, violent, and the search for a name, a code in which to record experience, makes the natural world decidedly un-homely (as in *The Collected Works of Billy the Kid* and many of the poems in *The Dainty Monsters* [Ondaatje, *Collected*, *Dainty*]). Solecki reads *The Man with Seven Toes*, for instance, as inaugurating a performative mode of reading where the reader is in the state of the woman traveling harrowingly through the desert, plagued by ravenous beasts, the words on the page our culture to her nature: "Ondaatje's structuring . . . increase[s] the number of narrative possibilities that each lyric creates, to the point that the reader simply does not know what to expect from poem to poem" (Solecki, "Point Blank" 14). The second poem's opening: "Entered the clearing and they turned / faces scarred with decoration / feather, bones, paint from clay / pasted, skewered to their skin" (Ondaatje, *The Man with Seven Toes* 11), Solecki reads as creating "a sense of immediacy" via the ellipsis of the subject in the opening line, which puts us, with "shocking directness," in the space of the action itself (Solecki, "Point Blank" 141). The "exotic" images take this further, the "cumulative effect" being to "indicate the disorientation of the woman and to achieve that of the reader" (Solecki, "Point Blank" 141).

But there is a slippage in this reading that is not there so clearly, as I see it, in the writing. Solecki earlier states that Ondaatje's removing the story of a woman, based on the historical figure of Mrs Eliza Fraser, shipwrecked off the Queensland coast of Australia in 1836, and captured by aborigines, from its original context to "an unspecified time and place" has the "overall effect" of "focus[ing] attention on the story's essential content, the effect upon an individual of her confrontation with a totally alien landscape and mode of being" (Solecki, "Nets and Chaos" 138). Yet the poems in *man* themselves render little that might be called essential or timeless content, confronting us with a violence of explosively physical details that assert the intricate commonality (not the total alienness) of woman, land, and imagined journey or poetic going. The woman's rape by the aborigines is inseparable from their slaughter and eating of animals, "shocked into death . . . / alive / alive . . . in their mouths" (Ondaatje, *The Man with Seven Toes* 16) where death and life are horribly—for her—intertwined, as her later violation by her white convict rescuer (Potter) repeats: "evening. Sky was a wrecked black boot / a white world spilling through. / Noise like electricity in the leaves. / . . . cock like an ostrich, mouth / a salamander / thrashing in my throat. / Above us, birds peeing from the branches" (Ondaatje, *The Man with Seven Toes* 32).

An early reviewer presages Solecki's wishful displacement from the equation woman as land to man as conflict-with-the-land that makes the woman's body the means of the shift and exploration. For this reader the poem "represent[s] a loss of the conscious self and a descent into the feared subconscious [*sic*] . . . But Mrs X [the name designating Mrs Fraser within the poem] is only exhausted, drained, sunburned. The man, already prison-branded and tattooed, loses three of his toes and gets his mouth badly cut (both castration analogies within the poem)" (Lane 154). If only—and perhaps this is felt particularly acutely by the female reader—it were so simple. Castration in Lacanian terms is "an effect of language on living beings" (Soler 53), the fraught imbrication of nature and culture that nourishes the European worldview. It is not something that is only experienced by a man. It refers, rather, to our being born prematurely, ahead of our ability to use (or be used by) language, which afterwards leaves us wondering what we lost, and anxious as to the price that was—and will be—paid for linguistic competence. This means that nature, and the maternal body with which it is contiguous, is nostalgically idealized or viewed with and as a bitter enmity (Tennyson's "red in tooth and claw"); we can only view nature through linguistically enabled and disabled lenses. As George Bowering observes, Ondaatje's early poetry explores this paradox: "Deep in the fields / behind stiff dirt fern / nature breeds the unnatural" (Ondaatje, *Dainty* 21, qtd. in Bowering 65) where a determined poetics goes in search of the un-homely, and where what is found troubles the status of poetic endeavor (see Bowering; Solecki, "Nets and Chaos").

Yet the journey into the nightmare of wilderness and society figured in *The Man with Seven Toes* resists being read (as Lane reads it) as a parable about the dark night or troubled sleep of civilization. As Solecki notes, its closing in subjunctive mood is unsettling rather than reassuring for the reader: "God bring you all some tender stories/ and keep you all from hurt and harm" (Ondaatje, *The Man with Seven Toes* 42; Solecki, "Nets and Chaos" 147), the lullaby evoking a woman's—or a mother's—voice, that voice which we have just witnessed being horrifyingly turned inside out ("She was too tired even to call"; "to lock her head between knees / . . . drink her throat sweat, like coconut"; Ondaatje, *The Man with Seven Toes* 9, 35). In this sense there is no consoling or

authoritative framework apart from the one we make and find unmade as we are reading. But the sequence equally resists being read as a tale about nature's violent life, a
primitivism pure and simple. The "train" is a "low bird" from the outset (Ondaatje, *The
Man with Seven Toes* 9) and Mrs X's red dress both is and is not a desert flower.
"Stripped off like a husk" it is thrown back a "dress," and Potter's eyes later "stam-
mer"—a word for a bodily struggle with language—at its "sudden colour" (Ondaatje,
The Man with Seven Toes 12, 18). What neither critic notes is the way the poetic rendition of the story is another violence in which the reader, and the critic, cannot help but
be engaged. The woman makes the journey, and becomes the journey, her ravaged
body the sign that makes the land a work in progress, an instance of the war of colonization. Words are swallowed as if live in the reader's throat as the subject/object distinction which ordinarily sustains readerly distance is annulled ("like to you a knife
down their pit, a hand in the warm/ the hot the dark boiling belly and rip" (Ondaatje,
The Man with Seven Toes 16); so the rape and feasting devour subjective borders for
Mrs X. On the penultimate page she, rescued, becomes the parchment of a map or page
of living, brutal history: "She slept in the heart of the Royal Hotel / . . . / She moved fingers onto the rough skin, / . . . / sensing herself like a map, then / lowering her hands into
her body" (Ondaatje, *The Man with Seven Toes* 41). But this communion allows no
safety; it is the scene of nature in its war with culture, animal with machine, the violence of a remorseless contest of which the woman as map, the poem's mapping of her,
is a trace. Her trait—the living out of the message encoded by her name (Mrs X)—is
that of being caught in this crossfire: "In the morning she found pieces of a bird /
chopped and scattered by the fan / blood sprayed onto the mosquito net, / its body leaving paths on the walls / like red snails that drifted down in lumps. // She could imagine
the feathers / while she had slept / falling around her / like slow rain" (Ondaatje, *The
Man with Seven Toes* 41).

As I propose above, Ondaatje uses architecture as a figure for work in progress
and as attempt to accidentalize his questioner's intrusions. The journey from *The Man
with Seven Toes* to *Handwriting* does seem to have taken us from the general of a
nameless woman in the desert, ravaged by beasts, and the insistent strangeness of the
early poetry (a kind of anti-domestication), to the particular of a war-torn Sri Lankan
history, albeit one made available through the journeys and shifting confines of ancient
myth. *Handwriting* seems to map a new kind of agreement between the discovery and
perception of the natural world and poetic language, which now appears more openly as
a search for working code with which to value transience, and thus history, the performative contours of a particular name. This journey homeward that is aware of its enabling divisions is given a more expansive treatment in Ondaatje's *Anil's Ghost*. In the
novel Anil, the protagonist, enacts a homelessness we recognize, the world citizen's
payoff: she lives for her work which involves traveling historically as well as geographically into the contested country of the past, which yields some unconsoling truths
about belonging. Anil must investigate the corpses of the politically murdered of Sri
Lanka, her native country, from which she has sought exile, and to which she returns.

Her chosen homelessness is precisely rendered through the imagery of the un-homely places where she works and stays, as in the independence that is fought for and grudgingly conferred by her brother's second name: "In her present house in Colombo there was a small pool cut into the floor for floating flowers. It was a luxury to her. Something to confuse a thief in the dark. At night, returning from work, Anil would slip out of her sandals and stand in the shallow water, her toes among the white petals, her arms folded as she undressed the day, removing layers of events and incidents so they would no longer be within her. She would stand there for a while, then walk wet-footed to bed" (Ondaatje, *Anil's Ghost* 67). Similarly, in "House on a Red Cliff" in *Handwriting*: "The flamboyant a grandfather planted / having lived through fire / lifts itself over the roof / unframed / the house an open net / where the night concentrates / on a breath / on a step / a thing or gesture / we cannot be attached to" (Ondaatje, *Handwriting* 67).

An echo of the earlier turn to a dreamlike resolution, in *Secular Love*, from a poetry earlier still obsessed with woundings and violent cartographies as a mode of action, this later poetry reminds me of Lacan's turn, late in his teaching life, to James Joyce, as a means of engagement with whose work he undid all his former theories in the elaboration of symptom—the suffering imposed by language—as *sinthome*, a kind of writerly labor of self-redemption (Lacan 1976–77; see also Tillet 37; Thurston; Rabaté 154–82). *Sinthome* also has the meaning, in my reading, of an opening of the house of subjectivity to its original conditions, its contract with weather, land, history, air, what Susana Tillet calls "a definitive suspension" of motivating or protective questions (Tillet 37). A symptom can be earlier read, in Lacan, as the form of each individual's pact with language—the price paid in the body for the divisive yet necessary converse enabled by the father's name—and in Ondaatje's earlier work this division is projected outward, alienating man via woman, animals and land. Yet in the later work alienation is brought inward, paradoxically once again by means of movement through a landscape, but now a landscape whose mythology is not so clearly violated, appropriated or disowned. It seems to be given its own space, rather.

Writing, for the late Lacan, is a way of making and remaking a home in language, a riddling that does not deny the enjoyment of the sin or fall—or love for crafting language—that keeps us from feeling quite at home, keeps us at odds with our nature. And Ondaatje has remarked in interview, on the relation between an author and the material of his work, his characters: "A lot of my own world gets into their stories. It's probably a major illness" (Ondaatje qtd. in Freedman 1; Ondaatje qtd. in Bök 114). Lacan's central insight was that what we call linguistic health—for example, ease of communication—is bought at the price of other freedoms which speak as symptoms via the unique knotting of each language user's being in and through the demands of the socius. Each individual pays, uniquely, for the privilege of estrangement that sustains a common language. In the late Lacan of the *sinthome*, naming becomes a creative working with the knots and holes of our real treaty with this field, the particular configuration of our suffering and enjoyment in its going (see Rabaté 181). Read against the earlier work *Handwriting* seems notable for not reading as the articulation of a trick, a joke, the record of an outlaw or a monster, however self-stylised, but simply doing what it says: returning language to pen to body, tracing the intimate converse of past and present that travels through the word, the page, the hand: "Last ink in the pen. / My body on this hard bed. / The moment in the heart / where I roam restless, searching" (Ondaatje, *Handwriting* 74).

WORKS CITED

Barbour, Douglas. "Controlling the Jungle: A Review of *The Dainty Monsters.*" 1968. *Spider Blues: Essays on Michael Ondaatje.* Ed. Sam Solecki. Montréal: Véhicule, 1985. 111–20.

Barbour, Douglas. *Michael Ondaatje.* New York: Twayne, 1993.

Bök, Christian. "Destructive Creation: The Politicization of Violence in the Works of Michael Ondaatje." *Canadian Literature* 132 (1992): 109–24.

Bowering, George. "Ondaatje Learning to Do." *Spider Blues: Essays on Michael Ondaatje.* Ed. Sam Solecki. Montréal: Véhicule, 1985. 61–69.

Cooke, John. *The Influence of Painting on Five Canadian Writers: Alice Munro, Hugh Hood, Timothy Findley, Margaret Atwood, and Michael Ondaatje.* Lewiston: Edwin Mellen, 1996.

Freedman, Adele. "From Gunslingers to Jazz Musicians." *The Globe and Mail* (22 December 1979): Entertainment 1.

Freud, Sigmund. "Screen Memories." 1899. *The Freud Reader.* Ed. Peter Gay. London: Vintage, 1995. 117–26.

Glickman, Susan. 1985. "From 'Philoctetes on the Island' to 'Tin Roof': The Emerging Myth of Michael Ondaatje." *Spider Blues: Essays on Michael Ondaatje.* Ed. Sam Solecki. Montréal: Véhicule, 1985. 70–81.

Hutcheon, Linda. "Crypto-Ethnicity." *PMLA: Publications of the Modern Language Association of America* 113.1 (1998): 28–33.

Julien, Phillipe. *Jacques Lacan's Return to Freud: The Real, the Symbolic, and the Imaginary.* Trans. Devra Beck Simiu. New York: New York UP, 1994.

Lacan, Jacques. Le Séminaire XXII: Problèmes cruciaux pour la psychanalyse. Seminar of 6 January 1965. Unpublished paper.

Lacan, Jacques. "Le Séminaire XXII: R.S.I." *Ornicar?* 2 (1975): 87–105; 3 (1975): 95–110; 4 (1975): 91–106; 5 (1975): 15–66.

Lacan, Jacques. "Le Séminaire XXIII: Le Sinthome." *Ornicar?* 6 (1976–77): 3–20; 7 (1976–77): 3–18; 8 (1976–77): 6–20; 9 (1976–77): 32–40; 10 (1976–77): 5–12; 11 (1976–77): 2–9.

Lane, M. Travis. "Dream as History: A Review of *The Man with Seven Toes.*" 1970. *Spider Blues: Essays on Michael Ondaatje.* Ed. Sam Solecki. Montréal: Véhicule, 1985. 150–55.

Leclaire, Serge. "Unconscious Inscription: Another Memory." *Psychoanalysis, Creativity, and Literature: A French-American Inquiry.* Ed. Alan Roland. New York: Columbia UP, 1978. 75–84.

Marks, Zita M. "Borromean Knot." *A Compendium of Lacanian Terms.* Ed. Huguette Glowinski, Zita Marks, and Sara Murphy. London: Free Association Books, 2001. 38–41.

Moretti, Franco. *The Way of the World: The* Bildungsroman *in European Culture.* London: Verso, 1987.

Mundwiler, Leslie. *Michael Ondaatje: Word, Image, Imagination.* Vancouver: Talonbooks, 1984.

Nobus, Dany. "Rumpelstiltskin's Revenge: On the Importance of Proper Names in Psychoanalysis." *The Letter: Lacanian Perspectives on Psychoanalysis* 9 (1997): 84–101.

Ondaatje, Michael. *Anil's Ghost.* London: Picador, 2000.

Ondaatje, Michael. *Handwriting.* London: Picador, 1998.

Ondaatje, Michael. *Secular Love.* Toronto: Coach House P, 1984.

Ondaatje, Michael. *Rat Jelly and Other Poems, 1963–78.* London: Marion Boyars, 1980.

Ondaatje, Michael. *The Collected Works of Billy the Kid.* Toronto: Anansi, 1970.

Ondaatje, Michael. *The Man with Seven Toes.* Toronto: Coach House P, 1969.

Ondaatje, Michael. *The Dainty Monsters.* Toronto: Coach House P, 1967.

Rabaté, Jean-Michel. *Jacques Lacan: Psychoanalysis and the Subject of Literature.* New York: Palgrave, 2001.

Ragland-Sullivan, Ellie. "Lacan's Seminars on James Joyce: Writing as Symptom and 'singular Solution'." *Psychoanalysis and . . . .* Ed. Richard Feldstein and Henry Sussman. New York: Routledge, 1990. 67–86.

Solecki, Sam. "An Interview with Michael Ondaatje." 1984. *Spider Blues: Essays on Michael Ondaatje.* Ed. Sam Solecki. Montréal: Véhicule, 1985. 321–32.

Solecki, Sam. "Introduction." *Spider Blues: Essays on Michael Ondaatje.* Ed. Sam Solecki. Montréal: Véhicule, 1985. 7–11.

Solecki, Sam. "Nets and Chaos: The Poetry of Michael Ondaatje." 1977. *Spider Blues: Essays on Michael Ondaatje.* Montréal: Véhicule, 1985. 93–110.

Solecki, Sam. "Point Blank: Narrative in *The Man with Seven Toes.*" *Spider Blues: Essays on Michael Ondaatje.* Ed. Sam Solecki. Montréal: Véhicule, 1985. 135–49.

Soler, Colette. "The Symbolic Order (II)." In *Reading Seminars I and II: Lacan's Return to Freud.* Ed. Richard Feldstein, Bruce Fink, and Maire Jannus. Albany:
   State U of New York P, 1996. 47–55.

Thurston, Luke. "Ineluctable Nodalities: On the Borromean Knot." *Key Concepts of
   Lacanian Psychoanalysis.* Ed. Dany Nobus. New York: Other P, 1998. 139–63.

Tillet, Susana. "The Symptom: From Freud to Lacan." *Analysis* 8 (1998): 26–37.

Yates, Frances. *The Art of Memory.* Chicago: U of Chicago P, 1966.

Ondaatje's *The English Patient* and Questions of History

Steven Tötösy de Zepetnek

In this paper, I discuss the historical background of Michael Ondaatje's *The English Patient* and Anthony Minghella's adaptation of the novel to film. Ondaatje's novel is fiction and the "truth" value of the historical background of this or any fictional text is of problematic and questionable relevance in the reading of literature or in the study of literature (that is, in most areas of literary study while in areas such as the sociology of literature this may not always be the case). However, research in audience studies shows that readers of fiction—or viewers of films—are voraciously interested in the "real" story of fictionalized persons and events. Indeed, in the case of *The English Patient* this has been the case and both the novel's and its filmic version's media coverage, reviews, web pages generated and internet chats, and follow-ups such as new novels, the (re)discovery of historical material, etc., suggest the readers' and viewers' interest in the historical background of the fictional renditions. In addition—as criticism of the novel and its adaptation to film shows—Ondaatje's fictionalization of historical material raised questions in the minds of readers and viewers with regard to the problematics of social responsibility, history, and writing. It is in this context and perspective that I relate the novel's "Almásy theme" and its historical background to the author's treatment of the historical data and to the author's notion of the Other. The context of the Other is based on the suggestion that Ondaatje's concept in the Almásy theme is both specific (the cosmopolitan Central European) and universal.

The English Patient was published in 1992 and won the Booker Prize in the same year and it also received a number of other awards such as the Trillium Prize. In 1996 it was released as a film, produced and directed by Anthony Minghella, with the cooperation of Ondaatje, and received seven Oscars (for a web site containing selected sources about the novel as well as the film, go to the Booker Prize Winners Web Site <http://www.brothersjudd.com/webpage/bookerrev.htm#englishpatient>).

In her study "Michael Ondaatje and the Problem of History," Ajay Heble observes that "Ondaatje has repeatedly been engaged in an attempt to incorporate marginal figures out of the historical past into a non-historical genre" (97). While this observation is written with reference to Ondaatje's *The Collected Works of Billy the Kid* (1970) and *Coming through Slaughter* (1976), it applies to *The English Patient* as well. Several characters in the novel are indeed such "marginal figures out of the historical past." At the same time, we should acknowledge that Ondaatje's method of using "marginal figures" from history does not make his prose works "historical" novels in any sense of the word. On the contrary, his postmodern use of the historical produces poetic fiction that "manages" history, as Heble observes: "The force of Ondaatje's texts thus resides in their ability to articulate a tension between . . . an insistence on what Ondaatje calls 'the truth of fiction'—on his imaginative account of the past as being narratively faithful to the way things might have been" (98).

The English Patient is a literary, that is, fictional text that succeeds in representing life—underlining its fullness, complicatedness, inexplicability, fragmentation, and its subtextual richness which cannot be represented by traditional uses and linear narrative of historical "facts." Thus, an interpretation of the interrelation between the historical subtext, its fictional rendition, and in the latter the perception of the Other may be useful for readers and viewers of Ondaatje's work. Some critics say that Ondaatje's work, in general, is postmodern (see, e.g., Bjerring). To me, it is certain that his prose is lyrical and poetic, just as Alberto Manguel suggests "prose exquise, polie avec la précision et la beauté d'une marqueterie" (80). In addition, I propose that Ondaatje's notions of historicity, his use of historical data behind the fiction, and his notions of the Other can be best analysed within the framework of comparative cultural studies (see Tötösy, "From Comparative" <http://clcwebjournal.lib.purdue.edu/clcweb99-3/totosy99.html>, 2003 "From Comparative"). Ondaatje's concern with the historicity of his novel is evident on a different level too: After I had begun my research on Almásy right after the book's publication, I wrote a letter to Ondaatje asking him about his knowledge about the "real" history of Almásy. Some months later (see below), Ondaatje explained to me that, beyond the sources he cited in his "Acknowledgements" in *The English Patient* (305–07), he was unaware of the history of any of the characters of his novel (Ondaatje's telephone calls to Tötösy, 5 April and 20 April 1993). He explained that he had never heard or read about the history and/or questions concerning Almásy in Hungarian and German sources, he did not know that Lady Clayton East Clayton died in plane crash one year after her husband's death (see below), etc. On the other hand, Derek Finkle, in an article entitled "A Vow of Silence" suggests that Ondaatje has always been cognizant in most exacting terms of historical backgrounds in his writing. We simply do not know whether or how much Ondaatje researched and knew about the historical background of Almásy. As it will become evident and as I explain below, the historical background of the novel and knowledge about it is of some importance, and so from several perspectives.

In *The English Patient,* Almásy, the Hungarian aristocrat (if not in precise rank: see below, certainly in demeanor, behavior, and contacts), cartographer, explorer, aviator, military and intelligence officer (spy?) is depicted as the Other in the novel. The reader does not know for a long time who the "English" patient is. But when we find out that the patient is Almásy and that he may be Hungarian, the mystery of the Other is not diminished. This construction of elusiveness is both cumulative and specific. For instance, Ondaatje's use of the metaphor félhomály (semi-darkness, dusk, half-light, twilight) he borrows from the Hungarian—in Hungarian poetry, this is an often-used and established concept—can be understood as a metaphorical replication of elusive origins we find in one of Almásy's texts: "The Arab children were wonderfully amused when I spoke to them in their own language. A little girl immediately asked me if I were an Egyptian. When I said no, the choir of children shouted: 'You are lying, lying, you are

Egyptian, we can see it from your skin!' I took my sunglasses off and asked them whether Egyptians had blue eyes. The crowd became silent and finally the little girl decided: 'Your mother was Egyptian'" (Almásy, *Rommel seregénél Líbyában* 87; my translation).

It is the undetermined-ness, un-definability, elusive-ness, the Otherness, that characterizes in many ways the Almásy theme of the novel and the film. But how and what is this Almásy theme? The historical data about the "English Patient" Almásy are oblique and they are analogous to the fictional Almásy of the novel—and this may be one of the reasons of my own and many other readers' fascination with the novel and its historical background. Count László Ede Almásy de Zsadány et Törökszentmiklós, second son of the renowned ethnographer, zoologist, and Asia-explorer György Almásy (1864–1933), was born 22 August 1895 in the family's castle, Borostyánkö, and died in Salzburg 22 March 1951 (see Schrott and Farin; Török 1992, 21–22, 1998; *Encyclopaedia Hungarica* vol. 1. 41–42, 250; *Magyar életrajzi lexikon* 23). The place of his birth, Borostyánkö, today Bernstein in Burgenland, Austria, is of interest in itself, as related to displacement and the Other: the Austrian federal state Burgenland is a construct of areas from provinces previously on Hungarian territory since the arrival of the Magyars (Hungarians) in the Danube Basin in the ninth century A.D., an area that was ceded to Austria following the Treaty of Trianon after the First World War (for the history of Borostyánkö/Bernstein, see *Encyclopaedia Hungarica* 250). Today, Bernstein Castle is a hotel and the property of Andrea Berger, born Almásy, the daughter of László Ede Almásy's brother, János.

Almásy's merits include the discovery of the lost and legendary oasis Zarzura in the Lybian desert, the discovery of prehistorical paintings in the caves of the Uweinat mountains, the cartography of the Lybian desert (his name is preserved in an area called "Djebel Almasy"), the development of civil aviation in Egypt and the building of the Al-Maza airport, scientific and geographical data accumulation in Egypt, the Sudan, Kenya, Tanganyika, Uganda, Abessynia, and Tripoli, and a good number of papers and books published in Hungarian, French, and German about his travels, discoveries, and experiences in the Second World War (for a partial list of his texts, see the Works Cited below). In his youth, he studied engineering at the University of London and was employed for a period by the Austrian car manufacturer Steyr. In 1949 he established a distance-flight world record by towing a glider plane from Paris to Cairo. Just before his death in 1951 in Salzburg, he was appointed director of the Desert Institute in Cairo (for biographical literature see *Encyclopaedia Hungarica* vol. I. 41–42, 250; *Magyar életrajzi lexikon; Révai nagy lexikona;* Bagnold; Brenner; Kasza; Kospach; Kröpelin; Murray; Perlez; Schrott and Farin; Seubert; Török, "Almásy" 21–22; Weis; note: Schrott and Farin list scientific literature where Almásy's Africa exploration and cartography is described, 18–19). In addition to Ondaatje's novel and Minghella's film, Almásy's life inspired four more novels: John W. Eppler's *Rommel ruft Kairo: Aus dem Tagebuch eines Spions* (Gütersloh, 1959) and his *Geheimagent im Zweiten Weltkrieg: Zwischen Berlin, Kabul und Kairo* (Preussisch Oldendorf, 1974), Hans von Steffens's *Salaam: Geheimkommando zum Nil 1942* (Neckargemünd, 1960), and Zsolt Török's *Salaam Almásy: Almásy László életregénye* (Salaam Almásy: A Fictional Biography of László Almásy. Budapest, 1998) (see Schrott and Farin 19).

I begin with questions about Almásy's identity with regard to his aristocratic title, count. While Hungarian encyclopedias and genealogical sources do not leave any doubts about Almásy's aristocratic rank, János Gudenus and László Szentirmay—whose book about the fate of Hungarian aristocrats after the Second World War is acknowledged as an authoritative source—suggest that Almásy could not have been an aristocrat (I add here that while in English "aristocracy" often means nobility in general, in the continental European context aristocracy means the ranks of titled nobility such as baron, count, duke, etc., while other non-titled nobility is differentiated). Gudenus and Szentirmay take their source from Peter Bokor's book *Zsákutca,* where Bokor writes that Count Almásy was assigned to the German army as a liaison officer and that in July 1944 he helped Vince Görgey, a Royal Hungarian army officer to escape to Berlin with the aid of the German SS (35). With reference to the question of count or no count, Gudenus and Szentirmay's suggestion is that Almásy was a member of the branch of the Almásy family that did not receive the title of count and remained in the ranks of the middle nobility (although other sources published between the two world wars list consistently this branch as "counts," see, e.g., *Révai nagy lexikona* Supplement A–Z. 49–50.). Gudenus and Szentirmay write: "In the aristocratic line of the Almásy family there was no László. Surely the reference is to László [de] Almásy, the renowned Africa explorer and discoverer, whom the Hungarian General Staff, in his rank as a reserve officer of the Royal Hungarian Army, assigned to General Rommel as a desert expert. After the war he was exonerated and cleared of war crimes. In Egypt he is regarded highly and several institutes are named in his honor" (Gudenus and Szentirmay 106; my translation; for the court documents of his trial as a war criminal, see Népbíróságok Országos Tanácsa [People's National Tribunal] No. 1428–1947, Budapest City Archives).

In my research about Almásy and his title, after going through Hungarian genealogical literature, I received confirmation from Szabolcs de Vajay, a noted Hungarian genealogist and expert of the history of the Hungarian aristocracy and lower nobility that László and his branch of the Almásy family were not granted the title like the other branch that received the title in 1771 (see, e.g., Kempelen I: 75–78; Nagy I: 19–23; Vajay, personal letter, 24 October 1994, Geneva, Switzerland). On the other hand, there is evidence that Almásy received the title orally from the last Emperor of Austria-Hungary, Karl, during or just after the ill-fated attempt of the emperor in 1921 to drive with Almásy from Switzerland to Hungary to reclaim his throne as King of Hungary. Almásy's rank and title of count was not recognized by the Hungarian parliament, the legal location where ranks and titles of nobility were examined and subsequently registered until 1947 (see, e.g., Schrott and Farin 7–8). I am not aware of any documentation suggesting that Almásy attempted to have his title recognized legally. In any case, Almásy used the title and Hungarian sources published between the two world wars—such as the *Révai nagy lexikona*—listed him with the title of count. Indeed, genealogical sources refer to several cases where Emperor Karl bestowed titles and nobility orally in the last days of the Austro-Hungarian monarchy; in some cases this has been recognized officially, in some it has not. In the case of Almásy, although the rank and title have not been officially recognized, their use by Almásy is not necessarily an act of usurpation, at least in my opinion. What is of interest for my discussion, again, is the elusive nature of the matter, as with many things of and about Almásy, in real life and in Ondaatje's novel.

Questions and misinformation about Almásy abound; for example, in the otherwise authoritative and often-quoted book about German military counter-espionage in the Second World War, where its author, Gert Buchheit, writes:

> Who was this Count Almasy? Laszlo Almasy, Count of Szombathely, was born about 1895 in the castle of Bernstein in Burgenland, then still in Hungary. The Almasys are ancient Hungarian magnates, whose title of count was abrogated after their participation in the 1849 Kossuth revolution. Despite of it all, the Almasys were committed monarchists. Janos, the older one of the two brothers, married a sister of Prince Esterházy, who almost went bankrupt after he bought the stables of the exiled Emperor Karl in 1918 for safekeeping until the return of the monarch. It was in this milieu that Laszlo Almasy grew up. He became a commissioned officer, a well-known gentleman rider and later an exceptional gentleman driver. It was in this capacity that he participated in the epoch-making drive from Mombasa to Cairo with Prince Liechtenstein. When Emperor Karl attempted a Putsch from Switzerland [into Hungary], Almasy drove his monarch in a secret, thirty-hour drive through Austria. (Buchheit 234; my translation; the original German is without Hungarian diacritics)

Buchheit further recounts Almásy's desert travels and discoveries in Africa, his military career, his war years and intelligence work with General Rommel. He closes with "And what has happened to Count Almasy? He is supposed to have died a few years after the Second World War in Egypt" (Buchheit 238; my translation). Buchheit's description suggests that he did not do much research on Almásy and he is unfamiliar with Hungarian history, that is, when it comes to detail. For instance, nobility in Hungary could not be abrogated for any reason (for a historical and legal explanation of this, see Ölyvedi Vad 68–75); the Almásys could not possibly have been counts of Szombathely, since the Middle Ages the seat of a bishopric where as such the church was the only landowner; Buchheit also confused Sir Robert Clayton East Clayton (baronet) with an engineer by the name of P.A. Clayton, who was a companion of Almásy and the baronet (see Buchheit 239; Almásy, *Récentes . . .* 43), etc. Nevertheless, the interesting factor here is again the question about Almásy's elusive identity, an analogue to his fictional counterpart in the novel. Plus, if it is indeed true that Ondaatje was not aware of Almásy's historical data as he claims, his construction of the fictional Almásy in its elusiveness and the Other thus overlapping with the said historical data confronts us with a remarkable coincidence—although I have to admit I am not sure how to interpret such a coincidence.

Along with the questions about his origin and as yet not researched activities of his German counter-intelligence activities with General Rommel, Almásy's historical life includes curious incidents that point to an interesting marginality strikingly similar to his fictionalized story in Ondaatje's novel. Of interest are, for example, Almásy's own chapter five of his *Récentes explorations*, "Herodote et les récentes explorations du Desert" or his discovery of Hungarians who settled in Egypt in the sixteenth and again in the eighteenth centuries on an island on the Nile (yet another aspect of "history," the Other, and elusiveness) Almásy's ethnographic and anthropological discovery of Hungarians in Egypt was the result of a chance encounter with an Arab sheik, who, upon learning that Almásy was Hungarian explained to him that he, too, was "Hungarian" (*magyar*). As it turns out, there were in 1996 about 14,000 such *magararab*-s (Hungarian Arabs) in Egypt in the areas of the Wadi Halfa, Cairo, Assuan, and Kom Ombo, descendants of two waves of immigration: the first in the sixteenth century consisting of soldiers captured during the Ottoman-Turkish and Hungarian wars and settled there by Suleiman II and the second in the seventeenth century of settlers who moved there on their own (see Almásy, *Levegöben ... homokon* 104–08; *Encyclopaedia Hungarica* Vol. 2. 389).

Almásy first traveled to Africa in 1926 when he organized a hunting expedition with Prince Antal Esterházy to the Sudan. In 1929 he organized another expedition with Prince Ferdinand von Liechtenstein, this time by automobile from Mombasa to Alexandria. In 1931 he attempted to fly from Hungary to Egypt with a small airplane but crashed in Syria (yet another "coincidence" between history and fiction?). His serious and scientifically-oriented cartographic, historical, and anthropological travels on the Nile with Sir Robert Clayton began after 1931. Clayton was "a young aristocrat taken by sports, who had a pilot's licence, and who was out to do adventure. Sir Robert came to see me in Hungary and offered his collaboration enthusiastically" (Almásy, *Récentes explorations* 4; my translation). Robert Clayton was born in 1908, fifth and last baronet of Marden and of Hall Place (*Burke's Peerage* 535). He was a British aristocrat who was interested in geographical discovery and in travel. Immediately after his marriage on 29 February 1932, the young aristocrat "set out with Count L.E. de Almasy to explore the unknown are of the Lybian Desert north of the Gilf Kebir, and to find the legendary lost oasis called Zerzura. After being lost for several days in the desert and suffering hardships the expedition returned without achieving its object. A full account of the adventure, a map, and illustrations were published in *The Times* of July 6, 1932. In a few weeks Sir Robert was dead. He developed a disease similar to infantile paralysis, and though respiration was induced by an automatic apparatus he died on September 1, at the age of 24" (*The Times*, "Obituary" 12).

Zarzura is mentioned by Herodotus and in the *One Thousand and One Arabian Nights*, in the latter as the "city of copper." And then, in 1933, Almásy and his group discovered the oasis Zarzura and the discovery was presented in 1934 in London, at the

British Geographical Society's meeting, by Wing-Commander H.W.G.J. Penderel and Dr. Richard A. Bermann, Almásy's companions (Bermann 450–63). The members of the successful expedition were Almásy, Dr. László Kádár, a geographer and geologist of the University of Debrecen (Hungary), Hans Casparius, a photographer, the Jewish-Austrian journalist and writer Dr. Richard Bermann, Commander Penderel, two Sudanese chauffeurs, and a cook. Bermann, in turn, is also of interest: the surname Bermann was a pseudonym, his real surname was Arnold Höllriegel, and he was a well-known author in Austria who died in exile in the USA in 1939. He published the description of the discovery in Zürich in 1938, in a volume entitled *Zarzura. Die Oase der kleinen Vögel* (*Zarzura: The Oasis of the Small Birds*) (on Höllriegel, see *Richard A. Bermann alias Arnold*). In Penderel's and Bermann's descriptions of the expedition, it was Almásy's research and guidance that made the expedition a success (see Bermann 453). Kádár published his memoirs in 1972 in which there is a detailed description of the Zarzura expedition and Almásy's work and activities.

The historical data about Lady Clayton East Clayton born Dorothy Mary Durrant (Katherine Clifton in the novel) is less elusive than those of Almásy, but they are equally striking in the context of the novel. For example, for the fictional Katherine Clifton "there was a line back to her ancestors that was tactile, whereas he [Almásy] had erased the path he had emerged from" (*The English Patient* 170). Dissimilar to Almásy, the historical data about Lady Clayton is clear: she was "a very experienced pilot . . . [she] was also a talented sculptor, and her home, as well as the vicarage of Leverstock Green [her father, Arthur Durrant, was the vicar there], contained many examples of her work" (*The Times*, "Obituary" 12). She accompanied her husband in several desert expeditions and after his death she expressed that "I am only carrying on my husband's work. We always did this sort of thing together. He left with his work unfinished. I want to try and finish it off" (*The Times*, "Obituary," 12). However, her own expedition in the Lybian desert after the death of her husband, where she flew her own plane, was unsuccessful. There is no indication in the accounts whether she accomplished this expedition with Almásy; in her brief account of the expedition, she writes that she was accompanied by a Commander Roundell (*The Times*, "The Lost Oasis" 11). That Lady Clayton and Almásy knew each other from previous expeditions with her husband is obvious; however, in 1933 when Lady Clayton East Clayton organized an expedition with Commander Roundell, Almásy and his group had a parallel expedition at the same time (see Penderel 455; Bermann 457–58). After her return to England in May 1933 from this expedition, she lead another expedition to Lapland. Five days after her return to England, on 15 September 1933, she fell to her death during a short flight at Brooklands. Inexplicably, Lady Clayton appeared to have climbed out of the cockpit and fell out of the plane (*The Times*, "Lady Clayton Killed" 10f). The accident has never been explained although an official inquest was held (*The Times*, "The Brooklands Accidents" 19a). Lady Clayton Dorothy Durrant's scientific interests and knowledge, her interests in aviation, her artistic talents as a sculptor, and her risk-taking attest to her exceptionality as an individual and as a woman of her time. It may be of interest why her friends nicknamed her "Peter" (*The Times*, "Lady Clayton East Clayton. A Correspondent Writes" 14c). These exceptional qualities, in the context of her time, are not recognizable in *The English Patient*, in the novel or in the film.

Almásy's history becomes difficult to chart after 1939, when the Second World War and its preceding political and societal upheavals began to wreck havoc everywhere. In 1936 and 1939, Almásy was a flying instructor in Egypt and this is the time when he was active in the development of Egyptian aviation. However, already in 1935 his activities in Northern Africa became an issue with the secret and intelligence services of England, Egypt, and Italy, as well as Germany (see Shaw; Schrott and Farin 12–17). As we know, Almásy was a reserve officer of the Royal Hungarian Army and he was first drafted to active duty, followed by an assignment to the German army, to the "Desert Fox," General Rommel, who was campaigning on his mythologized battles in North Africa. Obviously, Almásy must have been assigned to desert duty in the capacity of an intelligence officer owing to his expertise of the Sahara and North Africa. Most sources about Almásy's activities in the latter part of the 1930s and then during the war when he was with the German army appear to agree that it is virtually impossible to establish whether Almásy was or was not a Nazi sympathizer although there is evidence that he approved of Hitler's economic and social policies (see Schrott and Farin). At the same time—that elusiveness again—Raoul Schrott and Michael Farin write when describing the film made of the 1926 Sudan expedition of Almásy and Liechtenstein that while the film and the people in it exude the arrogance of colonialism, only Almásy appears camera-shy and detached (8). There are, however, voices who tell another story as I describe below.

As to my notion of the "Almásy theme" of Almásy and Otherness, Almásy's history with General Rommel is equally suggestive as well as elusive: He had, allegedly, a homosexual relationship with the general. Rommel's and Almásy's relationship has been reported after the release of the film in 1996 by a nephew of the general, who lives in Italy today (see Schrott and Farin 16). This has been confirmed, third-hand, from another source: I came into correspondence with Richard Bond of Arlington, Massachusetts, whose great-uncle, Marshall Bond Sr.—brother-in-law of the industrialist William Boeing—met Almásy and explorer, hunter, and author Count Zsigmond Széchenyi in 1927 in Egypt when Bond was on an expedition there (see Bond, *Gold Hunter* 181). Richard Bond's father was Marshall Bond Jr., son of Marshall Bond Sr., whose grandfather was Judge Hiram G. Bond. The Bonds have had a fascinating history altogether and much of their stories and achievements are written down in Marshall Bond Jr.'s books. For example, Marshall Bond Sr.'s dog "Jack" while he was prospecting in the Klondike in 1898 is "Buck" in Jack London's *The Call of the Wild*, in which the story begins in the Santa Clara Valley near San Francisco on Judge Miller's fruit ranch: "Judge Miller" is of course Judge Hiram G. Bond. Marshall Bond Sr., an engineer and outdoorsman, was hired in 1927 by a newspaper to write a report on traveling by riverboat from Aswan to Khartoum. According to Richard Bond, based on his recollections of his father's stories he was told, Almásy seized the opportunity of the contact with the

American in order to attempt to raise funds for his expeditions but neither he (Marshall Bond Sr.) nor the Boeings invested in Almásy's ventures because they considered him unreliable (although a socially most acceptable and delightful person). A further although much later connection between the Marshall Bond Jr. and the Almásys occurred in 1963, when Bond met János Almásy (László's brother) in Czechoslovakia on a camping trip with other aristocratic companions and then visited him in 1964 in Bernstein Castle (see Bond, *Adventures with Peons, Princes, and Tycoons* 108–12) and again between Marshall Bond Jr. and Jean Howard, the British intelligence officer assigned to Almásy during the Second World War (Bond, *Adventures with Peons, Princes, and Tycoons* 110–12). Richard Bond also wrote that according to his uncle, the personal papers of Almásy, kept in Szombathely, were destroyed during the war in a fire. As to the story of Almásy's homosexuality, Richard Bond wrote that this was reported to his grandfather by Count Karl Coudenhove in a letter already in 1927 and that Almásy has always been very discreet about it (Richard Bond, email correspondence July 1997, Arlington; unfortunately, Bond indicated to me that he does not have the letters). Bond also writes that "Jean Howard the analyst assigned to study him by the British Secret Service however considered him an enigma. He seems to me politically to have been a loyal Hungarian conservative serving an accommodationist government. As a scientific explorer before the war he had worked for whoever paid best. Laszlo Almasy could be described both literally and figuratively as a used car dealer" (Richard Bond, email correspondence July 1997; Jean Howard's forthcoming work on the history of Second World War British espionage and Almásy has been announced in Schrott and Farin [18]; I am not aware of its publication as of yet).

Now I discuss briefly the controversy about the Nazi connections of Almásy that erupted internationally after the release of the film (interestingly, the controversy occurred in the media and on the web only and I am not aware of scholarship dealing with the question with regard to *The English Patient*). As far as I am aware, my 1994 article in *ECW: Essays on Canadian Writing* was the first English-language publication about Almásy's historical background (see Tötösy, "Michael Ondaatje"): in December 1992 I sent Ondaatje a copy of my then forthcoming paper about Almásy's historical background and thus he was aware of Almásy's history. Several months later Ondaatje called on the telephone and argued that my attention to Almásy's historical background is misplaced. On my part, I argued that regardless whether he, Ondaatje, knows or does not know anything about the history of his protagonist, because of Almásy's—and, indeed, his family's—prominence in Hungarian, Egyptian, and to a smaller extent in German history of cartography, geographical exploration, and aviation, the novel would garner much interest in many quarters (Ondaatje's telephone calls to Tötösy, 5 April and 20 April 1993). I also met Ondaatje briefly at the Frankfurt Book Fair in October 1993, where he was invited for the release of the German translation of *The English Patient* and he re-confirmed that he has received and read the paper and that he disagrees with my unearthing of Almásy's historical background. Yet, it is a mystery to me why Ondaatje and Minghella would not anticipate and consequently attempt to preempt the storm that erupted with the release of the film. The storm about and the international media coverage of the film—including massive activity on the world wide web—was the allegation that Almásy was a Nazi sympathizer and that Minghella and Ondaatje should not have glorified such a figure, no matter how minor. Obviously, this was and is a serious and important aspect of the novel and the film and I now discuss some of its implications as I see them.

One of the most interesting aspects of the novel to me is Ondaatje's construction of a fictional individual, who is in-between and peripheral and the consequences of this locus, namely Almásy's rejection of homogeneity, national self-referentiality (particularly prominent in Hungary), and its exclusionary results. The negative impact of nationalism is ubiquitously felt everywhere. While I understand and admit that the preservation of national identity may have had justification in history, in contemporary times this belief construction leads us nowhere except to the like of the Tutsi and Hutu wars or the wars of the former Yugoslavia. In my opinion, contemporary culture demonstrates that the most interesting and valuable objects of art—and I dare to put this type of valuation on cultural products—are those which emanate from in-between, multicultured creators like an Ondaatje. If we had empirical evidence on the most important contemporary novels, for instance, I propose that a very high number of texts were by thematics of counter-hegemonical content and produced by culturally and individually in-between and non-mainstream, that is, "peripheral," authors. Contemporary culture and cultural production suggests that national self-referentiality and prioritization towards cultural homogeneity should be a matter of the past (of course, reality proves this otherwise but that is another story). Again, to me Ondaatje's novel represents the possible world of the non-nationalistic, non-self-referential Central European Hungarian—a stereotype, of course—being fully aware of the rarity of such in real life. This is the more outstanding and worthy of further attention in my mind because of the aforementioned controversy that erupted with regard to the historical background of Ondaatje's fictional hero, Almásy. In brief, I very much like Ondaatje's invention of the "international bastard" Almásy and the suggestion that there are Central Europeans and Hungarians who step outside, consciously, of the nationalist and self-referential paradigm so common and stereotypical of them (for the notion of "international bastards," see Ondaatje in Wachtel, Ondaatje, and Gibson 62).

Elizabeth Pathy Salett published in the Wednesday 4 December 1996 issue of the *Washington Post* an opinion piece, "Casting a Pall on a Movie Hero." Salett describes her father's—who was consul-general of Hungary in Cairo before the Second World War—encounters with Almásy in Cairo and concludes: "*The English Patient* calls itself a work of fiction. But in fact, what the film's director-writer does is to take a real story and a real person, minimize the meaning of his activities and recast him as a passionate, loving hero. *The English Patient,* which was constructed as a beautiful, romantically lyrical film, is amoral and ahistorical. The film's presentation of a moral equivalency between the Germans and Allies trivializes the significance of the choices men like Almásy made and the enormous consequences of their actions and alliances" (C6).

Salett's opinion of the film demonstrates several factors which have bearing on my discussion here: 1) An audience response to the interrelationship of "fact and fiction"; 2) A personal opinion and perception, where fiction is rated below historical "accuracy" and "fact"; and 3) The publication of the opinion in an internationally read newspaper demonstrates the systemic and media-accorded importance to artistic representation in fiction. It remains without saying that the apparent success of the film influences the popularity and sale of the novel, as the case is in most instances of filmic adaptation of a literary text. This systemic factor with regard to the interrelationship between different media processing of the same artistic product is significant by itself. But it has further dimensions: with regard to the perception of ethical dimensions as suggested by Salett, Ondaatje responded to the criticism in a letter to *The Globe and Mail*:

> From Homer to *Richard III* to the present, literature has based its imaginative stories on historical event. We read those epics and literary works to discover, not the facts of the Trojan War, but the human emotions discovered in the story. If one writes a novel and pretends it is nonfiction or makes a film and pretends it is a documentary, then the writer or filmmaker should be tested. However, *The English Patient* came out a few years ago as a novel and the film version is not a documentary. I wrote about an enigmatic desert explorer whose role when World War II broke out was to be a betrayer. In reality the facts are still murky and still uncertain—to some historians he was a spy, some others think he was a double agent. Whatever "spying" he did was witnessed and watched by the British Secret Service. *The English Patient* is not a history lesson but an interpretation of human emotions—love, desire, betrayals in war and betrayals in peace—in a historical time. It holds no sympathy for Nazis, in fact the most shocking scene in the film depicts a Nazi torture. It is about forgiveness, how people come out of a war. There are four other central characters who reflect and qualify the character of Almásy. The facts of the history behind *The Crucible* or *Richard III* is the raw material often chronicled by historians with a political dogma or party line to protect. Some are true, some are false. (Compare the histories of the War of the Roses or the Second World War written at the time and those written now—and they still continue to be revised.) It is what Shakespeare or Arthur Miller have written out of it that teaches us about the human condition. If a novelist or dramatist or filmmaker is to be censored or factually tested every time he or she writes from historical event, then this will result in the most uninspired works, or it just might be safer for those artists to resort to cartoons and fantasy. (Ondaatje qtd. in Saunders)

Salett's and Ondaatje's different opinion on the question of art in social discourse, is of course a crucial matter. It is not my intention to engage in the controversy whether *The English Patient* is a distortion of history or whether it is justified as it is as fiction. Suffice it to say that in my opinion both Ondaatje and Salett have a point. As

Ondaatje suggests and as we know, fictional descriptions of Napoleon or Julius Caesar have had the effect of mythologization in a positive context when the alternate opinion may be that they were mass murderers of the first order. Ondaatje is right in his opinion that the novel and the film are both fiction as artistic expression. Salett is right in her opinion in the context of social discourse that the glorification of an individual—even if in fiction—who, under whatever circumstances, supported Nazism would and must be ethically questionable: The history of the Nazi horrors is unique and too immediate, too near in time, and too raw for any audience still and hopefully will remain so. On the other hand, and here Salett's point of view gains on validity significantly, Ondaatje and Minghella could or should have paid attention to the said historical background concerning Almásy, as I suggested previously. The fact that the potentially explosive implication of the protagonist's historical background was not paid attention to may the result of either Ondaatje's opinion that fiction is fiction and this pre-empts any and all criticism of historical "facts" or it may have been a result of the rule that "most studies in film adaptation do concentrate on the creative processes involved, and especially the contribution of the film director, rather than that of other members of the team, e.g. the screenwriter" (Remael 390). In both cases, however, *The English Patient* case is illustrative. Despite the controversy that erupted around the main character's "historical" role and possible Nazi sympathies, the film received the award of best picture at the Oscars of 1997. I question the award, based on my agreement with such critics as Salett and the problematics of mythologizing the "wrong" marginal figure. On the other hand, the Hungarian "count" is marginal to the point where we cannot be absolutely certain about his Nazi sympathies. In fact, there are a number of sources in which the opposite is argued, namely that Almásy was sheltering a Jewish-Hungarian family is his apartment in Budapest and that Almásy, using his connections and uniform with medals displayed, has saved several Jewish-Hungarian families during the final days of the war in 1944, during Eichmann's and the Hungarian Nazi Arrow Cross Party's terror and murder of Hungarian Jews (see Offman <http://www.salon.com/books/log/1999/04/05/almasy/index.html>). In sum, we can observe that the conventions of fiction and art and the systemic properties of artistic communication mediate the "historicity" of "facts." In other words, fiction—whether in word or image—claims its own space and its own system. On the other hand, this is not the last word about *The English Patient:* only time will be the true judge. Thus, ultimately, "history" will decide about both the artistic value of the novel and the film. As to the question whether social responsibility is or should be a factor in the case of fiction, the debate remains.

In closing my discussion, I take a brief excursion to yet a further aspect of Otherness of the Almásy theme of the novel and the film, namely that of ethnicity. Winfried Siemerling, in his article "Das andere Toronto. Mündliches Wissen in Michael Ondaatjes *In the Skin of a Lion,*" deals with the question of ethnicity and its situation in English-Canadian historical discourse. His argument, namely that Ondaatje subverts the English-Canadian mainstream in his novels by drawing attention to the Other, is explained thus: "The experience of the immigrant does not yet infiltrate the public perception of the host culture with the acquisition of the foreign tongue by the individual. The interweaving of the searcher and narrator Patrick with the world of the foreign carries the fictional imprint of what was left out until now from possibilities of historicity while the success of the novel also builds bridges... in Ondaatje's writing is that possibility of history raised in an awakened voice that was left in the dark in the dominant texts of history" (Siemerling 180–81; my translation).

In *The English Patient*, Almásy's fictional position, that is, his indeterminability and elusiveness, overlaps with his "real" position of historical marginality and Otherness. This characteristic has extended to Almásy's position in the available critical readings of the novel, too. For instance, Kip has been noted as an example of Ondaatje's exploration of Otherness; yet the critical reaction to Almásy's position in the novel has been lacking. Val Ross's editorial in the *Globe and Mail*, "Minefields of the Mind," draws interesting and well-crafted observations about the novel. Ross points to "Kip, the young Indian," and Caravaggio, "an immigrant whose name is rich with sensual allusions, whose name sounds as absurd among the Anglo-Scots of Toronto as, say, 'Ondaatje'" (Ross C1–C2), but she makes no reference to Almásy. Similarly, Alberto Manguel's paper "Le poète anonyme" in the journal *L'Actualité* or Douglas Barbour's "Michael Ondaatje's Sensuous Prose Seductive" in *The Edmonton Journal*—to point to some selected instances—have no reference to Almásy. Somehow I doubt that this is a result of not wanting to preempt the readers by giving away the story. Could it be that we are dealing with yet another situation of the Other, a situation that the Almásy theme represents as I discussed here, in his historical situation as well as in Ondaatje's the novel and, then, again, on the landscape of criticism?

Note: Versions of this article have been published previously in Steven Tötösy de Zepetnek, *Comparative Literature: Theory, Method, Application.* Amsterdam: Rodopi, 1998. 159–72; in Steven Tötösy de Zepetnek, "Social Discourse and the Problematics of Theory, Culture, Media, and Audience" in *Language and Beyond: Actuality and Virtuality in the Relations between Word, Image and Sound.* Ed. Paul Joret and Aline Remael. Amsterdam: Rodopi, 1998. 231–40; and in Steven Tötösy de Zepetnek, "Michael Ondaatje's *The English Patient:* 'Truth Is Stranger than Fiction'," *Essays on Canadian Writing* 53 (1994): 141–53.

WORKS CITED

Almásy, László. *Autóval Szudánba. Az elsö autó-utazás a Nílus mentén (Driving in the Sudan: The First Automobile Drive along the Nile).* Budapest: Franklin, 1928.

Almásy, L.E. de. Reports in *The Sudan Notes and Records* (April 1930); (September 1935); (January 1936).

Almásy, László. *Az ismeretlen Szahara (The Unknown Sahara).* Budapest: Franklin, 1934; 1935.

Almásy, L.E. de. *Récentes explorations dans le désert libyque (1932–1936)*. Caire: Schindler, 1936.

Almásy, László. *Levegöben...homokon...(In the Air...On Sand...)*. Budapest: Franklin, 1937.

Almásy, Ladislaus von. *Unbekannte Sahara. Mit Flugzeug und Auto in der Lybischen Wüste (Unknown Sahara: With Airplane and Automobile in the Lybian Desert)*. Ed. Hans Joachim von der Esch. Leipzig: Brockhaus, 1939; 1940; 1942; 1943.

Almásy, Ladislaus von. *Die Strasse der Vierzig Tage (The Road of Forty Days)*. Leipzig: Brockhaus, 1943.

Almásy, László. *Rommel seregénél Líbyában (With Rommel's Army in Lybia)*. Budapest: Stádium, 1944.

Bagnold, Ralph A. *Sand, Wind and War: Memoirs of a Desert Explorer*. Tucson: U of Arizona P, 1990.

Barbour, Douglas. "Michael Ondaatje's Sensuous Prose Seductive." *The Edmonton Journal* (11 October 1992): D8.

Bermann, Richard A. "Historic Problems of the Lybian Desert: A Paper Read with the Preceding [Penderel] at the Evening Meeting of the Society on 8 January 1934." *The Geographical Journal* 83.6 (1934): 450–63.

Bjerring, Nancy B. "Deconstructing the 'Desert of Facts': Detection and Anti-detection in *Coming through Slaughter*." *English Studies in Canada* 16.3 (1990): 325–38.

Bokor, Peter. *Zsákutca (Dead end)*. Budapest: Minerva, 1985.

Bond, Marshall, Jr. *Adventures with Peons, Princes, and Tycoons*. Oakland: Star Rover House, 1983.

Bond, Marshall, Jr. *Gold Hunter: The Adventures of Marshall Bond*. Santa Fe: U of New Mexico P, 1968.

Booker Prize Winners (1999): <http://www.brothersjudd.com/webpage/bookerrev.htm#englishpatient>.

Brenner, Wilhelm. *Ein Wüstenforscher aus dem Burgenland* Special Issue of *Burgenländische Heimatblätter* 57.1 (1995).

Buchheit, Gert. *Der deutsche Geheimdienst. Geschichte der militärischen Abwehr (German Military Intelligence: A History of Military Counter)*. München: Paul List, 1967.

Burke's Peerage. Ed. Peter Townend. 104th ed. London: Burke's Peerage, 1967.

Encyclopaedia Hungarica. Ed. Lászlo Bárdossy. Calgary: Hungarian Lexicon Foundation, 1992. Vols. 1-3.

Finkle, Derek. "A Vow of Silence." *Saturday Night: Canada's Magazine* (November 1996): 90–98, 138.

Gudenus, János and László Szentirmay. *Összetört címerek. A magyar arisztokrácia sorsa és az 1945 utáni megpróbáltatások (Shattered Coats-of-Arms: The Fate of the Hungarian Aristocracy and the Ordeals after 1946)*. Budapest: Mozaik, 1989.

Heble, Ajay. "Michael Ondaatje and the Problem of History." *CLIO: Journal of Literature, History, and the Philosophy of History* 19.2 (1990): 97–110.

Höllriegel, Arnold. *Zarzura*. Zürich: n.p. 1937.

Kádár, László. "Visszaemlékezés Almásy László expedíciójára a Líbiai-sivatagban" ("Recollections of László Almásy's Expedition in the Lybian Desert"). *Magyar utazók, földrajzi felfedezök (Hungarian Travellers and Explorers)*. Budapest: Akadémiai, 1972.

Kasza, József. *A homok atyja*. Budapest, 1995.

Kempelen Béla, *Magyar nemes családok (Noble Families of Hungary)*. Budapest: Grill, 1911–1932.

Kospach, Julia. "Jenseits von Afrika." *profil* 12 (1997).

Kröpelin, Stefan. "Die Wüste des englischen Patienten." *Die Zeit* (18 April 1997).

Magyar életrajzi lexikon (Encyclopedia of Hungarian Biography). "Almásy György," "Almásy László Ede." Budapest: Akadémiai, 1981. 23.

Manguel, Alberto. "Le poète anonyme." *L'Actualité* 18.8 (15 May 1993): 78–80.

Minghella, Anthony. *The English Patient: A Screenplay*. New York: Hyperion-Miramax, 1996.

Murray, G.W. "Ladislaus Almásy." *The Geographical Journal* 117 (June 1951): 253–54.

Nagy Iván, *Magyarország családai czímerekkel és nemzedékrendi táblákkal (Noble Families of Hungary: Genealogies and Coats-of-Arms)*. Pest, 1857–1868.

Offman, Craig. "Nazi or Hero?" *salon.com Books Web Site* (1999): <http://www.salon.com/books/log/1999/04/05/almasy/index.html>.

Ondaatje, Michael. *The English Patient*. Toronto: McClelland & Stewart, 1992.

Ölyvedi Vad, Imre. *Nemességi könyv (The Book of Nobility)*. Szeged: Várnay, 1907.

Penderel, H.W.G.J. "The Gilf Kebir: A Paper Read with the Following at the Evening Meeting of the Society on 8 January 1934." *The Geographical Journal* 83.6 (June 1934): 450–63.

Perlez, Jane. "The Real Hungarian Count Was No 'English Patient'." *The New York Times* (17 December 1996).

Remael, Aline. "The Case of the Screenplay and Film Adaptation. The British New Wave: 'Saturday Night and Sunday Morning'." *Language and Literature Today*. Ed. Neide de Faria. Brasília: U de Brasília, 1996. Vol. 1. 389–97.

Révai nagy lexikona (Révai's Complete Encyclopedia) "Almásy László Ede (Zsadányi és Törökszentmiklósi)." Budapest: Révai, 1935. Vol. 21, Supplement A–Z. 49–50.

Richard A. Bermann alias Arnold Höllriegel. Österreicher-Demokrat-Weltbürger. Ed. Deutsche Bibliothek. Frankfurt: Die Deutsche Bibliothek, 1995.

Ross, Val. "Minefields of the Mind." *The Globe and Mail* (10 October 1992): C1–C2.

Salett, Elizabeth Pathy. "Casting a Pall on a Movie Hero." *Washington Post* (4 December 1994). Rpt. *The Globe and Mail* (Ontario edition) (6 December 1996): C6.

Saunders, Doug. "Michael Ondaatje Responds." *The Globe and Mail* (Ontario edition) (6 December 1996): C5.

Schrott, Raoul, and Michael Farin. "Schwimmer in der Wüste. Vorwort. Bibliographie. Editorische Notiz." *Ladislaus E. Almásy. Schwimmer in der Wüste. Auf der Suche nach der Oase Zarzura.* Comp. and ed. Raoul Schrott and Michael Farin. Innsbruck: Haymon, 1997. 6–22.

Seubert, Franz. "L.E. Almasy." *Die Nachhut* 7.25–26 (1973): 43–46.

Shaw, W.B. Kennedy. *Long Range Desert Group.* London: Greenhill, 1945.

Siemerling, Winfried. "Das andere Toronto. Mündliches Wissen in Michael Ondaatjes *In the Skin of a Lion.*" *Mündliches Wissen in neuzeitlicher Literatur.* Ed. Paul Goetsch. Tübingen: Gunter Narr, 1990. 171–83.

The Times. "The Brooklands Accidents. Inquests on Three Victims. Death by Misadventure" (22 September 1933): 19a; "Lady Clayton East Clayton" (16 September 1933): 13; "Lady Clayton East Clayton. A Correspondent Writes" (19 September 1933): 14c; "Lady Clayton East Clayton" (22 September 1933): 15b; "Lady Clayton Killed. An Aeroplane Accident" (16 September 1933): 10f; "The Lost Oasis. Across the Sand Sea. Posthumous Narrative" (16 September 1933): 11–13, 14; "Obituary. Lady Clayton East Clayton. Traveller and Explorer" (16 September 1933): 12.

Török, Zsolt. *Salaam Almásy. Almásy László életregénye* (*Salaam Almásy: A Fictional Biography of László Almásy*). Budapest: Eötvös, 1998.

Török, Zsolt. "Hungarian Explorer Count László Almásy was the Real 'English Patient.'" *Mercator's World: Magazine of Maps, Exploration, and Discovery* 2.5 (1997): 42–46.

Török, Zsolt. "Almásy László Ede." *Magyarok a természettudomány és a technika tükrében* (*Hungarians in the History of the Natural Science and Technology*). Ed. Ferenc Nagy. Budapest: Akadémiai, 1992. 21–22.

Tötösy de Zepetnek, Steven. "From Comparative Literature Today Toward Comparative Cultural Studies." Comparative Literature and Comparative Cultural Studies. Ed. Steven Tötösy de Zepetnek. West Lafayette: Purde UP, 2003. 235–67.

Tötösy de Zepetnek, Steven. "From Comparative Literature Today toward Comparative Cultural Studies." *CLCWeb: Comparative Literature and Culture* 1.3 (1999): <http://clcwebjournal.lib.purdue.edu/clcweb99-3/totosy99.html>.

Tötösy de Zepetnek, Steven. "Social Discourse and the Problematics of Theory, Culture, Media, and Audience." *Language and Beyond: Actuality and Virtuality in the*

Relations between Word, Image and Sound. Ed. Paul Joret and Aline Remael. Amsterdam-Atlanta, GA: Rodopi, 1998. 231–40.

Tötösy de Zepetnek, Steven. "Cultures, Peripheralities, and Comparative Literature." *Comparative Literature: Theory, Method, Application.* By Steven Tötösy de Zepetnek. Amsterdam-Atlanta, GA: Rodopi, 1998. 121–72.

Tötösy de Zepetnek, Steven. "Michael Ondaatje's *The English Patient*: 'Truth Is Stranger Than Fiction'." *ECW: Essays on Canadian Writing* 53 (1994): 141–53.

Wachtel, Eleanor, Michael Ondaatje, and Anne Gibson. "Michael Ondaatje." *Writers & Company.* Ed. Eleanor Wachtel. Toronto: Alfred A. Knopf, 1993. 49–63.

Weis, Hans. "Die Feldforschungen von Graf Ladislaus Eduard Almasy (1929–1942) in der östlichen Sahara." *Mitteilungen der Österreichischen Geographischen Gesellschaft* 132 (1990): 249–56.

A Selected Bibliography of Critical Work about Michael Ondaatje's Texts

Steven Tötösy de Zepetnek

Barbour, Douglas. *Michael Ondaatje*. New York: Twayne, 1993.

Bethell, Kathleen I. "Reading Billy: Memory, Time, and Subjectivity in The Collected Works of Billy the Kid." *Studies in Canadian Literature / Etudes en Littérature Canadienne* 28.1 (2003): 71–89.

Bök, Christian. "Destructive Creation: The Politicization of Violence in the Works of Michael Ondaatje." *Canadian Literature* 132 (1992): 109–24.

Bölling, Gordon. "Metafiction in Michael Ondaatje's Historical Novel *In the Skin of a Lion.*" *Symbolism: An International Journal of Critical Aesthetics* 3 (2003): 215–53.

Bush, Catherine. "Michael Ondaatje: An Interview." *Essays on Canadian Writing: Michael Ondaatje Issue*. Ed. Karen E. Smythe. Toronto: ECW, 1994. 238–49.

Carey, Cynthia. "Reinventing (Auto)Biography: The (Im)Possible Quest of Michael Ondaatje in Running in the Family." *Commonwealth Essays and Studies* 24.1 (2001): 41–51.

Cheetham, Mark A. "Obscure Imaginings: Visual Culture and the Anatomy of Caves." *Journal of Visual Culture* 1.1 (2002): 105–26.

Clarke, George Elliott. "Michael Ondaatje and the Production of Myth." *Studies in Canadian Literature* 16.1 (1991): 1–21.

Cook, Rufus. "'Imploding Time and Geography': Narrative Compressions in Michael Ondaatje's The English Patient." *Journal of Commonwealth Literature* 33.2 (1998): 108–25.

Cook, Victoria. "Exploring Transnational Identities in Ondaatje's *Anil's Ghost.*" *Comparative Cultural Studies and Michael Ondaatje's Writing*. Ed. Steven Tötösy de Zepetnek. West Lafayette: Purdue UP, 2005. 6–15.

Cooke, John. *The Influence of Painting on Five Canadian Writers: Alice Munro, Hugh Hood, Timothy Findley, Margaret Atwood, and Michael Ondaatje*. Lewiston: Edwin Mellen, 1996.

Curran, Beverley. "Ondaatje's The English Patient and Altered States of Narrative." *Comparative Cultural Studies and Michael Ondaatje's Writing*. Ed. Steven Tötösy de Zepetnek. West Lafayette: Purdue UP, 2005. 16–26.

Dawson, Carrie. "Calling People Names: Reading Imposture, Confession, and Testimony in and after Michael Ondaatje's The English Patient." *Studies in Canadian Literature / Etudes en Littérature Canadienne* 25.2 (2000): 50–73.

Delbaere, Jeanne. "'Only Re-Connect': Temporary Pacts in Michael Ondaatje's *The English Patient.*" *The Contact and the Culmination.* Ed. Marc Delrez and Bénédicte Ledent. Liège: L3-Liège Language and Literature, 1997. 45–56.

Duffy, Dennis. "A Wrench in Time: A Sub-Sub-Librarian Looks beneath the *Skin of a Lion.*" *Essays on Canadian Writing* 53 (1994): 125–40.

Ellis, Susan. "Trade and Power, Money and War: Rethinking Masculinity in Michael Ondaatje's *The English Patient.*" *Studies in Canadian Literature* 21.2 (1996): 22–36.

Emery, Sharyn. "'Call Me by My Name': Personal Identity and Possession in *The English Patient.*" *Literature-Film Quarterly* 28.3 (2000): 210–03.

Fagan, Cary. "Where the Personal and the Historical Meet: Michael Ondaatje." *The Power to Bend Spoons: Interviews with Canadian Novelists.* Ed. Beverly Daurio. Toronto: Mercury, 1998. 115–21.

Fledderus, Bill. "The English Patient Reposed in His Bed Like a (Fisher?) King: Elements of Grail Romance in Ondaatje's *The English Patient.*" *Studies in Canadian Literature* 22.1 (1997): 19–54.

Forshey, Gerald E. "*The English Patient*: From Novel to Screenplay." *Creative Screenwriting* 4.2 (1997): 91–98.

Fraser, Robert. "Postcolonial Cities: Michael Ondaatje's Toronto and Yvonne Vera's Bulawayo." *Studies in Canadian Literature / Etudes en Littérature Canadienne* 26.2 (2001): 44–52.

Ganapathy Dore, Geetha. "The Novel of the Nowhere Man: Michael Ondaatje's *The English Patient.*" *Commonwealth Essays and Studies* 16.2 (1993): 96–100.

Ganapathy Dore, Geetha. "Mapping Continents: The Journey Home in Salman Rushdie, Michael Ondaatje and Bharati Mukherjee." *Commonwealth Essays and Studies* 17.1 (1994): 3–9.

Garvie, Maureen. "Listening to Michael Ondaatje." *Queen's Quarterly* 99.4 (1992): 928–34.

Goldman, Marlene. "Representations of Buddhism in Ondaatje's *Anil's Ghost.*" *Comparative Cultural Studies and Michael Ondaatje's Writing.* Ed. Steven Tötösy de Zepetnek. West Lafayette: Purdue UP, 2005. 27–37.

Goldman, Marlene. "'Powerful Joy': Michael Ondaatje's *The English Patient* and Walter Benjamin's *Allegorical Ways of Seeing.*" *University of Toronto Quarterly: A Canadian Journal of the Humanities* 70.4 (2001): 902–22.

Gorjup, Branko, ed. Michael Ondaatje/*Notte senza scale/A Night without a Staircase.* Ravenna: Longo; 2001.

Guneratne, Anthony R. "Virtual Spaces of Postcoloniality: Rushdie and Ondaatje." *Contemporary Postcolonial and Postimperial Literature in English* (2004): <http://www.postcolonialweb.org/canada/literature/ondaatje/guneratne5.html>.

Härting, Heike. "Diasporic Cross-Currents in Michael Ondaatje's *Anil's Ghost* and Anita Rau Badimi's *The Hero's Walk*." *Studies in Canadian Literature / Etudes en Littérature Canadienne* 28.1 (2003): 43–70.

Heble, Ajay. "Michael Ondaatje and the Problem of History." *CLIO: Journal of Literature, History, and the Philosophy of History* 19.2 (1990): 97–110.

Heble, Ajay. "'Rumours of Topography': The Cultural Politics of Michael Ondaatje's *Running in the Family*." *Essays on Canadian Writing: Michael Ondaatje Issue.* Ed. Karen E. Smythe. Toronto: ECW, 1994. 186–203.

Hilger, Stephanie M. "Ondaatje's *The English Patient* and Rewriting History." *Comparative Cultural Studies and Michael Ondaatje's Writing*. Ed. Steven Tötösy de Zepetnek. West Lafayette: Purdue UP, 2005. 38–48.

Hillger, Annick. "'And this is the world of nomads in any case': *The Odyssey* as Intertext in Michael Ondaatje's *The English Patient*." *Journal of Commonwealth Literature* 33.1 (1998): 23–33.

Hsu, Hsuan. "Post-Nationalism and the Cinematic Apparatus in Minghella's Adaptation of Ondaatje's *The English Patient*." *Comparative Cultural Studies and Michael Ondaatje's Writing*. Ed. Steven Tötösy de Zepetnek. West Lafayette: Purdue UP, 2005. 49–61.

Ibarrola-Armendariz, Aitor. "Boundary Erasing: Postnational Characterization in Michael Ondaatje's *The English Patient*." *Tricks with a Glass: Writing Ethnicity in Canada*. Ed. Rocío G. Davis and Rosalía Baena. Amsterdam: Rodopi; 2000. 37–57.

Ismail, Qadri. "Discipline and Colony: *The English Patient* and the Crow's Nest of Post Coloniality." *Postcolonial Studies* 2.3 (1999): 403–36.

Jaireth, Subhash. "Anthony Minghella's *The English Patient*: Monoscopic Seeing of Novelistic Heteroglossia." *UTS Review: Cultural Studies and New Writing* 4.2 (1998): 57–79.

Jewinski, Ed. *Michael Ondaatje: Express Yourself Beautifully*. Toronto: ECW, 1994.

Kella, Elizabeth. *Beloved Communities: Solidarity and Difference in Fiction by Michael Ondaatje, Toni Morrison, and Joy Kogawa*. Uppsala: Uppsala UP; 2000.

Kemp, Mark A. R. "Italy and the Ruins of Western Civilization: Michael Ondaatje's *The English Patient*." *Nemla Italian Studies* 21 (1997): 131–55.

Kjellsmoen, Hilde Stuve. "Mapping the Desert as 'A Place of Faith': A Reading of *The English Patient* by Michael Ondaatje." *Postcolonialism and Cultural Resistance*. Ed. Jopi Nyman, and John A. Stotesbury. Joensuu: Faculty of Humanities, University of Joensuu, 1999. 110–16.

Kliman, Todd. "Michael Ondaatje: Cat Burglar in the House of Fiction." *The Hollins Critic* 31.5 (1994): 1–14.

Kranz, David L. "*The English Patient*: Critics, Audiences, and the Quality of Fidelity." *Literature-Film Quarterly* 31.2 (2003): 99–110.

Kyser, Kristina. "Seeing Everything in a Different Light: Vision and Revelation in Michael Ondaatje's *The English Patient*." *University of Toronto Quarterly: A Canadian Journal of the Humanities* 70.4 (2001): 889–901.

Lernout, Geert. "Michael Ondaatje: The Desert of the Soul." *Kunapipi: Journal of Postcolonial Writing* 14.2 (1992): 124–26.

Lernout, Geert. "Multicultural Canada: The Case of Michael Ondaatje." *'Union in Partition': Essays in Honour of Jeanne Delbaere*. Ed. Gilbert Debusscher and Marc Maufort. Liège: UP of Liège, 1997. 181–90.

Lewis, Tanya. "Myth-Manipulation through Dismemberment in Michael Ondaatje's *The Man with Seven Toes*." *Studies in Canadian Literature / Etudes en Littérature Canadienne* 24.2 (1999): 100–13.

Llarena, Ascanio, María Jesús. "The Work of Michael Ondaatje: A Metafictional Return." *Canadística canaria* (1991–2000): *Ensayos literarios anglocanadienses*. Ed. Juan Ignacio Oliva, Elena Sánchez, Luz González, and Isaías Naranjo. La Laguna: U of La Laguna; 2002. 121–39.

Llarena-Ascanio, Maria Jesus. "Michael Ondaatje's Use of History." *The Guises of Canadian Diversity: New European Perspectives*. Ed. Serge Jaumain, and Marc Maufort. Amsterdam: Rodopi, 1995. 19–26.

Lowry, Glen. "The Representation of 'Race' in Ondaatje's *In the Skin of a Lion*." *Comparative Cultural Studies and Michael Ondaatje's Writing*. Ed. Steven Tötösy de Zepetnek. West Lafayette: Purdue UP, 2005. 62–72.

Lowry, Glen. "Between *The English Patient*s: 'Race' and the Cultural Politics of Adapting CanLit." *Essays on Canadian Writing* 76 (2002): 216–46.

Matthews, S. Leigh. "'The Bright Bone of a Dream': Drama, Performativity, Ritual, and Community in Michael Ondaatje's *Running in the Family*." *Biography: An Interdisciplinary Quarterly* 23.2 (2000): 352–71.

Maver, Igor. "Creating the National in the International Context: The Postmodernity of Michael Ondaatje's Fiction." *Commonwealth Essays and Studies* 17.2 (1995): 58–66.

MacIntyre, Ernest. "Outside of Time: Running in the Family." *Spider Blues: Essays on Michael Ondaatje*. Ed. Sam Solecki. Montréal: Véhicule P, 1985. 315–19.

Maynard, John. "On Desert Ground: Ondaatje's *The English Patient*, Durrell, and the Shifting Sands of Critical Typologies." *Deus Loci* 5 (1997): 66–74.

Morgan, Maggie M. "*The English Patient*: From Fction to Reel." *Alif: Journal of Comparative Poetics* 18 (1998): 159–73.

Murkherjee, Arun. "The Sri Lankan Poets in Canada: An Alternative View." *Toronto South Asian Review* 3.2 (1984): 32–45.

Orr, Jeffrey. "Coming Through Language: Intersemiotic Translation and Michael Ondaatje's *Coming Through Slaughter*." *Journal of Language and Literature* 2.1 (2003): 18–27.

Penner, Tom. "Four Characters in Search of an Author-Function: Foucault, Ondaatje, and the 'Eternally Dying' Author in *The English* Patient." *Canadian Literature* 165 (2000): 78–93.

Pesch, Josef. "Cultural Clashes? East Meets West in Michael Ondaatje's Novels." *Across the Lines: Intertextuality and Transcultural Communication in the New Literatures in English.* Ed. Wolfgang Klooss. Amsterdam: Rodopi, 1998. 65–76.

Pesch, Josef. "Globalized Nationalisms: Michael Ondaatje's Novels and (Post)Colonial Correctness." *Zeitschrift für Kanada Studien* 17.1 (1997): 96–109.

Pesch, Josef. "Mediation, Memory, and a Search for the Father: Michael Ondaatje's *Running in the Family.*" *Zeitschrift für Anglistik und Amerikanistik: A Quarterly of Language, Literature and Culture* 45.1 (1997): 56–71.

Pesch, Josef. "Post-Apocalytical War Histories: Michael Ondaatje's *The English Patient.*" *ARIEL: A Review of International English Literature* 28.2 (1997): 117–39.

Pollmann, O.W. "Canadian Patient: Visit with an Ailing Text." *Antigonish Review* 113 (1998): 149–59.

Presson, Rebekah. "Fiction as Opposed to Fact: An Interview with Michael Ondaatje." *New Letters* 62 (1996): 81–90.

Provencal, Vernon. "The Story of Candaules in Herodotus and *The English Patient.*" *Classical and Modern Literature: A Quarterly* 23.1 (2003): 49–64.

Provencal, Vernon. "Sleeping with Herodotus in *The English Patient.*" *Studies in Canadian Literature / Etudes en Littérature Canadienne* 27.2 (2002): 140–59.

Randall, Don. "The Kipling Given, Ondaatje's Take: Reading Kim through *The English Patient.*" *Journal of Commonwealth and Postcolonial Studies* 5.2 (1998): 131–44.

Renger, Nicola. "Cartography, Historiography, and Identity in Michael Ondaatje's *The English Patient.*" *Beings in Transit: Traveling, Migration, Dislocation.* Ed. Liselotte Glage. Amsterdam: Rodopi, 2000. 111–24.

Roberts, Gillian. "'Sins of Omission': *The English Patient* and the Critics." *Essays on Canadian Writing* 76 (2002): 195–215.

Rundle, Lisa. "From Novel to Film: *The English Patient* Distorted." *Border/lines* 43 (1997): 9–13.

Sadashige, Jacqui. "Sweeping the Sands: Geographies of Desire in *The English Patient.*" *Literature-Film Quarterly* 26:4 (1998): 242–54.

Saklofske, Jon. "The Motif of the Collector and Implications of Historical Appropriation in Ondaatje's Novels." *Comparative Cultural Studies and Michael Ondaatje's Writing.* Ed. Steven Tötösy de Zepetnek. West Lafayette: Purdue UP, 2005. 73–82.

Sanghera, Sandeep. "Touching the Language of Citizenship in Ondaatje's *Anil's Ghost.*" *Comparative Cultural Studies and Michael Ondaatje's Writing.* Ed. Steven Tötösy de Zepetnek. West Lafayette: Purdue UP, 2005. 83–91.

Sarris, Fotios. "*In the Skin of a Lion*: Michael Ondaatje's Tenebristic Narrative." *Essays on Canadian Writing* 44 (1991): 183–201.

Scobie, Stephen. "The Reading Lesson: Michael Ondaatje and the Patients of Desire." *Essays on Canadian Writing* 53 (1994): 92–106.

Siemerling, Winfried. *Discoveries of the Other: Alterity in the Work of Leonard Cohen, Hubert Aquin, Michael Ondaatje, and Nicole Brossard.* Toronto: U of Toronto P, 1994.

Siemerling, Winfried. "Oral History and the Writing of the Other in Ondaatje's *In the Skin of a Lion.*" *Comparative Cultural Studies and Michael Ondaatje's Writing.* Ed. Steven Tötösy de Zepetnek. West Lafayette: Purdue UP, 2005. 92–103.

Simmons, Rochelle. "*In the Skin of a Lion* as a Cubist Novel." *University of Toronto Quarterly: A Canadian Journal of the Humanities* 67.3 (1998): 699–714.

Smythe, Karen E. "Listen It: Responses to Ondaatje." *Essays on Canadian Writing: Michael Ondaatje Issue* 53 (1994): 1–10.

Snelling, Sonia. "'A Human Pyramid': An (Un)Balancing Act of Ancestry and History in Joy Kogawa's *Obasan* and Michael Ondaatje's *Running in the Family.*" *Journal of Commonwealth Literature* 32.1 (1997): 21–33.

Solecki, Sam. "It Runs in the Family: A Reading of Michael Ondaatje's *Secular Love.*" *University of Toronto Quarterly: A Canadian Journal of the Humanities* 70.2 (2001): 633–52.

Solecki, Sam. "Making and Destroying: *Coming Through Slaughter* and Extremist Art." *Spider Blues: Essays on Michael Ondaatje.* Ed. Sam Solecki. Montréal: Véhicule, 1985. 246–67.

Stenberg, Douglas-G. "A Firmament in the Midst of the Waters: Dimensions of Love in *The English Patient.*" *Literature-Film Quarterly* 26.4 (1998): 255–62.

Sugunasiri, Suwanda H. J. "'Sri Lankan' Canadian Poets: The Bourgeoisie that Fled the Revolution." *Canadian Literature* 132 (1992): 60–79.

Summers-Bremner, Eluned. "Reading Ondaatje's Poetry." *Comparative Cultural Studies and Michael Ondaatje's Writing.* Ed. Steven Tötösy de Zepetnek. West Lafayette: Purdue UP, 2005. 104–14.

Thomas, Bronwen. "'Piecing Together a Mirage': Adapting *The English Patient* for the Screen." *The Classic Novel: From Page to Screen.* Ed. Robert Giddings and Erica Sheen. Manchester: Manchester UP; 2000. 197–232.

Tötösy de Zepetnek, Steven. "Ondaatje's *The English Patient* and Questions of History." *Comparative Cultural Studies and Michael Ondaatje's Writing.* Ed. Steven Tötösy de Zepetnek. West Lafayette: Purdue UP, 2005. 115–31.

Tötösy de Zepetnek, Steven. "Social Discourse and the Problematics of Theory, Culture, Media, and Audience." *Language and Beyond: Actuality and Virtuality in the Relations between Word, Image and Sound.* Ed. Paul Joret and Aline Remael. Amsterdam: Rodopi, 1998. 231–40.

Tötösy de Zepetnek, Steven. "Cultures, Peripheralities, and Comparative Literature." *Comparative Literature: Theory, Method, Application.* By Steven Tötösy de Zepetnek. Amsterdam: Rodopi, 1998. 121–72.

Tötösy de Zepetnek, Steven. "Michael Ondaatje's *The English Patient*: 'Truth is Stranger than Fiction'." *Essays on Canadian Writing* 53 (1994): 141–53.

Turci, Monica. "People In-Between: Running in the Family as Fictional Autobiography." *Borderlands: Negotiating Boundaries in Post-Colonial Writing.* Ed. Monika Reif-Hülser. Amsterdam: Rodopi; 1999. 247–54.

Turcotte, Gerry. "Response: Venturing into Undiscoverable Countries: Reading Ondaatje, Malouf, Atwood, and Jia in an Asia-Pacific Context." *Australian Canadian Studies* 15–16 (1997–98): 65–72.

Uusipaikka, Kaisa. "Appropriating the Confessional: Michael Ondaatje's *Running in the Family* as Post-Colonial Autobiography." *Tales of Two Cities: Essays on New Anglophone Literature.* Ed. John Skinner. Turku: U of Turku P, 2000. 59–76.

Van Wart, Alice. "Turning *The English Patient* into a Film." *Pop Can: Popular Culture in Canada.* Ed. Lynne Van Luven, Lynne and Priscilla L. Walton. Scarborough: Prentice Hall Allyn and Bacon Canada; 1999. 117–22.

Verhoeven, W. M. "Naming the Present/Naming the Past: Historiographic Metafiction in Findley and Ondaatje." *Shades of Empire in Colonial and Post-Colonial Literatures.* Ed. C.C. Barfoot and Theo D'haen. Amsterdam: Rodopi, 1993. 283–99.

Verhoeven, W.M. "Playing Hide and Seek in Language: Michael Ondaatje's Historiography of the Self." *American Review of Canadian Studies* 24.1 (1994): 21–38.

Vigurs, Rochelle. "On Rock and Book and Leaf: Reading Ondattje's *Handwriting*." *Studies in Canadian Literature / Etudes en Littérature Canadienne* 26.2 (2001): 71–90.

Waldman, Nell. "Michael Ondaatje (1943–)." *ECW's Biographical Guide to Canadian Poets.* Ed. Robert Lecker, Jack David, and Ellen Quigley. Toronto: ECW, 1993. 271–77.

Waldman, Nell. "Michael Ondaatje and His Works." *Canadian Writers and Their Works.* Ed. Robert Lecker; Jack David, and Ellen Quigley. Toronto: ECW, 1992. 359–412.

Whetter, Darryl. "Ondaatje's 'International Bastards' and Their 'Best Selves': An Analysis of *The English Patient* as Travel Literature." *English Studies in Canada* 23.4 (1997): 443–58.

Williams David. "The Politics of Cyborg Communications: Harold Innis, Marshall McLuhan, and *The English Patient*." *Canadian Literature* 156 (1998): 30–55.

Younis, Raymond Aaron. "Nationhood and Decolonization in *The English Patient*." *Literature-Film Quarterly* 26.1 (1998): 2–9.

A LIST OF MICHAEL ONDAATJE'S WORKS

The Dainty Monsters. Toronto: Coach House P, 1967.

The Man with Seven Toes. Toronto: Coach House P, 1969.

The Collected Works of Billy the Kid: Left Handed Poems. Toronto: Anansi, 1970. New York: Vintage International, 1996.

Sons of Captain Poetry. Toronto: Mongrel Films / Canadian Film-Makers' Distribution Centre, 1970. 35 min.

Carry on Crime and Punishment. Toronto: Mongrel Films / Canadian Film-Makers' Distribution Centre, 1972. 5 min.

The Clinton Special. Toronto: Mongrel Films / Canadian Film-Makers' Distribution Centre, 1972. 71 min.

Rat Jelly. Toronto: Coach House P, 1973.

Coming Through Slaughter. Toronto: Anansi, 1976. New York: Vintage International, 1996.

Elimination Dance. Ilderton: Nairn Coldstream, 1978.

Claude Glass. Toronto: Coach House P, 1979.

There's a Trick with a Knife I'm Learning to Do: Poems 1963–1978. Toronto: McClelland and Stewart, 1979. New York: Norton, 1979.

Rat Jelly and Other Poems: 1963–78. London: Marion Boyars, 1980.

Tin Roof. Lantzville: Island Writing Series, 1982.

Running in the Family. Toronto: McClelland and Stewart, 1982. New York: Norton, 1982. New York: Penguin Books, 1984. New York: Vintage International, 1993.

Secular Love. Toronto: Coach House P, 1984. New York: Norton, 1985.

Two Poems. Mt. Horeb: Perishable P, 1986.

In the Skin of a Lion. Toronto: McClelland and Stewart, 1987. New York: Knopf , 1987. New York: Penguin Books, 1988.

The Cinnamon Peeler: Selected Poems. New York: Knopf, 1991. New York: Vintage, 1997.

The English Patient. Toronto: McClelland and Stewart, 1992. New York: Knopf, 1992. New York: Vintage Books, 1993. New York: Random House, 1996.

Handwriting: Poems. Toronto: McClelland and Stewart, 1998. New York: Knopf, 1999.

Anil's Ghost. Toronto: McCelland and Stewart, 2000.

Bioprofiles of Contributors to *Comparative Cultural Studies and Michael Ondaatje's Writing*

Victoria Cook teaches Canadian literature at the University of Central Lancashire. Cook's interests include transnational theory with regard to representations of the process of identification, individual and national identity, and the discourse of multiculturalism in contemporary English-Canadian fiction. Her recent publications include papers in *Etudes Canadiennes* (2002) and in *AFEC: Association Française d'Etudes Canadiennes* (2002).

Beverley Curran teaches cultural studies and translation in the Department of Creativity and Culture at Aichi Shukutoku University in Nagoya, Japan. Curran's papers, interviews, and reviews have appeared in collections and journals including *Canadian Literature* (1998), *Style* (1999), *a/b: Auto/Biography Studies* (2000), *He Said She Says: An RSVP to the Male Text* (Ed. Mica Howe and Sarah Appleton Aguiar, 2001), and *Ecopoetry: A Critical Introduction* (Ed. J. Scott Bryson, 2002). *Rezubian nikki*, Curran's translation of Nicole Brossard's *Journal intime* was published in 2000.

Marlene Goldman teaches Canadian literature at the University of Toronto. Goldman has published papers on Canadian authors including Michael Ondaatje, Timothy Findley, Margaret Atwood, Aritha van Herk, Jane Urquhart, and Alice Munro, and her work has appeared in journals such as *Studies in Canadian Literature* (1990), *Canadian Literature* (1999, 1996, 1993), *Essays on Canadian Writing* (1998), and *Modern Fiction Studies* (2002). Currently, Goldman is working on the motif of haunting in English-Canadian fiction.

Stephanie M. Hilger teaches comparative literature and German at the University of Illinois at Urbana-Champaign. She has published articles on eighteenth-century constructions of gender and class in *Seminar* (2001), *Colloquia Germanica* (2001), *The Lessing Yearbook* (2001), *Neophilologus*, and *College Literature*. Currently, she working on her book project, *Textual Politics: Women Authors Rewrite the Enlightenment*.

Hsuan Hsu is visiting scholar with the American Academy of Arts and Sciences. In his Ph.D. dissertation, *Scales of Identification: Geography, Affect, and American Literature 1803–1901*, completed recently at the University of California Berkeley's Department of English, Hsu details the ways in which literary works by Brockden Brown, Poe, Melville, James, and Norris produce and/or question collective identifications at different geographical scales. Hsu has published papers on American literature and culture in *Early American Literature* (2001), *The CEA Critic* (2003), and *Nineteenth Century Studies* (2003).

Glen Lowry is working on the publication of his Ph.D. dissertation, *After the End/s: CanLit and the Unravelling of Nation, "Race," and Space,* he completed at Simon Fraser University. Lowry has published work in *Essays on Canadian Writing* (2002) and in *West Coast Line* (2002). He has also edited, with Sook C. Kong, *CanAsiaPacific,* a special issue of *West Coast Line,* on the interrogation of new boundaries in Canadian writing and cultural practices (2001). Lowry is a poet and photographer and his poetry has appeared in *Prairie Fire* (2001) and *dandelion* (2002).

Jon Saklofske, after completing his Ph.D. in English at McGill University in 2003, teaches literature at the University of Manitoba. His interests include early American literature, twentieth-century Canadian literature, and the function of media interaction in William Blake's composite designs. While most of Saklofske's explorations of Blake are based in eighteenth-century studies, he hopes to use his findings as a foundation for further investigations of the tensions and relations between words and images in composite forms of expression over the past century. Saklofske's publications include papers on Canadian Native writing in *Humanity and Society* (1995) and on Blake and Gray in *Word and Image* (2003).

Sandeep Sanghera immigrated to Canada in 1975 from India and she has lived since in Vancouver, Kyoto, and Toronto. A free-lance editor, Sanghera's areas of interest include Caribbean poetry, expatriate Canadian writings, and literature from India. She has published her work in *Kansai Time Out* (1999) and *The Hart House Literary Review* (2001). Sanghera is at work on her first novel examining the echoes of Indian classical dance and flamenco.

Eluned Summers-Bremner teaches gender and sexuality in the arts, media and performance, and technologies of the body with the Department of Women's Studies at the University of Auckland. Her current interests include the interface between psychoanalysis, cultural memory, and performance, and the emergent subjectivities and readerships of late-capitalist technologies of communication. Summers-Bremner has published numerous papers on literary, psychoanalytic, and performance-related topics, in journals such as *New Formations* (2001), *Feminist Studies* (2001), and *Hypatia* (2000). She is currently at work on two book-length projects: one on the hysterics of place and the other on metropolitan memory.

Winfried Siemerling teaches comparative Canadian literature at the Université de Sherbrooke. Siemerling's more recent publications include *Discoveries of the Other: Alterity in the Work of Leonard Cohen, Hubert Aquin, Michael Ondaatje, and Nicole Brossard* (1994) and he has published papers in journals such as *Tendances actuelles en histoire littéraire / Contemporary Trends in Canadian Literary History* (2002), *Callaloo: A Journal of African-American and African Arts and Letters* (2001), *Journal of Indo-Canadian Studies* (2001), *Literary Review of Canada* (2000), *Canadian Literature*

(2000), *Texte: Revue de Critique et de Théorie Littéraire* (1998), and *REAL: Yearbook of Research in English and American Literature* (1998).

Steven Tötösy de Zepetnek's areas of scholarship are in comparative culture and media studies (see at <http://clcwebjournal.lib.purdue.edu/totosycv.html>). At the University of Alberta 1984–2000, since 2000 Tötösy lives in Boston and is teaching concurrently comparative media and culture studies at the University of Halle-Wittenberg, Germany. Author of numerous papers and books published on both sides of the Atlantic and in Asia, Tötösy is editor (founding) of *CLCWeb: Comparative Literature and Culture* <http://clcwebjournal.lib.purdue.edu/> and editor of the monograph series of Books in Comparative Cultural Studies, both published by Purdue University Press.

Index